VICTOR CHANDLER

—

PUT YOUR
LIFE ON IT

VICTOR CHANDLER

—

PUT YOUR LIFE ON IT

Reach Sport

www.reachsport.com

Reach **Sport**

w w w . r e a c h s p o r t . c o m

First published as a hardback in Great Britain and Ireland in 2021 by Reach Sport,
5 St Paul's Square, Liverpool, L3 9SJ.

www.reachsport.com
@Reach_Sport

Reach Sport is a part of Reach PLC.
One Canada Square, Canary Wharf, London, E15 5AP.

Hardback ISBN: 978-1-914197-11-6
Paperback ISBN: 978-1-914-197-82-6
eBook ISBN: 978-1-914197-12-3

Photographic acknowledgements:
Victor Chandler personal collection.
Every effort has been made to trace copyright.
Any oversight will be rectified in future editions.

Printed and bound by CPI Group (UK) Ltd,
Croydon, CR0 4YY.

CONTENTS

CONTENTS

For Billy and Jonnie, Harry and Lucy,
and, of course, Caroline.

7

ACKNOWLEDGEMENTS

Put Your Life On It is not a novel. It's a true story – the incredible story of Victor Chandler and his father and grandfather – and Victor has been the central contributor throughout. He's shared countless memories and anecdotes, from his childhood and youthful misadventures to the high-rolling heyday of the betting ring in the 1980s, his dramatic move offshore and his audacious attempts to take on the big Far Eastern gamblers. It's been a long but exhilarating journey and, in the early stages, I was lucky enough to be assisted by many of the older Chandler family members and friends. Sadly, not all of them are still alive to witness the outcome. I'm thinking of Victor's mother Betty and her cousin Benno Miller, the ineffably charming Gerry Albertini, Victor's Aunt Frances and his legendary Uncle Ronnie, who was, truthfully, 'the greatest gentleman of them all.' One riotous night in the Dunraven Arms in Adare with Ronnie and his friend Dave Cahill will live forever in the memory. There were also immensely helpful contributions from Victor's old colleagues Bobby Edwards, Tommy Lawrence and Alan Mills, and from the lovely Carole Masters, who sadly died in 2021.

I also want to thank another cast of characters who are still very much alive. None more so than Bill Tye, who was wonderful company and provided me with numerous insights on racecourse bookmaking, especially at Cheltenham, and Richard Thomas who has been such a

ACKNOWLEDGEMENTS

great friend and ally down the years. Then, too, I must mention Victor's and his father's lifelong friend and confidante Charlie Maskey, along with Mike Carlton, Michael Buckley, Victor's Irish cousin Ronnie and the inimitable Butch Beaton-Brown. I should also like to thank James de Wesselow for doing everything he could, and the team at Reach – Steve, Paul, Rick, Adam and Harri – for getting it over the line.

Barney Curley, Victor's friend and rival for almost 40 years, was kind enough to write a brief foreword to the book but, alas, he died before publication.

Finally, I can not stress enough how much I owe to my wife Sara. The last few years have not been easy for her, or for me, but without her unflagging support and encouragement, there would have been no book.

Jamie Reid
May 2021

FOREWORD

"Victor's reputation as one of the great modern bookmakers is fully deserved. We took each other on for many years and he was always honourable, fair and resolute. I used to bet with his father too. They were both always gentlemen and they had perfect manners. There was so much atmosphere along the rails and on the racecourse in that era, and those of us who lived through it can say 'we saw the best.'

It would have been very easy for Victor to quietly disappear with the demise of the on-course betting market. But he was one of the pioneers of the bookmaking industry moving online. He was blessed with vision and he was confident enough to stand out from the crowd.

The strength of the brand, Victor Chandler, that he created is a fitting testament to his character and his career."

Barney Curley
July 2020

"I am shocked, shocked! to find that
gambling is going on in here.

– Claude Rains as Captain Louis Renault in
Casablanca (1942).

"Son ... you only have a short time.
Make sure it's a good time."

– Anon

Prologue

I n the summer of 1966, the 15-year-old Victor Chandler, whose father was one of Britain's leading bookmakers, was expelled from Highgate School. The miscreant had been caught climbing out at night to meet girls and going down to the Flamingo Club in Soho. It wasn't his first offence. Victor senior, who had been a pupil at the North London public school in the 1930s, was not amused, but as far as 'Young Victor' was concerned, expulsion was a blessed release. "I hated school," he says with an intensity that would be hard to exaggerate. "I was put off it at an early age. All my childhood, I was always more interested in the forbidden. It was so much more fun."

At Highgate, they saw things rather differently, and in a phrase that was as unintentionally comical as it was pompous, described the teenager as "trying to live in a sort of James Bond world," which, according to Victor's housemaster Norris Butcher, "just won't do."

Some of Victor's friends would say that he's always lived in a sort of James Bond world in the course of a 40-year career pursuing high life and fast times as one of the biggest and boldest bookmakers the game has ever seen. There's his fearless love of a gamble, mirroring Bond's battle with the villainous Le Chiffre in Casino Royale, and his willingness to pit his wits against a long line of maverick personalities in locations ranging from Cheltenham and Royal Ascot to Hong Kong,

Macau and Singapore. He also shares 007's penchant for good food and wine and bespoke tailoring, not to mention – especially when he was younger – up to 30 or 40 cigarettes a day.

Yet, in other respects, Chandler couldn't be less like an Ian Fleming stereotype. More Len Deighton's anti-hero Harry Palmer, immortalised on screen by Michael Caine. Gravel voiced from years of smoking, Victor's roots lie in the East End of London, not Eton or Fettes, and unlike Mister Bond there's no streak of Scottish Calvinism in his make-up or sadomasochistic interest in pain. He's shy on the surface and with people that he doesn't know well yet, he loves company and sociable gatherings, and he's a charming and extremely generous host. But while he may give the impression that life is all a laugh, to be enjoyed and never taken too seriously, he occasionally shows glimpses of a much tougher side and an inner steeliness that he has had to draw on many times, often just in order to survive until the next race.

The Chandler saga is by no means a seamless narrative of triumph and good fortune. It illustrates that if you want to live life to the full, you must never be afraid to stray beyond the tramlines of what others may consider to be acceptable behaviour. At the same time, some of Victor's experiences are a stark reminder that adventurous options have consequences, and some of his choices have resulted in considerable pain both for himself and those around him.

Ironically, Chandler never intended to be a bookmaker at all. It was only the premature death of his father, aged 50, which propelled him into the family business. Not long before he died, Victor senior concluded that bookmaking was a dying profession. He also feared that his prodigal son would never make anything of himself at all.

He was wrong on both counts.

VICTOR CHANDLER

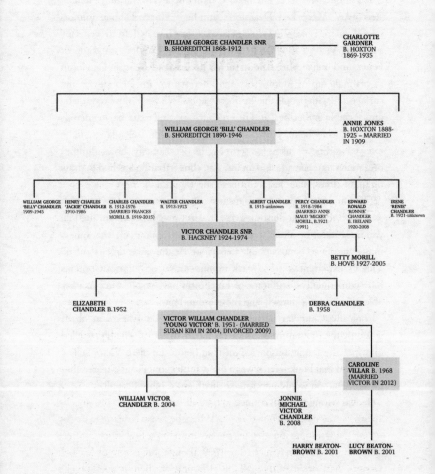

WILLIAM GEORGE CHANDLER SNR
B. SHOREDITCH 1868-1912

CHARLOTTE GARDNER
B. HOXTON 1869-1935

WILLIAM GEORGE 'BILL' CHANDLER
B. SHOREDITCH 1890-1946

ANNIE JONES
B. HOXTON 1888-1925 – MARRIED IN 1909

WILLIAM GEORGE 'BILLY' CHANDLER
1909-1945

HENRY CHARLES 'JACKIE' CHANDLER
1910-1986

CHARLES CHANDLER
B. 1912-1976 (MARRIED FRANCES MORILL B. 1919-2015)

WALTER CHANDLER
B. 1913-1913

ALBERT CHANDLER
B. 1915-unknown

PERCY CHANDLER
B. 1918-1984 (MARRIED ANNE MAUD 'MICKEY' MORILL, B.1921 -1991)

EDWARD RONALD 'RONNIE' CHANDLER
B. IRELAND 1920-2008

IRENE 'RENIE' CHANDLER
B. 1921-unknown

VICTOR CHANDLER SNR
B. HACKNEY 1924-1974

BETTY MORILL
B. HOVE 1927-2005

ELIZABETH CHANDLER B.1952

DEBRA CHANDLER
B. 1958

VICTOR WILLIAM CHANDLER 'YOUNG VICTOR' B. 1951- (MARRIED SUSAN KIM IN 2004, DIVORCED 2009)

CAROLINE VILLAR B. 1968 (MARRIED VICTOR IN 2012)

WILLIAM VICTOR CHANDLER B. 2004

JONNIE MICHAEL VICTOR CHANDLER
B. 2008

HARRY BEATON-BROWN B. 2001

LUCY BEATON-BROWN B. 2001

Chapter One

The Duellist

A silver-grey Mercedes was gliding through a Cotswold landscape of dream-like beauty. Smoke was hanging in the air, dry stone walls lined the narrow country roads, and away to the north-west, patches of early spring sunshine were breaking through the clouds behind the Malvern Hills.

The time was shortly before 11am on Tuesday 14th March, 2000, and the atmosphere was hopeful and optimistic. There was a sense of winter finally drawing to an end, and of longer, brighter days ahead. The mood inside the Mercedes was tense, eager and expectant. Tuesday the 14th was the opening day of Cheltenham's National Hunt Festival, and Victor Chandler was on his way to do battle with the punters.

VC was the man. The player. The number one bookie in the ring and, for almost 25 years, he had spent two or three days each week standing outside on the racecourse in all weathers and running the firm's credit and on-course book. When he wasn't racing, he'd be laying and trading on the telephone from his old Linhope Street office in Marylebone. Since May 1999, though, the centre of Victor's business had moved offshore to the 24-hour sports betting operation he had set up in Gibraltar. The new company, Victor Chandler International, had revolutionised the UK gambling market by offering – two years before Gordon Brown abolished betting duty – tax-free wagering online and by phone in a multitude of different languages and currencies, from English to Chinese, and euros to yen.

But no matter how big or far flung his interests had become, the National Hunt Festival, with its passionate atmosphere and intoxicating betting market, remained the most important date in Victor's calendar. He'd been going to the Cotswolds in March – and to Royal Ascot in June – every year since 1975, and there was no other racecourse in the world he loved as much. The Millennium Festival would mark a historic turning point for VC, as it was to be the last time that he would stand up at Cheltenham to front the Chandler business in person.

As the old century slipped away, a whole racing and bookmaking culture was slipping away with it. A colourful, guileful, person-to-person world, based around customs, codes and practices dating back to the Edwardian era and beyond. Victor's father and grandfather were steeped in that world and it was a constant backdrop throughout the early years of young Victor's life. By 2000, things were already changing, and 20 years later, it's all but vanished, except for a few wild, defiant days each year at Cheltenham and a handful of other Festival meetings. Replaced by the undeniable convenience and oppressive sterility of computers. The leviathans of the contemporary betting ring are not bold individuals like Victor Chandler and his forebears, nor Stephen Little or William Hill. They are the internet betting exchanges, like Betfair. The indispensable trading platform of the modern age. Permitting professionals to sit and watch the action at home on satellite TV or through their phones or computer screens while wagering with anonymous fellow bookies and punters in cyberspace. Backing horses, dogs, golfers, football teams or whatever to win or, if they prefer, to lose. Making amateur bookmakers of us all and permitting the callowest racecourse layers to simply follow the online herd with no need for them to ever pit their wits against the public or back a judgement of their own.

Victor had seen the changes coming, gradually cutting back on his racecourse pitches in order to concentrate on the volume of online trading, and his move offshore in 1999 was as seminal a moment for the traditional bookmaking industry as the rise of Betfair. But the story of the Chandler dynasty is, in part, an evocation of, and tribute to, that earlier vanishing world. A hail and farewell to the old ways and the old faces. And a last call for more than 200 years of gambling society.

Everton, Victor's private driver, steered the Mercedes onto the main road from Stow-on-the-Wold and then continued down Fish Hill and onwards through Broadway. Daffodils lined the green grass verge where local schoolchildren waited to greet the Cheltenham-bound Queen Mother with their usual bouquets, and more smoke trails climbed high from the tall chimneys of the Lygon Arms Hotel. There were other smart motors on the road now too. Bentleys, Range Rovers, Jaguars. And in the sky up above them, the first helicopters were starting to arrive from the south.

Victor was in the back seat of the Mercedes. His mobile phone in one hand, the racing pages spread out on his lap. Sitting next to him was his second cousin and right-hand man Peter Beaton-Brown, or 'Butch' as he was known in the firm, and up front next to Everton was Charlie Maskey, a former *Sporting Life* journalist and lifelong friend of the Chandler family. A second car bringing other members of the firm's racecourse team was following behind. The men were all smartly suited and immaculately groomed. Their ties hand-made, their shoes buffed to a lustrous sheen, and their watches and signet rings glinting discretely. There is nothing flash about Chandler, who is as far removed from the old caricature image of a bookie in a loud check suit as his father and grandfather were before him. But dressing well was a firm and family tradition. "The racecourse is a piece of theatre," says Butch, "and the rails where Victor used to stand is the most conspicuous stage of them all."

Once upon a time, all the rails bookies – and plenty of the cash or boards bookmakers too – wore made-to-measure suits and shoes. But by the end of the 20th century, standards were changing and older bookmaking figures who remembered the great sartorial days of the

VICTOR CHANDLER

1940s and '50s were unimpressed by those contemporary layers who turned up for work in anything less than a whistle and flute. Victor Chandler senior used to say that it was "no crime being skint," but that "only a fool looks poor before the racing has even begun."

Young Victor's panache and savoir-faire was much appreciated by his regular customers. It reminded them that he was not just any bookie or impersonal corporate figurehead. His father was one of the most handsome and charismatic men on the Turf. As well as his bookmaking pitches, he owned a gambling club in Mayfair, and its launch coincided with that great crossover era in the 1960s, when the same London party or opening might include a glamorous young actress or model, a society photographer, a dissolute journalist or two, a couple of gangsters and several members of the House of Lords.

Victor's grandfather, William George or Bill Chandler, was an even bigger character. Roguish, visionary and daring, and one of the biggest bookie-gamblers in British sporting history. Bill founded Walthamstow Greyhound Stadium, owned No.1 Wardour Street in London's West End, and ran an illicit casino in the basement of the Piccadilly Hotel during the blackout in WW2.

Young Victor's success came about from combining his grandfather's nerve and his father's style, and then adding to them a dash of sophistication all his own. You could never quite pin Chandler down. One day he was the bon vivant and old Soho bohemian with a fund of fabulous stories about the artist Lucian Freud. The next he was sponsoring a big race at Ascot, hosting some of the top owners and trainers in the country and contributing thousands to charity. The day after that, he was being accused of laundering money for the drug smuggler and gangster Brian Wright. His mobile phones were always ringing. He was always just about to jet off on another trip, and another pack of Camels or Marlborough Reds were always close to hand. Above all else, though, Victor Chandler was a gambler. "The biggest on the track," reckoned Charlie Maskey, who has known him since he was a child. "He wanted to back every winner and lay every losing favourite too."

18

The Mercedes rolled on across the vale country and then hit a slow-moving traffic jam inching through the picturesque village of Winchcombe. Victor had little time to enjoy the view. He had been talking on the phone virtually non-stop since the journey began. Only the previous evening some of the callers had been enjoying his company and hospitality over dinner at the Dormy House Hotel. The big bookie and his biggest punters temporarily united in a bacchanalian truce. Today, though, the appreciative dinner guests have transformed into Western Long Riders and, having loaded up their Winchesters and Colt 45s, are intent on taking the bookmaker's money. And, as usual, Victor seems only too willing to accommodate them. It's a moot point which of them is wearing the black hats but, as the shrewdest gamblers must surely recognise, there is a strategy behind Chandler's apparent willingness to please.

There used to be 20 fiercely competitive races over the three days at Cheltenham (before the meeting expanded to four days and eventually 28 races in 2005), and it was unimaginable that the favourites would win all of them. Victor always believed that any horse, no matter its reputation, should be 2-1 just to jump round in a steeplechase let alone win something like the Cheltenham Gold Cup. The Chandler approach was to lay the short-priced favourites to his high-rolling clients and try and back some of the longer-priced horses – whose odds he believed underestimated their chances – with his rivals elsewhere in the ring.

With so much money circulating, there were always value betting opportunities at the Festival. The test of a bookie's skill lay in deciding precisely which favourites to lay and which other runners to back on their own, and the firm's, account. In 1990, Victor had been well behind on day two of the meeting after short-priced favourites won the first two races. But they were followed by 20-1, 12-1 and 40-1 winners, and by the time of the last race, the Mildmay of Flete Challenge Cup, the bookmaker was ready to back a long shot. The figures compiled by the firm's 'speed boys' highlighted a 100-1 outsider called New Halen, whose potential appeared to have been overlooked by the market. Victor instructed two of his on-course team to put £1,000 each way on New Halen, and watched Bobby Edwards and Tommy Lawrence hurry off to the lower end of the ring and place two bets of £50,000 to £500 each way. Bookmakers promptly slashed the odds to 66-1. Cheltenham was New Halen's 14th run of the season but he was nothing if not genuine and, after regaining the lead at the tenth fence, he jumped the last in front and ran on up the hill to score by eight lengths. "The whole of our staff were going wild with delight," said Victor. "We had seriously overstood the favourite, First Bout, and performed the double whammy, backing New Halen to win £125,000."

But as well as trying to pick winners at big prices, Victor also had to be on the lookout for the market movers. The sudden significant gambles on horses that might have been plotted up by crafty owners and trainers, and were probably much better than their form figures suggested. "To survive at Cheltenham you had to be able to dodge the bullets," said Butch. "If we were with a horse and the firm was backing it, we'd lay a majority of the bets off. If we were against it, we'd maybe let the bets mount up. There can be anything up to a million-pound swing on the week. Get it right and it's Chateau Laffite and Chablis Premier Cru. Get it wrong and it's scrambled eggs on room service."

Victor stresses that at Cheltenham, "you had to have a game plan," and while he may have taken the big decisions himself, "it was a whole team that put a card together in the morning and we considered everything." The state of the going was usually their first consideration. How accurate was the official ground description, and was the surface really good or good to soft, or was it fast or even heavy? Some horses are crucially ground-dependent and, as regular racegoers know, a whole season's preparation can be wasted if the conditions at Cheltenham go against them.

The racecourse was always awash with rumour, speculation and gossip, much of it emanating from the weighing room. The bookmakers heard all the stories and, in those less reproving times, it was common knowledge that the shrewdest oddsmakers made use of inside information to help them make their book. But while proper intelligence was worth paying for, Victor felt that anyone depending on jockeys and trainers for tips was liable to end up in the poorhouse. "I was a big believer in speed figures, and I had my own clock man and form man, and I still think that times and the form book are generally more important than information. But what I did respect was money. And nothing was more significant than when somebody really sharp was prepared to put more than their usual maximum on the line."

The financial moves that Chandler watched out for sometimes featured five and even six-figure enquiries from the biggest gamblers in the game. Some of whom might be 'Arbers' or Arbitrage punters seeking to make gains by backing several different outcomes with rival bookmaking firms and staking large sums in pursuit of small percentage profits. But they might just as easily involve a canny racing-mad priest from County Cork or Westmeath who normally had no more than £50 on a horse but suddenly wanted to treble his stake. VC would accept the bet but the firm would then 'be all over' the horse, going back through its form and maybe calling up someone they knew connected to the stable to see if there was anything they'd missed.

Chandler is notoriously unpunctual, but no matter what time he got to bed during Cheltenham week, he was usually up as early as any stable lad and would begin his day by checking his emails and overnight phone messages from Gibraltar, before turning to that day's card and form in the *Racing Post*. Alan Mills, a silver-haired South Londoner who worked for Victor and his father before him for over 35 years, was a regular member of the firm's Festival line-up. Mills was another early riser who liked to head off for an invigorating run towards Snowshill before returning to the Dormy House for a hearty breakfast. Victor doesn't do jogging. Not now. Not then. Not ever. Sometimes he had breakfast in his bedroom, sometimes he joined the others in the restaurant, but by 10.30am, the majority of the 10-strong party would be showered, shaved, dressed and ready for action. There would then follow the inevitable 10 or 15-minute wait before VC arrived downstairs "with a mobile clamped to each ear," recalled Mills, "and wanting to know why we hadn't left already."

At this stage of the day, every one of them was determinedly sober. It was no coincidence that some of the firm's most successful clients were teetotallers. Victor entertained guests every night during Cheltenham but, other than one disastrous experience when he was young, he never drank during the daytime when he was working.

By 11.30am, as the Mercedes began the ascent of Cleeve Hill, the level of telephone activity had briefly settled down and, in Butch's words, "Victor always went quiet for five or 10 minutes. It was like the scenes at Rorke's Drift at the beginning of Zulu. You can't see them yet, and you can't hear them either, but you know they're out there."

As more helicopters swept overhead, the convoy of traffic – private cars, taxis, coaches, buses and stretch limousines – reached the top of the Cotswold escarpment. And there, spread out beneath them at the foot of the ridge, lay the beautiful, seductive and time-honoured racecourse. The O.K. Corral of British gambling. Victor reached for his cigarettes. Butch smiled nervously.

It was time to go to work.

Chapter Two

Irish Eyes

Flags snapped and fluttered in the breeze, advertising hoardings rattled against the white-painted running rails, and a pervasive aroma of fried onions drifted down from the fast-food kiosks at the top end of the track. Punters were already packing into the bars, boxes and hospitality areas, and everywhere you looked, glasses were being tipped back, bottles drained and more orders placed. It was all talk, talk, rumour, rumour, gossip, intrigue and speculation.

The Victor Chandler high rollers were looked after in a box up in the grandstand while the medium rollers were accommodated in the firm's pavilion in the tented village. Guests and account holders mingling freely and everyone revelling in the general air of mounting anticipation. Old hands and familiar faces, some of whom were racing at Cheltenham in Victor's father's time, sought Young Victor out for a word, a joke, a tip, or tried to draw him into a huddle to discuss a private financial accommodation.

Butch was part of a six-strong team deputed to run the betting operation in the tent, accepting both cash and credit wagers. Some punters wouldn't leave the marquee all day, preferring to follow their money on the television screens to fighting for a position outside. Butch, dapper in his Knightsbridge countryman's gear – posing charmingly for a *Tatler* photographer one minute, setting up a hefty credit line

23

for a trainer the next – was in his element looking after them, though requests for bets of £20,000 or over would have to be relayed up to the rails for approval. Not that everyone was a high roller. One year, Prince William came into the tent in the company of the Grand National-winning owner Trevor Hemmings, who was his host for the day. The Prince said that he'd like to have a fiver each way on the next race and proceeded to hand over £5. As his granny and great-grandmother would have known, it had to be politely explained to him that £5 each way actually required a stake of £10. The extra fiver was duly produced, but the horse lost.

The first race was off at 2pm, and shortly after 12.30pm, Victor and the boys – his clerk Bill Tye and his outside men Bobby Edwards, Steve Wilson, Tommy Lawrence and Alan Mills – left the tent and headed up past the parade ring, through the stands and out across the concourse to the betting ring. There used to be over 150 bookmakers at Cheltenham, around 20 of them standing on the rails that separate the Members Enclosure from the cash or boards bookmakers in the cheaper Tattersalls Enclosure next door. Theoretically, the rails bookies, just as in Victor's grandfather's day, dealt predominantly in credit betting with known clients and account holders, including hedging bets with the trade. In practice, many of them also dealt in huge amounts of cash. From January 2001, they would be able to advertise their prices on a board too, though older punters – used to bookmaking's labyrinthine ways – still preferred a confidential enquiry about a horse's odds.

Victor's father was a boards bookmaker and he had the prestigious number one pitches at all the main southern tracks. Young Victor, like his grandfather in the 1930s and '40s, was a rails bookie and, like Bill Chandler before him, had acquired a reputation for taking the biggest cash or credit wagers. By 2000, though, the level of racecourse trading was already dipping in the face of the Betfair revolution and, with head office having moved to Gibraltar, Cheltenham and Royal Ascot were the only remaining occasions when VC was guaranteed to be there himself.

With a few greetings and acknowledgements from old friends and rivals – John Banks, Stephen Little, Colin Webster, Michael Simmonds of Heathorns, all of them trying to sell the same product in the same crowded marketplace – the Chandler team settled down on their pitch. VC was in pride of place, Bill standing on one side of him, Bobby looking after the satchel full of cash, and Steve, Tommy and Alan working the floor. Steve's job was to lay off the firm's liabilities and place hedging bets around the ring. Tommy and Alan's role to place Victor's bets, some of them personal, some what he called 'insurance' at the best possible odds right up to the off.

Still of crucial importance in that era were the tic-tac operators or 'top men' like the legendary Mickey Fingers and his colleague Micky Stuart, whose father was an Italian ice cream salesman in Brighton before the war. Micky's racecourse nickname was 'Hokey', an abbreviation of 'Hokey Pokey', which is what the Italians used to call an ice cream cornet or a cone. The tic-tacs wore white gloves for easy identification and carried a series of 'twist cards' in their gloved hands, coloured red, white and blue and all pertaining to betting movements on each race. The bookies had to pay the tic-tac men to be able to make use of this knowledge, each of them receiving a call sign to enable them to send and receive messages around the ring. Victor's call sign was 'medal', meaning Victoria Cross or VC, and the tic-tacs banged their heart with their fist, miming pinning a medal on their chest, when they wanted to relay a message to him. Ancient and Dickensian it may have been, but the system had worked effectively for generations and was as integral a part of a day's racing and bookmaking as the big double-sided ledger in which Bill Tye recorded the bets.

Bill, who was born in Poplar, London, in 1956, left his grammar school at the age of 16 already in love with the whole world of racing, betting and odds making. His father had done a bit of street bookmaking in the days before the shops were legalised, and a formative experience for Bill came when he was walking out of the main entrance of Walthamstow Stadium with his dad one night in the mid-1960s. "Look, son," said Bill senior, pointing at a row of smart cars, including a Bentley and a couple of Jaguars, parked by the entrance. "Now look over there." Across the road, Bill saw a queue of about a 100 people waiting at the bus stop. "Those cars," continued his father, "they belong to the bookmakers. The people waiting for the bus? They're the punters."

Bill's choice of career was decided there and then. He started out working as a settler in London betting offices owned by William Massey and Wally Coomes, and by the age of 17, he was a shop manager. He first met Victor in 1983 and began clerking for him a few years later. "He's the steadiest man you'll ever work with," says VC. "A friend more than anything else, and with a fantastic knowledge of racing."

Bill's job at the races was detailed and painstaking and, like tic-tac, had changed little since 1900. Each race would be recorded on a different double-sided page in the big field ledger. At the top, Bill would write the names of the leading contenders, with the expected favourite in the right-hand column, and the bets placed would be entered under each horse. All the details had to be recorded by hand, including the initials of the punter, and it was customary for the win part of the bet to be recorded first, so a wager of say £10,000 at 4-1 placed by John Banks would be written as '£40,000 to £10,000, JB' and so on. The boards bookies may have taken a greater number of bets on a race but most of them were little more than £10, £20 and £30 a time. The rails layers took fewer bets in total, but they were for much higher stakes, and it was the clerk's job to continually keep a count in his head as regards how much they stood to pay out should a particular horse win, and to advise Victor of the firm's profit and loss position after each race.

VC's client list, burnished by the name and reputation he inherited from his father, comprised many of the top owners and trainers in racing, including numerous members of the Jockey Club. But he also laid bets to an eclectic cast of recreational gamblers, from the painters Lucian Freud and Francis Bacon, to City men, film producers, restaurant owners, football managers, actors, tipsters and journalists, such as the late and permanently potless Jeffrey Bernard.

In the 1990s, Chandler began duelling audaciously with some colossal Far Eastern speculators whose main passion was not racing, but football. But at Cheltenham, the core of his business still featured a small group of big-hitting Irishmen whose names were synonymous with the Festival meeting. There was the inimitable Barney Curley, who once trained as a Jesuit novitiate and was a hero to punters on both sides of the Irish Sea. Curley had been devastated by the death of his son Charles in a car accident in 1995, and in the years that followed, had increasingly devoted himself to his charity, Direct Aid for Africa. But Barney was still partial to a bet come March.

Then there was the imposing Dubliner Noel Furlong, a carpet dealer and self-made millionaire who won the World Series of Poker in Binion's Horseshoe in Las Vegas in 1999. Dublin Noel liked to play for high stakes on the racecourse too, and was never afraid to go all-in at Cheltenham.

And then there was JP McManus, the Sundance Kid of racing legend, domiciled not only at Kilmallock in County Limerick, but also in Switzerland and Barbados.

Until the arrival down south of the fearless Scotsman Freddie Williams at the beginning of 1999, Victor, Stephen Little and Colin Webster, were the only bookies really prepared to look these gamblers in the eye and not flinch. The big hitters knew they had a realistic chance of getting on at the advertised price, and to a substantial sum. Little, an Uppingham-educated clergyman's son famous for his distinctive ankle-length fur coat, would be guided by his mathematical knowledge and the strength of the market. But VC, drawing on his family tradition as well as his own passion for racing and love of a bet, was happy to 'take a view', and the resulting dramas lit up the ring.

In the opening race at Cheltenham in March 2000, the two-mile Supreme Novices' Hurdle, a Grade One contest with 15 runners, there was a red-hot favourite. A horse wreathed in mystique and reputation – more reputation than actual ability as it turned out. A horse called Youlneverwalkalone. Running in the green and gold colours of the aforesaid JP McManus and trained on the Curragh by Christy Roche, a former English and Irish Derby-winning jockey and an instinctively crafty character – "but then why wouldn't he be, born in Tipperary?"

in the words of the mischievous Paddy Power founder Stewart Kenny.

Roche and JP had originally hoped to run Youlneverwalkalone in the 1999 Cheltenham Bumper (the champion National Hunt flat race) but a setback forced them to leave the horse out of their plans for that season. The gelding's novice hurdling career was deemed to be a stepping stone to big things, and as early as October at the Breeders' Cup meeting in Florida, well-informed Irishmen were telling their English confidantes that Youlneverwalkalone would be their Millenium Cheltenham banker.

"If you lay JP a bet and it wins, it's your fault," says Victor bluntly. He described the former bookmaker turned fabulously successful currency dealer – but still a good Catholic and philanthropist to boot – as a man "with a smile like Mother Theresa and the brain of Al Capone." By 2000, JP was no longer in the habit of betting in person with Victor on the rails. He might "come down to the pitch to say hello," as Bill Tye puts it. "But someone else close to him, sometimes his racing manager Frank Berry, would come up and do the business." Whatever the identity of the putter-on, the story in the ring half an hour before the race was that somebody had laid a bet of £150,000 to £100,000 on Youlneverwalkalone, the wager presumed to have been struck on the owner's behalf. Victor refused to accept that the 'good thing' deserved to be a 6-4 or even a 15-8 chance. It may have been unbeaten, but what had it beaten and how much would it find off the bridle when pressure was applied? Might the ground be a shade too firm for it and, as a half-brother to a three-mile Cheltenham Stayers' Hurdle winner, would the two-mile trip be too short?

The punters disagreed, and as the clock ticked down, Bill Tye's ledger was filling up with money for the favourite. McManus may have been lying low but from out of the crowd of punters, watchers and bookies runners, came two more mighty Irish racing personalities. Rich and powerful men, fresh from a winter sojourn in the sun. Bill Tye remembers one of them turning up at the pitch on the opening day in the early 1990s, unbuttoning his coat and tipping out a huge wad of cash – bricks of £50 notes – as "ammunition or something to be going on with." He was accustomed to betting in four or five figures and, over the years, his selections had always been shrewd and often successful.

VC, who had been expecting them, greeted the duo with a kind of nonchalant good humour, as if they were old acquaintances who just happened to have bumped into each other at the races. After a few moments, though, the Irishmen got down to business, and before they left to return to their box high up in the stands, Victor had laid a bet of £62,500 to £50,000 on Youlneverwalkalone, whose price had contracted to a best-priced 5-4 throughout the ring.

By now there were around 60,000 spectators gathered on Cheltenham racecourse, all of them clutching their betting tickets and living the dream, and an impassioned cry went up as the starter called the runners in and another Festival got under way. The bookmakers, whose hearts may have been beating just as fast as their customers but who had long taught themselves to conceal their emotions, trained their binoculars on the action. The elite rails layers standing tall on the highest steps of their pitches, their clerks and workmen gathered at their feet. Other bookies and punters followed the race on the giant TV screens opposite the grandstand.

At the top of the famous hill on the far side of the track, a group of half a dozen horses were still in with a winning chance, with Youlneverwalkalone – held up off what had been a relatively steady pace – in fourth or fifth. Close enough maybe, but not quite travelling as easily as a 5-4 favourite should be. They began to race downhill, a thrilling ballet of horses and riders flowing over the Cotswold turf, and then swung left handed into the home straight. And all of a sudden it looked as if the gambling Gods were looking down on Victor Chandler and not the favourite's backers, because despite the jockey Conor O'Dwyer's best efforts, Youlneverwalkalone was struggling and unable to overtake the leaders. And approaching the last hurdle, it was another Irish runner, Sausalito Bay, ridden by the great stylist Paul Carberry and sent off at the punter-friendly odds of 14-1, that hit the front. The future triple winner Best Mate ran on strongly to finish second, with the beaten favourite – the groans of his supporters still hanging in the air – a length and a quarter away in third.

The first swing of the pendulum had been in Victor's favour, his total payout on Sausalito Bay a mere £11,555, but there was no time to celebrate. At Cheltenham, the action moves at breakneck speed and decisions have to be taken continually. In the second race, the Arkle Trophy – the two-mile championship for novice chasers – there were 12 runners and another short-priced market leader to take on. Decoupage. Trained in Lambourn by the rotund and Wodehousian figure of Charlie Egerton and an impressive winner of his only two races over fences. But VC felt Decoupage was crucially short of experience and laid it repeatedly from 9-4 to 2-1 to 7-4 favourite. He was right again. Decoupage hit the third and seventh fences and then blundered badly two out, ending up in third place behind the 8-1 winner Tiutchev, trained by Nicky Henderson and ridden by Mick Fitzgerald. With another payout of little more than £11,000, Victor finished £43,000 up on the race.

Two down and the atmosphere around the pitch was electrifying. Racegoers already high on the Festival's addictive mix and an ever increasing number of them trying to place bets with VC and get the best odds. And now it was the big one. The Smurfit Champion Hurdle, worth £145,000 to the winner, and with the peerless Istabraq in the JP McManus colours bidding to become only the fifth horse in Cheltenham history to win the race for the third year running. On the eve of the Festival, there had been a scare when the champion was discovered in his box in the racecourse stables with a trace of blood in his nostrils. Was the great horse showing the first signs of burst blood vessels, suggesting his long and distinguished career was beginning to take its toll? Or had he just rolled over in his box in the night and sustained a harmless scratch?

The alarm caused the favourite's odds to drift. On the Tuesday morning, he was trading at 8-15, still a skinny price but better than the 1-3 he'd been expected to go off at 24 hours before. Not that his owner was backing him. Not this time. In 1998, the year of Istabraq's first tilt at the Cheltenham crown, JP McManus had attempted to place a £300,000 bet on him with Victor. The bookmaker had just been to the dentist in Gibraltar and was walking back to his office when he got a call from McManus on one of his several mobile phones, the one reserved for the really big hitters. The Irishman, polite and soft spoken as ever, explained that he'd like to have a little bet on Istabraq. "Oh, yes?" said Victor. "That's right," said JP. In fact, he'd like to back him to win a million pounds. "Oh, really", said Victor, trying to sound equally deadpan but his brain presumably whirring. It didn't whirr for long though. Istabraq may have been McManus's pride and joy and built up as the Irish banker but, in Victor's view, he had "never really done a time" and the bookmaker felt he just had to take him on. He didn't lay JP quite what he wanted but he did lay him £100,000 at 7-2, and the story was that the gambler got on more elsewhere.

Victor paid dearly for his opinion as Istabraq routed the opposition, romping home by 12 lengths, and the following year he served up a repeat performance, his owner's money down once again. But in March 2000, McManus wasn't playing. This time he was just watching and hoping and keeping his fingers crossed for his family treasure. But Noel Furlong was backing him.

'Dublin Noel', in his big brown overcoat, had made a theatrical appearance in the Chandler pavilion. The 62-year-old – a poker-playing, racing and greyhound-loving punter to his fingertips – had cleaned out the bookies to the tune of £500,000 in an epic gamble on his novice hurdler Destriero at Cheltenham in 1991. Nine years later, not many oddsmakers were prepared to accept his wagers, not even at the Festival. Victor was the exception. Furlong – who was born JJ Furlong but nicknamed 'Noel' because his birthday was on Christmas Day – wanted £150,000 on Istabraq at 1-2, and was accommodated.

Charlie Swan was in the saddle as always and, after being in touch with the leaders all the way and closing effortlessly three out, the champion drew away from the last and landed the hat-trick by four lengths. For most racegoers present, it was one of those unforgettable Cheltenham moments, whether they had backed the favourite or not.

"Go on, Charlie," they roared as the conquering heroes rounded the home turn, a great wave of emotion washing up over the crowd like the oncoming tide. But then the wave hit the equivalent of a concrete breakwater in the shape of the mercilessly unromantic bookmakers. Many of whom were hit hard by the result, even at such short odds, and forced to pay out through gritted teeth.

Victor was wounded, and Noel Furlong wasn't finished yet. He'd placed a £50,000 double with VC on Istabraq and the Irish steeplechaser Florida Pearl in Thursday's Cheltenham Gold Cup, and now his Champion Hurdle winnings were running on the Pearl at 9-2.

In the fourth race, the William Hill National Hunt Handicap Chase, Chandler laid just one £30 bet on the 11-2 winner, Marlborough, but personal wagers amounting to £8,000 on the 14-1 outsider Village King went west and those losses had to come off the field book. But with the punters on the back foot in the last two contests on the card, the firm ended the day £50,000 up.

Wednesday, though, began badly as Victor laid a £10,000 bet at 5-4 on Monsignor, hot favourite for the Sun Alliance Hurdle, at which point more punters came in for it. The 'jolly', trained by Jenny Pitman's son Mark, stormed home by eight lengths, leaving the firm with a £60,000 loss on the race. Much worse was to follow. In the second race, the Queen Mother Champion Chase, the favourite was the previous year's Arkle Trophy winner Flagship Uberalles, owned by Michael Krysztofiak and his wife Elizabeth, trained by Paul Nicholls, and successful in the Game Spirit Chase at Newbury a month before the Festival. VC respected his chances but had much less faith in Tony McCoy's mount Edredon Bleu, running in the Best Mate colours of Jim Lewis but beaten twice by Flagship Uberalles during the winter. Victor felt that Edredon Bleu was not an out-and-out two-miler and needed further, and laid a £50,000 bet on the horse at 4-1. The wager was placed by the Surrey-based businessman Clive Smith, a high-stakes punter, who made a fortune building municipal pay-and-play golf courses and selling them to the Japanese, and would go on to own the great dual Cheltenham Gold Cup winner Kauto Star.

Not perturbed by looking down the barrel of a £200,000 loss, VC trimmed Edredon Bleu half a point to 7-2 and then laid another serious bet on the seven-year-old to an Irish client. What followed was the most thrilling contest of the week as Edredon Bleu and Norman Williamson's mount, Direct Route, battled it out from the last fence, the pair of them neck and neck up the hill with McCoy at his strongest forcing Edredon Bleu home by a short head. Flagship Uberalles was a disappointing third. Victor had laid the favourite as well as the winner but his total losses on the race were still a few pounds shy of £110,000.

In the build-up to the 26-runner Coral Cup, the day's big handicap, Barney Curley – distinctive as ever with his toothbrush moustache and slightly cock-eyed brown trilby hat – popped up at Victor's side. There were some bookmakers that Barney wouldn't hear of. Bookies that he raged at for not laying him what he thought were acceptable odds about his horses (and for their part, there were some bookmakers who had unprintable views about Barney), but Victor wasn't one of them. "When I was first starting out, he used to be very helpful to me," he recalls. "He'd discuss why he thought some horse's price was too big or too short, or tell me what he thought would win the Derby, or just point out some impending plot or other. Of course, the next day he'd often send somebody round to back a horse with us without me realising he was working for Barney. I suppose he just couldn't help being devious. He changed a lot after his son died, and that accident was a terrible thing. But the racecourse would have been a much duller place without him."

The Saturday before Cheltenham, Barney had won the Imperial Cup at Sandown with his own horse, Magic Combination, but had then refused to attend the trophy presentation afterwards. The race had been sponsored by the respected independent bookmaking firm Sunderlands, and Barney was indignant that the Sunderlands founder Pat Densham – a rear gunner on Sunderland flying boats in WW2, hence the company's name – had declined to lay him a bet on Magic Combination at his preferred price. Even so, Magic Combination was now lining up for the even more competitive Coral Cup with the prospect of landing the £50,000 bonus for any horse who could win both races.

As Barney negotiated with Victor in the thick of the rails melee, he launched into a long and not entirely coherent re-run of the Sandown dispute. "If it had been you," he said, "it would never have happened. I would have accepted the prize. But I'm not shaking hands with that monk." The latter comment apparently a slighting reference to Pat Densham's bald head and mildly clerical appearance. Victor did his best to nod and listen politely while simultaneously trying to deal with a throng of other punters desperate to get on. Eventually, Barney settled on odds of 8-1 and a bet of £56,000 to £7,000, but Magic Combination was never sighted, finishing no closer than 15th of the 26 runners, the prize going to the 33-1 outsider What's Up Boys.

The roller coaster continued in the fourth race, the RSA Chase won by the 9-2 shot Lord Noelie, ridden by Jim Culloty. The firm paid out £61,000 on the winner but still made a profit of £94,000 thanks to the defeat of the John and Sue Magnier-owned favourite Native Upmanship. Then in the seventh and last race of the day, the Festival Bumper, some of Victor's English clients piled into Nicky Henderson's runner, Inca, who was backed into 2-1 favourite. But to the bookmaker's intense relief, Inca finished second, beaten by Joe Cullen from the Willie Mullins stable who was returned at 14-1. "In the end, we did £82,000 on the day," recalled Bill Tye, but if Inca had won, it would have been much worse.

Chapter Three

Some You Lose

A t the end of each afternoon, VC and the rails team returned to the pavilion where they were looked on with a certain amount of awe and respect. They were the ones who had tasted combat, smelled the cordite and the gun smoke, and they were still standing. The firm's successful punters were toasting their good fortune too. The losers consoling themselves with a large Scotch and pleading discretely and sometimes not so discretely with Butch to advance them just a little more credit. 'What do you mean I've exceeded my limit? What's ten grand? Victor's known me for years. I always settle up in the end. I've told you there's this dog running in the sixth at Crayford tonight. It can't lose. It's a f******g bank job. What do you mean, forget it? That's what Victor says? You must be f****** kidding me. You're not? You can't be serious. You CAN NOT be serious....'

Other less abusive faces were busily availing themselves of the free hospitality. Owners, trainers, punters and journalists, with glasses of champagne in one hand and a selection of the caterers' teatime cakes, scones and egg and cress sandwiches in the other. Some of them put away slices of coffee sponge as if they couldn't be sure of eating again that week.

After the first traffic rush had cleared, it was time for the party to move on as Everton, who had been standing guard at the entrance to the tent, chauffeured Victor, Butch and Charlie Maskey back to the Dormy House for hot baths, showers, clean shirts and more drinks in the softly lit bar, followed by dinner at a special table in a secluded corner of the restaurant. Eight or more guests are invited to join the party each night. Enjoying Puligny-Montrachet with their monkfish and crab and then a Pomerol or Gevrey Chambertin of a particularly good year with the venison fillet and the duck.

But there was no dinner in the restaurant for Bill Tye, who had to have his upstairs in his room while he continued working. The clerk's job included making a tally of every account punter's position at the end of each day and relaying the details to head office the next morning so that limits would be known and cheques for winnings or statements requesting payment sent out on time at the end of the week. The more bets there had been, the longer it took, making Cheltenham and Royal Ascot easily the longest weeks of Bill's year.

Meanwhile, downstairs, they had just reached the coffee and brandy stage when Victor was approached by an attractive and smartly dressed woman, perhaps in her late fifties or early sixties. She had a husband in tow but he clearly knew his place and was lagging a few feet behind her. But when he was sure his wife couldn't see he waved at Victor from behind his wife's back. If she had her way, it seemed as if it might be something of a farewell salute. "I just want you to know, Victor, that he won't be playing any more," she said firmly. The husband grinned stupidly and mimed slitting his throat. "From now on, all the money is going into bricks and mortar. So that's an end to it." The husband looked tempted to indicate in sign language that it might not be the end of it and that, with any luck, he'd be betting again in a few months' time. But then he thought better of it.

Victor, who had got up from his chair, expressed his regret with a charming and self-deprecating shrug. Sums of money were not mentioned, not there, not then, protocol forbidding it, but the impression gained by the other guests was that the husband had not exactly been emptying Victor's pockets. More a case of the other way around.

Victor gallantly offered to buy them both a drink but the wife declined on both their behalves. The husband looked disappointed but then, with a final covert thumbs up sign to VC, obediently followed his wife upstairs to their room and a non-racing, non-gambling future. Or perhaps not.

Back in the bar, some of the guests had got the cards out and a poker game was starting. The dealer used to be a Gloucestershire farmer called Harold Hayden whose bucolic accent and manner concealed an accomplished hustler who regularly took money off visiting Festival racegoers. Tempted to try and play up their winnings or recover whatever losses they'd incurred on the racecourse earlier that day, the smart boys from London usually ended up paying the farmer instead. "If you want to find a c… in the country," he said to Victor one year (meaning a loser who can easily be fleeced), "you've got to bring him with you."

Thursday, the climactic day of the meeting, began with the Elite Racing Club Triumph Hurdle, which in the era of three-day Festivals used to have up to 30 runners and be one of the biggest betting races of the week. The crowd would be swelled with thousands of once or twice a year racegoers ranging from pub outings to expensively dressed City wives and their velvet-collar coated husbands enjoying the hospitality of Christie's or the Turf Club. Excited just to be there on Gold Cup day, and determined to enjoy themselves, they would kick off with a bigger bet than usual on the opening race. But Victor's biggest liability on the 2000 Triumph was not the frivolous wager of an occasional punter, but another carefully aimed arrow from a well-informed Irish client. Ringing up VC on his phone from his box, he asked for a thick each way bet at 10-1 on Christy Roche's runner, Young American. But this time the Irishman's luck was out as the former Aidan O'Brien trained gelding finished unplaced, victory going to the 7-1 favourite Snow Drop, owned by the Monaco-based commodity broker John Martin and trained in Chantilly by the debonair Francois Doumen. Ridden with the utmost confidence by the trainer's son Thierry, the French filly outran her 27 rivals, coming through to take it up at the final flight and staying on up the hill to win by two lengths. Victor, who was not blind to Snow Drop's chances, finished with a £16,000 profit on the race.

In April 1999, Victor and John Martin were part of a syndicate of four who won over a million pounds on Martin's globetrotting five-year-old Jim And Tonic in the Queen Elizabeth II Cup in Hong Kong. The chestnut gelding, trained like Snow Drop by Francois Doumen, was returned at 73-20 on course and won easily by three and a quarter lengths. The quartet's money had gone on at even bigger odds with the local illegal bookies.

Back at Cheltenham, a victory for the favourite in the first race on Gold Cup day was popular all round, not least with the trainer himself. Monsieur Doumen was never short of self-regard and his big hair and suave Gallic good looks charmed female racegoers of a certain age and county background. "Oh, Francois. You are brilliant," they cooed, thoughts of dogs and hunters swept aside as he sauntered along a corridor past the open doors of their private boxes. "Mais oui. Naturel-lement," he seemed to be saying. But sometimes his self-importance tripped him up.

Victor jokingly referred to Doumen as 'Captain Pompous', and there was a story along the rails about the day the Frenchman went to the Punchestown Festival where he was to be a guest in JP McManus's box. As he approached the entrance to the restricted area on the top floor of the stand, an attendant asked to see his badge.

"I am Francois Doumen," he said haughtily.

"That's grand, sir," said the attendant. "But could I just see your badge?"

"I am Francois Doumen," replied the trainer. "I come every year."

"Well then in that case, sir, you'll know that you need to have a badge to enter this area," continued the attendant.

"I'm Francois Doumen," shouted the Frenchman again.

At which point a couple of security men were about to jump on him, secure him in a half Nelson and escort him from the premises. Fortu-nately, the row had been overheard by guests of the bookmaker Justin Carthy, whose box was next door. They came out and smoothed things over and the decidedly unsmiling Francois was allowed to proceed into JP's hallowed company.

In the second race at Cheltenham, the three-mile Stayers' Hurdle, the market was headed by the English mare Lady Rebecca, who was sent off 5-2 favourite, and the hugely popular Irish challenger Limestone Lad, owned, bred and trained by the Kilkenny-based farmer James Bowe. VC took them both on, laying one bet of £70,000 to £20,000 about Limestone Lad who made a valiant attempt to make all the running but was caught close home by Madeleine Lloyd-Webber's horse Bacchanal. There was scarcely a single bet on the winner and, with Irish money going astray for the second race running, the result was a 'skinner' for the firm.

By the time the trophies were being presented for the Stayers', the runners in the 2000 Tote Cheltenham Gold Cup were entering the parade ring and the Blue Riband and centrepiece of another Festival was only 15 minutes away. The horse the public wanted to back was the 1999 winner and 9-4 favourite See More Business, who had won a second King George VI Chase at Kempton over Christmas. Despite reports of confidence running high in the champion's camp, VC laid a couple of £90,000 to £40,000 bets, one of them to an entrepreneur and regular client who had won over half a million off Victor at the 1994 Festival. He also laid bets of £22,500 to £10,000 as the odds contracted. Victor reasoned that there hadn't been any back-to-back Gold Cup winners since L'Escargot nearly 30 years before and that, at the age of 10, See More Business's powers may have been on the wane.

The joint-second favourites at 9-2 were Noel Furlong's fancy Florida Pearl and Richard Johnson's mount Looks Like Trouble, who had won as a novice at Cheltenham the year before. The wild card was the brilliant six-year-old Gloria Victis, trained by Martin Pipe and ridden by Tony McCoy and bidding to be the youngest Gold Cup winner since Captain Christy in 1974.

Running down the hill for the last time, five were still in contention and the race was anyone's. But as they jumped the third last fence, See More Business looked beaten, and, rounding the home turn, Gloria

Victis was narrowly ahead with Florida Pearl challenging and Looks Like Trouble close up. But then Gloria Victis fell heavily, and as it turned out, fatally, at the second last fence and it was the eight-year-old Looks Like Trouble who jumped ahead at the last and ran on strongly up the hill to land the prize by five lengths with Florida Pearl second and the 20-1 outsider Strong Promise in third place. See More Business finished fourth. Dodging the bullets fired by Noel Furlong and the favourite backers, the firm ended up £68,000 ahead, but the post-race atmosphere was subdued, with delight at Dickie Johnson's great victory tinged with sadness – and an unpleasant degree of bitterness in some quarters – at the fate of the novice Gloria Victis.

The Christie's Foxhunter Chase for amateur riders which followed the Gold Cup was tea-time for most punters. VC won just under £10,000 on the race but then it was the infinitely more dangerous Cheltenham Grand Annual Chase, a two-mile handicap with a reputation as a fierce betting heat. At the same stage the previous year, Bill Tye had recorded one of the biggest bets he'd ever written in the field ledger. A £900,000 to £200,000 on Space Trucker, trained on the Curragh by Jessica Harrington and ridden by Shay Barry. The punter was Noel Furlong and he was right on the money, just as he had been when Destriero won at the Festival in 1991, Space Trucker becoming Jessie Harrington's first-ever Cheltenham winner and triumphing by a length and a half. Fortunately for Victor, there were no Furlong-scale wagers this time around, though he did lay another big Irish punter a bet on the winner Samakaan, the 9-2 favourite ridden by Norman Williamson, and his total losses on the race were over £60,000.

The roller-coaster ride wasn't finished yet. In the sixth race, the old Cathcart Chase, a repeat victory for Mick Fitzgerald's mount, the 11-2 chance Stormyfairweather, was enough to see Fitzgerald claim the meeting's top jockey award. And with £60,000 worth of losing bets on the favourite Castle Sweep, it yielded the Chandler firm a surprising £54,000 profit.

And so it all came down to the last race of the day and the final race of the 2000 Cheltenham Festival meeting. The Vincent O'Brien

County Hurdle, another fiendishly tough two-mile handicap with 21 runners, plenty of whom had the look of plots and conspiracies by their connections. Christy Roche had two representatives this time and who was to say that they might not be working in concert to ambush the layers? The question was, which one of them was the number one gun? Was it the JP McManus-owned Afarad? Or was it Spokesman, running in the colours of Theresa McCoubrey, wife of the Belfast bookmaker Robert McCoubrey, one of JP's oldest gambling associates and friends. McManus had a second string too – Master Tern – trained not in Tipperary, but up in Cumbria by one of Ireland's favourite sons and greatest Cheltenham heroes, Jonjo O'Neill.

Victor had learned to be wary of Jonjo's Cheltenham runners, especially when the ex-jockey, eyes twinkling, insisted that they were no hopers really and were only running to please the owner and, as far as Jonjo could remember, were lucky to still be in possession of four legs and a tail. The more the trainer dismissed them, the more carefully VC weighed up their chances. But in the minutes leading up to the 'Getting Out Stakes', as the final race was traditionally known, he decided to keep Christy Roche's Spokesman on side and lay the other two. But then as the horses were milling around at the start, punters still queuing up frantically to have one last bet, a clear favourite began to emerge. Master Tern. Already laid by Victor at 8-1 and 17-2, his odds tumbled on the boards from 7-1 to 6-1 to 5-1 to 9-2. The plot suddenly unfolded. The coup revealed.

The race was run in fading light. Victor, still watching from the rails, was just lighting up a cigar – his usual celebratory smoke at the Festival's end – when he saw JP McManus's second colours – the green and gold with the blue cap – coming through to hit the front at the final flight. It was Master Tern. "Oh, no," he muttered. "Here he goes." The gamble came under pressure running up the hill but held on to win the race by a neck. Danegold, trained by the ex-Southampton and England footballer Mick Channon, was second and Spokesman finished third. "We've done our money," said Bill Tye as they went past the post.

But there was no shouting or swearing from VC. He just shrugged and smiled, though he did throw his cigar away not even half finished and hunted in his pocket for another Camel or Marlborough Red. "He was always an unbelievably good loser," says Bill. "If it hurt, he didn't show it," agrees Alan Mills. "The only way you'd know he'd had a particularly bad result would be from the number of extra cigarettes he lit up."

Bill Chandler had a catchphrase when the results went against him. "Turn it over," he'd say to his clerk, meaning the losing page in his big bookmaker's ledger. "Just turn over another page." His grandson, it seems, was similarly philosophical. At Royal Ascot in the summer of 1999, the firm had finished the week a million in front and Victor had handed out £5,000 cash bonuses to every man on the team. This time, "after visiting all kinds of places," as VC put it, the pendulum had swung the other way, and after taking care of the wages and the hotel bill and other expenses, and despite seeing hundreds of thousands of pounds worth of bets pass through the book, they had ended up with a profit on the meeting of less than £50,000. Bacon and eggs, if not an inevitable supper item, was at least an option. Though there would be no need to sell the Mercedes just yet.

As Everton steered his passengers away, the gambling foot soldiers trooping past them towards the buses, trains, hotels and bars, Victor was leaving the setting he loved best for another year and would not be racing at all in England, even as a spectator, until Ascot came around again in June. In the weeks following the National Hunt Festival, most journeymen bookies and punters would be chasing small-time profits and losses around the routine branch line of racetracks from Plumpton to Ludlow and Hereford to Bangor-On-Dee, the bigger rails layers joining them for Newbury and the start of the turf flat racing season at Doncaster and then for the Grand National meeting at Aintree. Once upon a time, that would have been Victor's regular beat too, whereas, incongruously, he was now swapping the sweet cigar-flecked air of a British racecourse for life behind a desk in a third-floor office thousands of miles away in the Mediterranean sun.

SOME YOU LOSE

Almost everybody who knows Victor well, believes he was never really comfortable in his executive exile, at least not once the excitement and satisfaction of pulling off the offshore move had passed. But if there were days when he felt trapped in the world of meetings, memorandums and IT conferences, and needed to be reminded where he came from and how he'd got there, he had inspiration close to hand. On the walls of his Gibraltar office, there were three photographs. One of them was a black and white photo of his grandfather, taken at a racecourse in the 1930s. Long coat, trilby hat, binoculars. The one behind Victor's chair was a black and white picture of his father at the races in the early 1960s. Long coat, trilby hat and binoculars. On the other wall was a colour picture of Young Victor at a racecourse in the 1990s. Dark glasses, jacket, tie, binoculars. No hat – you'd almost never see VC wearing a trilby – but, like the other two, a richly atmospheric image.

The Chandler story is a great family story. Fathers and sons. Grandfathers and grandsons. A generational tale of ambition and enterprise, rebellion and conflict. And a chronicle that, for all its ultra-modern flourishes, has its origins deep in the social and sporting history of Britain.

Chapter Four

The Old Man

William George Chandler, known to his friends as Bill and to his family as the Old Man or The Guvnor, lay dying in an upstairs room of his daughter-in-law's house in Theydon Bois on the north-eastern edges of London.

It was January 1946, the first shivering, fuel-starved winter after the war, and Bill Chandler was 10 years older than the century. A lifelong 60-a-day man, who always had a cigarette in his hand even though he only took two or three puffs, The Guvnor had cancer of the lung and bowel. In his prime, he had been a muscular 14 stone, strong and virile with a firm jaw and a keen eye. In his tailor-made suits and coats, and his brown trilby hats, he'd combined the aura of a captain of industry with the lingering menace of the actor Robert Newton, whose most famous roles were Long John Silver and Bill Sikes.

On Britain's racecourses, where even in an age of legendary book-makers he played for the highest stakes, they called him Leo The Lion. But now, at the end of his life, illness had reduced him to a pitiful skeleton and all those hats, coats and row upon row of suits, shirts and shoes lay idle and gathering dust. But with characteristic stubbornness, Bill Chandler was determined to end his days as he had lived them. He was a strict teetotaller who hadn't touched alcohol since he was a boy, but there was no way he was going to give up tobacco, even at this parlous stage in his existence, and he sat propped up on his pillows with a lighted cigarette in his hand, even as his body was wilting and fading from the effects of a lifetime's addiction.

Bill's daughter-in-law, Frances, had a 15-year-old younger brother called Barney who was later killed in an accident on an aircraft carrier in South Africa. The teenager often came and sat with the Old Man and kept him company, finishing as many of the half smoked cigarettes as he could. The family also resorted to placing bowls of water around the bed in an effort to catch the ash and the falling butts when he nodded off. The local GP, Dr Mackenzie, visited Bill on an almost daily basis and gave him liberal injections of morphine. Mackenzie was a betting man too, and sometimes he and Barney would sit up in the room and play cards, poker or gin rummy, with the patient.

Frances Chandler, or Frannie as she was known in the family, did most of the nursing, looking after Bill devotedly, even though she was heavily pregnant at the time with what would be her first child. Bill Chandler had fathered seven sons and one girl, and Frannie was married to Charles, the third of Bill's boys and the one who would take over the management of Walthamstow Stadium. A native East Ender, whose grandmother ran a wet fish business and literally laundered £5 notes, Frances Morill was born in 1919 and died a month short of her 96th birthday. She had two younger sisters, Betty and Maud, who would also go on to marry Chandler boys – Betty wedding Victor senior in 1948, and Maud or 'Mickey' marrying Percy in 1951.

Ash blonde and husky-voiced, Frances was a forceful character with no fear of Bill, who liked her all the more because of it. He reproached her for continually running up and down stairs to look after a sick old man, but he revelled in her company, and in between the bouts of drug-induced stupor, he talked to her about his life and times, frequently returning to a story about gold, which Frances remembered made him shake with laughter.

The frail figure in the bed was a stark contrast to the impression Bill made when Frances first met him before she and her husband were married. "When I first went out with Charles, I was only about 17 and, at the time, the Chandlers lived in this lovely big house up on Green Lanes in Harringay. Long gone now, of course. It was pulled down after the war. But back then, all the boys had to be there for lunch on Sundays, and I remember the first time Charles and I went there together. They had three maids who were dressed in black and white uniforms, like the Nippies at Lyons Corner House, and a chef who had cooked for Cecil B DeMille. Bill used to stand at the head of the table carving the joint. The young ones were all put right down at the end. I remember him calling out to me 'Hoy. You down there. Charlie's girl. How do you like your beef?'

The Old Man had great taste in food as well as clothes, and on Sunday mornings, black cabs used to come out to Green Lanes from the West End bringing things like baskets of fresh strawberries, peaches and asparagus. He didn't really show affection to his sons the way a modern father would. But then his wife had died when she was still very young – Victor's father wasn't even two years old at the time – and I don't think he was ever quite the same afterwards. He didn't really know what to do with all these children, which is why he sent the youngest of them off to boarding school and got on with running his business.

But they all respected him. He was as strong as a lion and he had this poker-faced smile. A bit like Young Victor, you'd never really know if he was winning or losing. One year, in the war, he drew the eventual winner in the Derby Sweep at the Victoria Sporting Club. Everyone was congratulating him after the race and it wasn't until a few days later that we found out he'd laid the same horse, Ocean Swell, to lose £120,000."

The take-out from the Ocean Swell bet would be more like £3million today. But then four and five-figure wagers were nothing to Bill Chandler, who was not only a fearless punter, but also a skilful card player who often played poker, Chemin de Fer and the old Western saloon game Faro until the early hours. "Victor's grandfather was a late-night clubs and gambling man," concurred Charlie Maskey. "He was also a hugely successful businessman." But unlike the rise of VC,

46

there was no family model or inspiration for Bill to work from. With minimal formal education, he made his way by virtue of his own prodigious energy, allied to a native intelligence that was quicker than most to spot the potential for a commercial opening.

William George Chandler was born in Shoreditch in 1890. His father, also William George, was 22 years old at the time, the same age as Bill's mother, Charlotte. Bill, who was the first born, had four sisters and a younger brother Henry who died of pneumonia aged 11 in 1908. William senior was a small-time street bookmaker who laid the odds behind Lord's Cricket Ground whenever play was under way. According to the memoirs of the rakish gambler and racehorse owner Robert Standish Sievier, cricket betting in the 19th century was big business. There were more bookies at Lords and the Oval than Royal Ascot, and they used to bet on every ball.

St John's Wood may have been William's place of work but the Chandler family home was in the less salubrious district of Hoxton, which in the late 19th and early 20th century was one of the toughest and most deprived areas of the capital. Census takers were scared to set foot there for fear of being robbed or attacked, and in Charles Booth's 1898 Poverty Map of London, the social reformer described Nile Street as 'a den of thieves and prostitutes.'

A hundred years later, Hoxton and Shoreditch had metamorphosed into an almost impossibly fashionable manor. Style file frontier towns where the first settlers, in the shape of conceptual art galleries and determinedly cool clubs and bars, arrived towards the end of the 20th century, to be followed by City money, rising property prices and wagon trains full of hipsters with more varieties of craft beer and artisan coffee, more waistcoats and beards and Peaky Blinders-style flat caps than in any other corner of London.

The prosperity is partly superficial. Hard times and low incomes still unite plenty of Hoxton's residents in the old blocks of post-war council flats dotted around between Pitfield Street and the City Road. But once notoriously rough quarters like the Nile – as the area around Nile Street was known – have been transformed out of all recognition. The tall, dark, 19th century buildings turned into super cool modern offices – all open plan with leather sofas, table football and exercise bikes. On the corner of Shepherdess Walk and Nile Street is an old six-storey block that was once the headquarters of the evocatively named Cairo Studios. Nowadays, it's the home of the Pulse Media and Content Marketing Agency, though they still display an original Cairo Studios poster on their front door showing a Valentino-style horseman against a backdrop of towers and minarets amid the desert sands. Further up the Nile, where the narrow street meets East Road, there are equally smart studios and loft spaces – ideal for upwardly creative millennials, provided their fees and commissions are soaring in proportion to the rents – and exhilarating views across the rooftops towards Liverpool Street and the City.

To many of the elderly men and women who remember Hoxton before WW2, the idea that anyone would pay serious money to live and work there seems totally absurd. In the 1920s and '30s, it was a place of poverty, rickets and rank bad housing. There were overcrowded tenements and narrow interconnecting thoroughfares with Dickensian names like Micawber Street and Peerless Street. "I can assure you it wasn't pleasant," testified Bobby Edwards, who grew up in the Nile and worked for Victor for over 30 years. "You had eight or 10 people living in two rooms with no running water. Gas lamps. Two toilets on the staircase that never worked and children walking around with no shoes on. I was glad when Hitler came and bombed it, and everybody else felt the same. As soon as you could afford to get out, you moved to Bethnal Green, and as soon as you could get out of there, you moved to Chingford or the Essex suburbs. Yet there are some houses there today that we wouldn't have paid two shillings for that have changed hands now for hundreds of thousands of pounds."

Gentrification may have had an unimaginable effect on the local property market, but long before the hipsters arrived, slum clearance and soulless post-war development had already destroyed the sense of community that Edwards and other former residents remember as the great redeeming feature of Hoxton life and hard times. The area between Nile Street and Hoxton Market was the beating heart of that community and it bustled like a slice of New York's Lower East Side. There were hawkers and costermongers, cabinet makers, printers, piano shops, flower sellers and itinerant hop pickers who went down to Kent each summer. There were cockles, whelks and mussels from the Thames Estuary, pie and mash shops and fish and chips. There was Bert Mintz Gents Clothier, Clarks' Scrap Metal Dealer and 'Daddy Burt's' Mission serving free meals to deprived children. Big Jim Spinks and his crew held court in the Admiral Keppel pub, and in 1937 there was a Nile street party for the coronation of King George VI.

The citizens of the Nile were not just native-born Cockneys. Some were Irish, some were Scotsmen who'd come south on the coal barges that came up the Grand Union Canal, and many were refugees and immigrants from as far away as Russia, Poland and Bessarabia. Some of them were skilled artisans and craftsmen. Some were market traders. One or two of them owned a horse and cart, but very few of them owned a motor car or a fridge. A lot of the men went through periods of unemployment. Some were street bookmakers and bookies runners. Some lent money. Some of them were prizefighters and some were villains. The Hoxton Mob, which Jimmy Spinks was part of, was one of London's most celebrated gangs, just like the fictitious Tommy Shelby's mob in Peaky Blinders, and forever in a state of uneasy alliance or competition with the Italians from Clerkenwell and Saffron Hill, and the Elephant Boys south of the river.

Gang membership involved moments of violence and high drama, but it also brought material rewards that were out of reach by honest means, and for some men it was the only option. Around the corner from the junction of Nile Street and East Road, there used to be a café called Jack's, which Bobby Edwards remembered being like a greasy spoon equivalent of the borough of Queens diner in Goodfellas, where Robert De Niro, Joe Pesci and Ray Liotta meet to talk business over breakfast. "Every morning you'd see all the characters sitting in there waiting to go to work. All the thieves and the rogues too. But then in the early days, and especially in the Depression, men were desperate to take home a wage. Bookmaking and racing was their best way to make money. And when you couldn't get any work, you went and tapped Bill Chandler for a job. He employed everyone from the Nile."

The Old Man was brought up there, just like Bobby Edwards, and when he was first married in 1908, he lived in Crondall Street on the Hoxton Market side of the East Road. Fifteen years later, he'd become a figure of prosperity and influence – 'the young Croesus of Hoxton' as a local paper described him – and was able to move his wife and family to that big Edwardian house on Green Lanes where Frances first met him in the 1930s. But Bill Chandler never forgot the Nile or the people who lived there. He looked after them when he could, and employed them as bookies runners or as workmen on his pitches at the racetracks and greyhound stadiums like Walthamstow and White City, and, on occasion, he called on them to make use of their strength and special skills to protect his enterprises.

If a working-class man with Bill's brain had been born and bred somewhere like New York or Chicago in the early 20th century, it's easy to imagine him ending up in industry and finance while maybe selling Prohibition whisky on the side. But the stifling nature of the British class system, and lack of formal opportunities for advancement, put the Stock Exchange and the City of London out of reach. There were no such barriers though to becoming a bookmaker, and for Bill it was a natural fit. He'd started collecting betting slips for his father at the age of 12, and in 1908, aged 18, he'd bet £1,000 on the turn of a card. So, inspired by his success and the evidence on all sides of a population enthusiastically in love with a flutter, Bill Chandler decided to lay the odds.

In early Victorian London, there were hundreds of off-course betting shops or 'listers', so-named for their lists of prices on horse racing, coursing and prize fights. They were closed down in 1853 on the order of the government, supposedly to protect innocent punters from dishonest bookies seeking to make off with their winnings, but really to placate anti-gambling sentiment and control the behaviour of the lower orders.

All that prohibition actually achieved was to create a vast, illicit off-course industry, which continued until the shops were legalised again in 1961. Throughout that period, betting on a racecourse was perfectly legal, and wealthy punters were free to have credit accounts with established firms and relay their wagers by telephone or telegram. But the thousands of working-class gamblers who also enjoyed a bet – but hadn't got the wherewithal to obtain credit or the time or the money to go racing – relied on the services of the illegals. Some of the book-makers operated from street corners, pubs, factory gates, barber shops and billiard halls. One of the most popular pitches in Shoreditch and Hoxton was the Eagle Tavern on Shepherdess Walk, formerly the site of the Olympia Theatre and Music Hall where Marie Lloyd, Gus Ellen and Sir Charles Hawtrey (no relation to the bespectacled Carry On star), once topped the bill.

In some cases, the illegal bookies and the legitimate credit and race-course firms were one and the same, and the bookmakers employed teams of runners who patrolled allotted patches of the towns and cities. The runner's job was to collect the written lines or bets and deposit them along with the stake money at the bookie's appointed office or HQ before racing began.

Alan Mills, who like Bobby Edwards, worked for both Young Victor and Victor senior before him, was a bookie's runner in South London in the 1950s. "I started out when I was 12 years of age," he recalls. "I was with Gibbs and Adams in Battersea, and to begin with I worked in the evenings, six days a week, collecting bets on the dogs. You carried these special clock bags, which had a kind of clock or machine inside them that timed the bets to guarantee they'd been placed before the off."

The prevailing view of governments and assorted moral guardians may have been that the shiftless workers shouldn't be encouraged to gamble, but in many areas, the local police – who were often on a retainer from the bookmakers – were happy to look the other way. For a consideration, they'd even provide advanced warning of the obliga-tory once-a-year raid, which was conducted purely for appearances sake. A stooge would be put up to be caught taking bets when the law arrived, and then fined by a local magistrate the next day; then everything would go back to normal, with the police and the bookies fraternising together as usual.

But street bookmakers who couldn't afford to keep the police happy found the going tough, and in cities like Birmingham, Manchester and Sheffield, as well as London, it was equally important to be able to deal with the local villains who might demand a share of a bookie's take in return for permitting them to operate on their territory.

Bill Chandler left school at 13 and worked briefly in a second-hand furniture shop, but he was already a bookie's runner, and when his father died in 1912, he took over his pitches. The 22-year-old, by now a married man and father, was quick to see that instead of putting all his efforts into collecting money for somebody else, it would be a lot more profitable to set up in business on his own. Branching out and employing his own runners and clock men required nerve, muscle and cunning, but by the early 1920s – having somehow obtained an exemption from wartime service on the grounds that his was a reserved occupation – Bill was a wealthy and established figure.

Ben Miller – better known as Benno – was Frances and Betty Chandler's cousin. A commission agent, who used to put money on for well-to-do gamblers who didn't want or didn't know how to deal with a bookmaker in person, Benno knew both Victor senior and Bill Chandler well. "To be a street bookmaker back then you needed to have eyes in the back of your head," he recalled before his death in 2014. "There weren't many A Levels among them, I can assure you. There was an element of Don Corleone about the Old Man, but what can I say? In those days, the situation leant itself to that. What's the line at the beginning of The Godfather? 'At the root of every fortune, there's a crime?'"

In the post-1918 world, with record attendances at racetracks and huge 'plungers' among the gambling fraternity, ambitious men like Bill Chandler could make a fortune if they were bold enough. Running his own East End street business, and buying up other businesses and incorporating them into his set-up, gave him the capital to start betting on the racecourse, and he soon acquired rails pitches at all the top tracks in the south along with other profitable places like Aintree, Doncaster and Lincoln. He already had a command of odds and percentages, but now he needed detailed knowledge of the Turf and its practitioners too.

"To begin with, he always bet primarily on the horses," said Benno, "and he loved taking on the money." The Cheltenham Festival was still in its infancy in the 1920s, and the biggest betting race of the year was the Grand National, closely followed by the Derby and the big flat racing handicaps like the Lincoln in March, and the Cesarewitch and Cambridgeshire – the so-called Autumn Double – at Newmarket in October. Going to the races was an established national pastime, like watching football and cricket, and betting was thriving, but then, in the mid-1920s, Bill Chandler diversified, and at exactly the right moment, as he spotted the commercial potential of the hottest new sporting craze.

In the 19th and early 20th centuries, the most popular betting medium – other than horse racing – was the now demonised sport of hare coursing, and in February each year, thousands of punters made their way to Altcar in Lancashire to watch and gamble on the Waterloo Cup. The coursing classic was inaugurated in 1836 by William Lynn, the proprietor of the Waterloo Hotel in Liverpool, and public interest was so great that Lynn decided to organise a horse race in the same week. The result was the Grand Liverpool Steeplechase, or the Grand National as it became known, and the first running of the National in 1839 actually took place on what should have been the last day of the Waterloo Cup, giving the greyhounds an extra 24 hours to recover before the final. Champion coursing dogs were accorded celebrity status, much like the triple Grand National winner Red Rum in the 1970s, none more acclaimed than the Irish dog Master McGrath, a triple winner of the Waterloo Cup between 1868 and 1871 who was presented to Queen Victoria at Windsor Castle. Coursing enthusiasts came from both town and country and were as likely to be gypsy travellers as miners, farmers and peers of the realm. Most of them stayed up on Merseyside for the week and the gambling went on night and day. The big bookmakers like Bill Chandler went up too, and over the three days of the meeting they could expect to field bets on a similar scale to Cheltenham in Young Victor's day.

In the USA, an imaginative impresario launched enclosed greyhound racing in a stadium, with the dogs chasing a mechanical hare. The new phenomenon made its debut in Britain in 1926 and was taken up by Brigadier-General Alfred Critchley, a Canadian ex-army officer who had served in both the cavalry and the Royal Flying Corps in WW1. Critchley, who was related by marriage to the press magnate Sir Max Aitken, later Lord Beaverbrook, formed a company called the Greyhound Racing Association, and on July 24th, 1926, the consortium staged the UK's first-ever greyhound race meeting with an electric hare at Belle Vue in Manchester. The following year, the GRA brought dog racing to London, moving into the renovated stadium at White City that had originally been built for the 1908 Olympics. Over 40,000 spectators flocked to the track for its opening run of fixtures, and Bill Chandler, who had acquired pitches there, realised that dog racing could be a winning bet.

More stadiums were opening up and down the country, their owners able to buy and develop land in those days before restrictive planning laws with a rapidity more akin to the Wild West than conservative Britain. The new London tracks included Harringay, Clapton and West Ham, and The Guvnor didn't just take bookmaking pitches, he bought shares. Alfred Critchley had described the dogs as "the poor man's racecourse" but Bill Chandler appreciated that easy-to-access betting and racing in the evenings after work – the seductive combination of gambling, sociability and spectacle beneath the floodlights – could also bring in thousands of new punters who might one day be prosperous ones and who should be looked after accordingly. So, as he explained to Frances in 1946, "I decided I'd build my own track."

Bill took his money out of Harringay and Hackney Wick, and for £23,000, bought a few acres of waste land in Walthamstow in North

East London, up where Walthamstow Avenue converged on the Chingford Road. The site was called The Billet and was named after the Crooked Billet pub and the adjacent 'flapping' or unlicensed dog track next door. It was little more than a field and some old sheds when Bill first took possession, but it was ideal for his purposes, and not just because men were already racing greyhounds there informally. The location was on the edge of a large and heavily populated urban area and had good transport links to Central London thanks to the recently extended Piccadilly Line.

Right from the outset, The Guvnor saw a future for the sport offering entertainment to all classes and sizes of wallet, including food and drink served in comfortable surroundings. "Some people have this idea that everyone at the dogs always wore flat caps and mufflers," said Frances. "That wasn't Bill's vision at all." At Walthamstow, Chandler was determined to see his dream realised to the highest standards. "I don't like it. Pull it down and try again," he told the builder he'd contracted to erect the first three-tier stand. The second version didn't satisfy him either, so they started again. "That's the type I want for my patrons' comfort," he said when they'd finally finished. "Now build another and better stand opposite it, and lay the track."

The finished article was a thing of wonder with two tea rooms, a cocktail bar and a dance floor where top bands like Geraldo And His Orchestra, and Al Collins and the Savoy Orpheans would come out and play after racing. But the most famous feature was the beautiful Art Deco facade with its clock tower and electric Totalisator board and the name WALTHAMSTOW STADIUM lit up in red capital letters. The iconic neon image of a racing greyhound would be added in 1952.

The official opening took place on Easter Saturday, April 15th, 1933, and the pioneer aviator Amy Johnson – the first woman to fly solo from England to Australia – was the guest of honour. It was a fine, dry weekend towards the end of the Depression and the champion jockey Gordon Richards was riding the favourite in the Rosebery Stakes at Kempton Park. Avid punters had the chance to watch the horses in the afternoon and then go on to the 'Stow' that evening, setting a precedent that would be followed by many thousands more over the next 75 years.

Chandler had also had the foresight to buy all the available land surrounding the stadium and his commercial acumen ensured that it was astutely developed. Some of it was singled out for private housing, with Bill retaining a share of the profits when the properties were sold. Another plot became the site of a thriving garage that was also family owned.

The Guvnor's investments were paying off handsomely. The money accruing was used not just to further his wardrobe or bankroll his expanding bookmaking concerns, but to support and take care of his extensive tribe of children. By 1933, there were eight of them, their ages ranging from 24 to nine. But while Bill Chandler's business career may have been a diamond-studded success story, his personal life had been marked by tragedy.

Chapter Five

Seven Brothers

Living in Hoxton in the first quarter of the 20th century, you would have been odds-against to reach the age of 50, and plenty of men and women didn't even see 21. Bill Chandler was 18 when his younger brother Henry died in 1908, and four years later the boys' father died, aged 44. Bill was now responsible not only for his mother Charlotte and his three sisters, he also had a wife and children of his own.

On February 14th, 1909, in the church of St John the Baptist in Hoxton, Bill had married the 21-year-old Annie Jones, whose father Walter was another small-time street bookmaker. At the end of that year, the couple had their first child, a son they christened William George junior, after his father and grandfather, and henceforth known as Billy. Between 1911 and 1924, seven more children followed. Jackie, Charles, Albert, Percy, Ronnie, Renie – the solitary daughter – and then finally Young Victor's father, Victor Senior. To begin with, all of them lived in the house in Crondall Street on the eastern side of Pitfield Street, going in the direction of Hoxton Market and Hoxton Square.

By 2018, there were no family members still alive who remembered Annie Chandler personally. But Frances and Betty's grandmother, Polly Craze, knew her and described her to her girls when they were growing up. "My grandma said that Annie was very beautiful with dark hair and deep blue eyes," recalled Frances. "It was obvious that Bill worshipped her."

It was said in bookmaking circles that all of Bill's gambling and speculation throughout his 17-year marriage was designed primarily to give Annie the best of everything, and by the summer of 1924, his affairs had prospered to the point where he was able to move his family out of Crondall Street to their new home in Harringay. Number 313 Green Lanes had particularly appealed to him as it added up to his lucky number, 7.

Harringay today is not the quiet residential enclave it would have seemed in Bill Chandler's era. Where number 313 once stood, there are blocks of post-war flats, a care home and a day centre for the deaf. Across the other side of the road is the Woodberry Downs estate, and around the corner is The Tower, the old Metropolitan Waterworks building which has become an indoor climbing centre. But in Portland Rise, on the west side of Green Lanes, there are still a few big old pre-war and 19th century houses: four storeys, complete with attics and basements for below-stairs staff, and large back gardens shaded by trees. The houses have all long since been converted into flats, but they at least give some idea of what number 313 must have looked like in its prime.

Young Victor's Uncle Ronnie Chandler never forgot the first time he ever went to the house. "I must have been about four years old. It was a lovely sunny afternoon and I was outside in this big back garden, sitting on the lawn. There were flower beds and roses, and there was an ornamental fish pond, and I remember looking up at the house and saying, 'Oh, I wish we could live somewhere like here.'"

"You are going to live here," Ronnie was told. But sadly, the family's domestic bliss was to be short lived.

Annie Chandler was literally swept off her feet by the move. The new house came complete with a gardener, a cook and three housemaids to help her. There was a brand new kitchen too. New cutlery, china, glasses and cooking utensils. New linen, new furniture, new everything.

The Old Man described it all to Frances in his dying days in 1946, but she always wondered whether Annie was quite so enthusiastic. "She was taken out of her former home and told she had to leave everything behind and taken off to this new one where everything was to be done for her. She liked the house alright but I think she missed her old things and never really enjoyed being waited on."

Annie's good nature and reluctance to impose on others was to prove fatal. In November 1925, not quite 18 months after moving to Green Lanes, she was pregnant once again. Bill Chandler never drove. He had a chauffeur-driven Buick, the favourite car of the Prince of Wales and future King Edward VIII. Early one winter morning, the chauffeur was bringing Annie back to the house after they'd been out to do the weekend shopping. Halfway up the front steps, Annie turned round to see the driver struggling with some boxes of groceries. She reached out to take one from him and carry it indoors but, as she did so, she slipped and fell. The following day she had a miscarriage and then, with bewildering speed, developed peritonitis and died. She was 37 years old.

Bill Chandler was devastated. "There's no doubt he was totally heartbroken," said Frances. "And I don't think he ever really got over it." Annie was buried in Manor Park Cemetery near Forest Gate in North East London. Young Harry Chandler and Bill's father were close by and the Old Man would end up there too when the time came.

"After my mother died, I think my father decided he couldn't really be a businessman and a family man at the same time," said Ronnie Chandler poignantly. There were already maids and nannies at Green Lanes. Now the Old Man, aghast at the prospect of having to bring up eight children on his own, including Ronnie, aged five, and Victor senior, aged 18 months, hired a full-time housekeeper too. Miss Grover, a small bird-like woman usually dressed in black, became the Green Lanes equivalent of Mrs Danvers, the intimidating housekeeper in Daphne du Maurier's novel Rebecca. The older boys – Billy, Jackie, Charles – couldn't stand her, but the younger ones didn't dare to challenge her authority.

Bill provided ample funds for the kitchen and larder to be generously stocked with food, but, as Ronnie explained, "Miss Grover had the keys, and when Dad was away, she often wouldn't let us in." The housekeeper appeared to have rationed the boys' provisions while treating herself to small but mouthwatering repasts in the privacy of her own room, and her meanness would eventually lead to a rebellion, with The Guvnor's eldest son walking out.

Frances wasn't at all surprised that Charles and his younger brothers Percy and Victor not only enjoyed courting the Morill girls, but also spending as much time as they could in the comfortable normality of their household in Woodford Green. "He (Bill) wasn't a typical father," agreed Betty's cousin, Benno Miller. "But the brothers still relied on him heavily and, in many ways, they had very fortunate lives."

On Sundays once a month, Bill would arrange for Mr Marsden, the barber at Simpsons of Piccadilly, to come out and cut the boys' hair. One of the third-floor rooms had been given over to them as somewhere they could do as they pleased without any interference from Miss Grover, and in the centre of the room was a full-sized billiard table. Joe Mack, a professional snooker player and keen racing man, often came round at weekends to iron the green baize, staying on afterwards for lunch. The boys had a gramophone up there too, and a collection of dance records, and Ronnie's job "was to wind it up for Billy and the older ones."

The Old Man may not have been around much during the week, and he may not have shown a tender side very often, but he was still a huge presence in the boys' lives. "He used to get up early and have breakfast with us before he went off to work," remembered Ronnie. "He always wore a suit, and a shirt with a stiff collar, and he had any number of suits and coats and ties. Before he went out, he'd wink at us and tell us we could go and look in his coat pockets, and if we found a sovereign, we could keep it. Sometimes we'd find more than one, and Percy, Victor and I would keep them without telling. Then the chauffeur would be waiting with the Buick and he'd wave us goodbye and we might not see him again for several days."

By the mid-1930s, sovereigns, half crowns, ten bob notes and a lot more were sticking to Bill like women to Prince Aly Khan. It wasn't just Walthamstow, which was booming, but greyhound racing generally that was proving a reliable source of income. So powerful was Bill Chandler, and so influential his contacts, that he had 10 different book-making pitches at White City alone, ranging from prime spots in the main ring to lesser joints in the cheaper enclosures. The GRA track had instigated the Greyhound Derby and other sought-after races, but up at the 'Stow', The Guvnor had decided that "to begin with, every dog should be owned by the stadium," said Frances. "There was no prize money, just a trophy. He believed there'd be less crookedness that way." To back up his enterprise, Bill had bought the kennels near Epping Forest which supplied Walthamstow with a lot of its runners in the early days. He also bought an 800-acre farm down at Etchingham in East Sussex, where he bred greyhounds very successfully. In other respects, though, "Dad wasn't much of a farmer," recalled Ronnie, laughing. "He thought he'd keep chickens there too, and have fresh eggs, so he bought 50 of them, but when he got them home he found they were all cockerels."

The chicken story was one of the very few instances when Bill Chandler came off worse in a business transaction. In 1934, he'd opened up an SP or 'starting price' office in Soho Square, and a year later he moved to Number One Wardour Street, in the heart of the West End. Bill was on the first floor but the ground floor was a branch of Barclays Bank, and their strait-laced manager and his staff objected to sharing their premises with a bookmaker. One day they rang up Bill and told him they were getting in touch with the building's owners and that he'd have to leave. "He just listened very quietly at first and didn't say much, then he put the phone down," said Benno Miller. "But at the end of that week, the bank got a call from him. He told them he'd just bought the whole place, including their lease, and that he was throwing them out instead."

From then on, Number One – on the corner of Coventry Street, only yards away from Piccadilly Circus and Leicester Square – became Bill's centre of operations, and where Barclays had been, he opened an amusement arcade and the Honeysuckle Milk Bar, which boasted it was 'open night and day.' They're both long gone but the outer shell of the building, which survived the Blitz, remains remarkably similar today to the way it would have looked 80 years ago.

There were numerous telephone lines at Number One, up-to-the-minute communications being as important to The Guvnor as they would become to his grandson. Bill showed his foresight again by creating what became known as 'The Blower' in tandem with Harry 'Snouty' Parker, another high-stakes rails and credit bookmaker. Snouty, whose family name was Stein, was the brother of Max Parker – who went on to own Ladbrokes – and another brother, Jack, was the father of the future Ladbrokes Chairman, Cyril Stein.

To protect their on and off-course interests, Bill Chandler and the Parkers needed a form of risk management in real time, and The Blower involved installing outdoor telephones on the rails at the major racetracks like Newmarket, Aintree and Epsom. The new phone service, which other bookies had to pay to use, enabled SP offices round the country to phone or 'blow' money back to the track, giving them a chance to hedge their off-course liabilities with the on-course market.

Bill was also a leading member of the Victoria Sporting Club in Wellington Street, just off the Strand. The wealthier bookmakers and a few privileged representatives of the racing press used it as an agreeable private setting in which to meet and talk business over a smoke and a drink. The Club was also where call-overs were held, which were competing shows of the latest bookies' prices on the big ante-post betting events like the Derby, the Lincoln Handicap and the Grand National.

At the races, Bill was renowned for carrying what the Greyhound Express described as 'astronomical amounts of white money,' and whether he was at Royal Ascot, White City or standing in the middle of a field at the Waterloo Cup, he paid everyone out in cash. He had both rails and boards pitches, and employed men to bet for him while he was working. In the 1930s, one of his biggest customers was the eccentric Miss Dorothy Paget, who owned Golden Miller, the greatest steeplechaser of the pre-war era. "She used to ring him up and ask for a £500 Yankee almost every other day," said Benno Miller. "'He's the only one who'll lay all my bets,' she'd say." Dorothy Paget seemed oblivious of the fact that her runners at the smaller meetings were often being stopped at the behest of Bill's bookmaking rival William Hill. But the profits from her innumerable losing wagers, and from other slow horses and dogs, contributed towards the costs of educating Bill's sons.

There may not have been many home comforts at Green Lanes, but as far as Ronnie Chandler was concerned, they were still vastly preferable to life at boarding school. "Myself, Percy and Victor's father were all sent away, and I think Vic was only six years old." The boys went first to a prep school for Highgate, which Bill had established was one of the principal public schools in North London, and Ronnie's memories of the early years in particular were predominantly of loneliness, homesickness and fear. "One day at prep school we all had to stand up and say what our fathers did. So I asked my brother Percy, 'What exactly does Dad do?' because I didn't really understand, and he said, 'he's a bookmaker.' So when my turn came, I stood up and said, 'my father makes books,' and, of course, everybody laughed. I always remember sitting down afterwards and feeling such a fool."

Unkind laughter was the least of Ronnie's worries at the bigger school. "It was very rough," he said, "and there were terrible beatings. I remember once the headmaster giving me six of the best. They had fagging and the prefects were allowed to beat the younger boys too, and they used to take a run at you with the cane. When you were sent for, you had to wait outside the room, and you'd hear it all going on next door with boys crying out, and you'd know that it was your turn next."

Ronnie and the other Chandler boys responded, as presumably The Guvnor had hoped they would, by standing up for themselves in the classical Tom Brown's Schooldays manner. "Victor's father, who was slightly smaller than me, boxed, swam and played water polo, and I boxed all the way from five stone upwards. In the end, I was the captain of the boxing team, and Dad used to send the Buick, or the big American station wagon he'd bought, to take the team to away matches."

Ronnie's only defeat in his whole school career came in 1935 in his final fight against a boy from Westminster. He'd felt ill beforehand and was subsequently found to have a temperature of 103, though he always gallantly refused to accept that his condition contributed to his opponent's victory. "It was in the Bath Club in Dover Street. The Old Man was there, and so was King George V, and after the match the King presented me with a medal."

The boys were sometimes allowed out on Sundays, when everyone continued to gather at Green Lanes for the big family lunch, and Frances first met Bill. The Old Man's presence ensured there could be no meddling by Miss Grover, so on that day, at least, the portions were plentiful and the food was of the highest quality. But no wine or beer was served, and until they were full-grown adults, the boys were all strictly prohibited from drinking alcohol.

Shortly before he was 16, Albert Chandler, who was born in 1911, was reputed to have been 'experimenting' with spirits. The news got back to the Old Man, and the following Sunday, when everyone sat down to their lunch, Ronnie remembered that "instead of putting a plate of food in front of Albert, the maid was instructed to just serve him with a bottle of Scotch instead. Everyone saw it, and there was an awful silence. Albert looked at it and blushed. The Old Man looked at him. 'I hear that's all you'll be needing,' he said. Albert was a lot more careful with his drinking from then on. But Father was such a strict teetotaller and everybody was frightened of him at times."

Benno Miller learned to be wary of Bill too. "I took his daughter Renie out dancing a couple of times when we were teenagers and he practically wanted to have me assassinated. He never trusted any boy she went out with. I suppose it was because he was such an old reprobate himself. It was the same with Jackie Chandler, the second eldest son, when he caught him with his hand in the till at Number One Wardour Street. Bill called up a detective he knew in the Met and got him to give Jackie a grilling. But then it takes a thief to catch a thief."

Bill's suspicion of men and male suitors was balanced by occasional striking acts of generosity towards his daughter and daughters-in-law. "I remember one Christmas at Green Lanes in the 1930s," said Frances. "There was a special cracker on the tree for all of us girls, and a very special one for Renie, and when she pulled it, a diamond necklace fell out."

Christmases aside, the best time for the Chandler children to catch their father in an attentive mood was during the long summer holiday. At the beginning of July, after Highgate School broke up, Bill moved his family down from London to Bournemouth, taking a set of rooms in the Highcliff Hotel, later the conference hotel of choice for assorted politicians, from Winston Churchill to Margaret Thatcher and Tony Blair.

The holidays in Bournemouth were the happiest times of Ronnie's childhood. "We were there for up to six weeks and we all so looked forward to Dad being there with us most of the time." The Highcliff was extremely comfortable and stylish, with a pianist in the foyer and its own private lift down to the beach. "All our meals were included too," added Ronnie, no doubt mindful of the contrast with Miss Grover's housekeeping.

With Bill Chandler in benign form, the boys could all relax and enjoy themselves. They swam and played tennis and beach ball, and there were plenty of girls to meet and dances to go to. Percy and Victor senior were both good looking young men, while Ronnie was a positive Adonis and almost as good a swimmer as he was amateur boxer. He made a big impact the year he won a swimming competition organised by the Mayor of Bournemouth. "There was a boat moored out beyond the pier," he remembered, "and you had to dive in and swim back to the shore. I won first prize." His reward, in those genteel times, turned out to be not cash or tickets to a show, but an ornamental cake-stand.

In the evenings, the boys wore whites and sometimes they'd accompany their father on a post-prandial walk through the town while he puffed on a cigar. By the mid-1930s, Bill Chandler was a very wealthy man who could afford to turn down an offer of £500,000 for Walthamstow Stadium, but the Depression had barely ended and others were less fortunate. "When Dad went out in Bournemouth, he'd often pass homeless men begging," said Ronnie. "The police were told to move them on but Dad would always give them money to spend on food or to buy a coat or shoes or whatever. He used to say that not everyone was as lucky as he'd been and that if you'd been through hard times yourself, you never forgot what it was like."

The Guvnor may have forbidden his sons from drinking, but given his occupation he can hardly have been surprised that by their mid-teens all of them were compulsive punters. Ronnie and Victor senior were often taken to Walthamstow by their father and given more sovereigns and half-crowns if they cleared up any litter they saw lying around in the car park or on the terracing. Both of them would grow up to own and bet on greyhounds, with Ronnie developing a special genius at training them. But it was the eldest son, Billy, who led the way at gambling, even preceding Victor senior into the bookmaking business.

Billy was the chosen one. The boy who had been given his father's name. The most confident and charismatic. The most loved. Like many a restless teenager, he clashed repeatedly with his strong-willed father, but it was the housekeeper that drove him away. He was only 15 when his mother died, but within three years, he'd moved out of Green Lanes for good. "He wouldn't stand for Miss Grover any longer," said Ronnie. One evening, when their father was out, Billy came home later than the others and wanted to make himself some bacon and eggs, but he found that the kitchen was locked and that Miss Grover had shut herself up in her room. Raging at the niggardly housekeeper one last time, he went upstairs, packed a bag and left.

The 18-year-old had more than enough talents to get by. He was charming and well dressed. He was passionate about racing and betting and had already made numerous friends in the milieu. And he was Bill Chandler's son. "He couldn't, or wouldn't, work with his father," said Frances. "So he set up in business on his own as a racecourse bookie." He was an instant success. "Young Billy was a character," said Benno Miller. "But he was canny with it. I remember him saying to one punter, 'you know too much for me.' But same as all the boys, if he liked you, you were in."

Billy had a great social life. He danced as well as he dressed and women were drawn to him. He had an affair with the actress Merle Oberon, who starred with Laurence Olivier in the 1939 film of *Wuthering Heights*, and one of his biggest clients was the millionairess Mrs JV 'Pat' Rank, whose betting was almost on the same scale as Dorothy Paget. "She only had to look into his eyes to double her stake," said Benno.

By the end of the decade, Billy, who had both rails pitches and an off-course office, was one of his father's biggest rivals, and Bill Chandler was extremely proud of him. "They hadn't fallen out entirely," said Victor. "Billy used to bet for grandfather at White City and look after all his pitches there. He would've been the natural successor if things had turned out differently." He may have lacked Bill's experience, but Billy's youthful charm attracted a new generation of punters. He'd married by now and he and his wife Elsa became friendly with the jockey Charlie Smirke and the Epsom trainer Hughie Wallington who, according to Benno, ran with a fast crowd. In 1935, Billy and Elsa moved down to Epsom, buying the Red House, a large, late Victorian property in Ashtead, less than half a mile away from the Derby start.

Ronnie, Percy and Victor senior idolised their older brother, who was equally fond of the three youngest boys in the family. Ronnie had little interest in flat racing but he'd always wanted to see the Grand National, and in 1933, thanks to Billy, he got his wish.

The Guvnor wasn't working up at Aintree that year as he was too busy supervising the imminent opening of Walthamstow, but Billy was there. The National took place on a Friday in those days, but it was late March, the Highgate school holidays had begun, and the 13-year-old Ronnie was at home. Unbeknown to the others, he'd been assiduously saving up money, and early on the morning of the race, he slipped out of Green Lanes undetected and took a taxi to Heston aerodrome where he'd booked a seat on a special Grand National day flight up to

Speke Airport on Merseyside.

Not wishing to alarm his father unduly, Ronnie had left a note behind, saying where he was going, and when The Guvnor found it, he telephoned Billy, who was staying at the Adelphi Hotel, once Liverpool and Cunard's finest and the prime destination for ocean-bound travellers and high-rolling racegoers on their way to Aintree. The relationship between Bill Chandler and his eldest boy may have been strained but Billy would do anything for his kid brother. He went out to meet him at the airport and then drove him around for the rest of the day, taking him to the races, feeding him, spoiling him and generally showing him a high time. "He was the greatest gentleman of them all," said Ronnie.

Bill sent the Buick to pick Ronnie up on his return. He didn't criticise him for his escapade and may well have admired him for his daring. Whether the boys all realised it or not, their father was always watching out for them in the background and he never flinched from taking whatever steps he thought necessary to protect his own and their future prosperity.

Chapter Six

Peaky Blinders

Nerve, style and proficient odds-making skills were all part of a big bookmaker's armoury in the 1920s and '30s. But back when Bill Chandler was approaching his zenith, physical strength and an ability to defend yourself if necessary was every bit as important. Bill was a strong man – Bill was Leo the Lion – and Dougie Tyler, a bookmaker at Walthamstow for almost 60 years, remembered him combining "physical power with a natural air of authority. He was a proper leader of men." He needed to be.

In the Depression, street bookmakers and their runners were often tailed to their homes by men desperate for a few shillings, while bookies on the racecourse would sometimes welch or run off before the last race without settling their debts to the ring. An even greater threat, though, came from the attentions of professional villains offering their own insidious form of protection.

The most powerful criminals in London and the south of England in the 1920s and '30s were Darby Sabini's Italian Mob. Their leader, Charles 'Darby' Sabini, was born in Saffron Hill in 1888. He was the illegitimate son of Ottavio Sabini, an Italian immigrant, and an English woman called Eliza Handley. The family's relationships were complicated and Darby used a variety of aliases, but he achieved lasting fame as a Sabini. There were five brothers in total, the others being Harry

Boy, who was born in Highbury in 1900, Joseph, Fred and George. English was their first language but the gang had a distinctly Sicilian flavour, and Darby and Harry Boy were particularly close to an Italian boxer called Pasquale Papa, who fought professionally under the name of Bert Marsh.

The Sabini's manor stretched from the Clerkenwell and Gray's Inn Roads to Back Hill, Summers Street and Leather Lane, but they also had interests throughout the West End. They drank in the Central Club, the Duke of York, the Griffin and the Yorkshire Grey, and on Sundays they faithfully attended mass at St Peter's Catholic Church off Clerkenwell Green.

The brothers had a number of uniformed and plain clothes police officers on their payroll and, emboldened by police protection, they specialised in extorting money from bookmakers. Layers who didn't cooperate or were too weak to defend themselves were put out of business, whether on the streets or at the races, and their pitches given to Sabini stooges. The gangsters had various none-too-subtle ways of imposing their will. A group of them might suddenly surround a bookmaker's pitch, making it impossible for the punters to get through and bet. Then there was the Sponge, the piece of wet cloth used to wipe out the odds next to a list of runners so that the bookmakers could chalk up their prices for the next race. Unlucky layers would have to pay for this service to be performed, otherwise some uninvited individual might suddenly wipe out their odds at a crucial moment. (The notorious hard man 'Mad Frankie' Fraser started out 'on the sponge' at the Epsom spring meeting in the 1950s).

Bookmakers would be forced to pay for chalk too, even if they'd brought their own, but the most profitable racket involved the 'tissue' or sheets of runners, without which the layers couldn't make a book. Leading figures like Bill Chandler and William Hill had their own sheets printed from the information available in the Sporting Life, but the smaller racecourse firms were compelled to buy their sheets directly from the Sabinis and their henchmen.

In 1926, Darby Sabini unsuccessfully sued the newspaper publisher

DC Thomson & Co for libel after they'd described him in print in a popular rag called *The Topical Times* as a 'prominent Turf villain.' Darby told the court he was employed by the Bookmakers and Backers Racecourse Protection Association, which he claimed was a legitimate, limited liability company. He said that his job was to sell lists of runners to bookies at five shillings a time and that he received £8 a week commission. But Thomson's counsel said that the bookmakers only took the sheets out of compulsion and fear, and the court believed them. The case was thrown out, leaving Darby with a large bill, but it did nothing to end the racket.

It was estimated that on bank holidays and high summer days at courses like Brighton and Yarmouth, the gangs could make £5,000 in an afternoon, and at Epsom on Derby Day the profits could be more like £20,000. Not surprisingly, the Sabinis faced challenges from fellow racketeers who also wanted a share of the lucrative trade. The most aggressive of the rival outfits were Billy Kimber's Birmingham – or Brummagem – Boys, who were in alliance with elements of the Elephant and Castle Mob from South London.

The combatants' favourite weapon in this battle for mob influence was the cut-throat razor, which became as potent a symbol of gang warfare in Britain as the Tommy gun or Thompson submachine gun in Chicago in the Roaring Twenties. Firearms were sometimes carried too, although they were used more sparingly than in the US, along with coshes, knives and bayonets. But nothing quite matched the lurid impression of a blade cutting suddenly and violently across a man's hands or face.

In the Boulting Brothers' 1948 film of Graham Greene's novel *Brighton Rock*, the role of Charlie the barman at the Four Feathers was played by Carl Ramon, a former Sabini 'soldier' whose job was also to advise Richard Attenborough and other cast members on the finer points of razor slashing. The weapon might be hidden in a top pocket or in the peak of your cap, like the Peaky Blinders, or if you were a cheaper hood like Pinkie Brown – Attenborough's character in Brighton Rock – it might just be a spare Gillette Safety wedged into a bar of soap.

Darby Sabini claimed he found 'cutting' distasteful and preferred to look away when the blood flowed, but he was a trained boxer and wasn't above carrying a gun for his protection. In April 1921, Billy Kimber went to see Darby on the Italian's home ground in Clerkenwell and ended up getting shot in the side, but when the police were called, he said he was unable to identify his attacker. Alfie Solomons, the Jewish bootlegger from Camden Town and sometimes ally of the Sabinis (brought flamboyantly, if not entirely accurately, to life by Tom Hardy in Peaky Blinders), later surrendered to the law and was charged with attempted murder. But his subsequent trial was a sham and swiftly wound up by the judge due to a lack of evidence.

The following month, two Jewish cab drivers who chauffeured the Sabinis were attacked by Kimber's men at Alexandra Park racecourse, and a couple of Jewish bookies who were in business with Solomons were set upon at Bath races. Then, in June 1921, the Birmingham Boys attempted to ambush what they thought was a Sabini convoy leaving Epsom at the end of Derby Day. But the wily Italians had slipped away earlier in the afternoon and Kimber's mob discovered they were attacking a car-load of their own men.

Gang fights and reprisals continued on and off the racecourse throughout the 1920s. In August 1925, there was a pitched battle between the Sabinis and the Elephant Boys in the Waterloo Tavern opposite Waterloo Station, and two years later, the Italians clashed openly with the Hoxton Mob in Ham Yard, the narrow West End thoroughfare leading off Windmill Street. The police reaction to these conflicts seemed to depend on who was paying them most at the time, but on the racetracks, the Jockey Club appointed a couple of ex-Army men – Major George Wymer and Major William Bebbington – in an attempt to patrol the ring and straighten things out.

By 1929, the BPA – or Bookmakers Protection Association – had been set up, introducing a hierarchy of sorts that became the much derided system known as Dead Man's Shoes. Racecourse bookmaking pitches were to be the property of individual families and would be handed down through successive generations. The only way new blood could muscle in would be when a family retired or died out with no surviving relative wishing to take over, and even then new applicants would have to enjoy a position of seniority on a waiting list that could take years to ascend.

It imposed an order of sorts, but it was a pretty restrictive and nepotistic system, and the Sabinis weren't happy with their share of the spoils. As the 1930s began, the Italians resumed their extortionate demands at the new greyhound stadiums and on the so called free courses, meaning the plots of common land adjacent to a racecourse but not controlled by the Jockey Club Stewards, at places like Brighton, Epsom, Salisbury and Lewes.

It was this subplot that Bill Chandler had to contend with as he went from street bookie to entrepreneur to rich man. Bill never paid protection money to anyone. He was careful not to antagonise the Sabinis unnecessarily while also cultivating their North London rivals Alf White and his family from King's Cross. (Alf White's son John went on to be a prominent racecourse bookmaker, and his son John junior is still in business to this day. At one point, VC dated John's daughter). He had good police contacts, including friendly detectives on the Flying Squad, which had been formed in 1918, but he also had his own crew, thanks to his background in the Nile, and he was not afraid to use it to back up his position.

One renowned character Bill could call on was known as Double Handsome, an ironic reference to his fearsome appearance, which was more Magwitch in *Great Expectations* than Rudolph Valentino. "I remember him when I was a boy," said Bobby Edwards. "He lived on his own and he wasn't perhaps the cleanest of men. Once he was entertaining a female friend and they were sitting on the balcony outside his flat. She kept saying, 'well, I'll just stay a little bit longer, but then I really must be going.' He gave a big laugh and says, 'you stay another half an hour my dear and I'll have a nice bit of bacon for my breakfast.'"

Double Handsome was a handy man to call on in a scrap, but Bill's principal minder was Charlie Maskey's father, who was known as

Charlie The Hammer. As Young Victor was told, the nickname had less to do with Charlie's early career as a blacksmith and more with his expertise at hitting Bill's enemies over the head in a fight. Charlie and The Guvnor were an imposing double act and they made a big impression on Bill's rival William Hill, who, like Chandler, laid huge bets to the biggest punters in the 1930s and '40s.

The Birmingham-born Hill was himself a powerfully built man who had served in the detested Black and Tans in southern Ireland during the War of Independence. In the 1930s, he started making a book at the Northolt Park pony racing track, which was tremendously popular at the time, and opened a London office in Jermyn Street. He wasn't an easy person to intimidate, but he was frightened of Bill Chandler. "My grandfather didn't get on with him for some reason," explained Young Victor, who was told all the stories. "William Hill owed him some money at one time, so Bill, who also had pitches at Northolt Park, went off to see him in his offices with old Charlie Maskey. When Hill heard they were coming he had himself locked in a cupboard."

The debt regarding bets that Chandler had hedged for Hill on course was settled, but not long afterwards, William Hill appeared at White City dogs attired in plus fours, which apparently didn't impress Bill Chandler and his fellow bookmakers.

The presence of Charlie The Hammer deterred most welchers and 'knockers', and also prevented gangs of pickpockets like the Broad Mob from bothering Bill on course. But The Guvnor was more than capable of fighting his own battles when he had to. "On one occasion in the '30s, he was involved in a confrontation with another man at the top of the Nile," recalled Bobby Edwards. "It was over money and he knocked the other fella down. By this point, Bill owned a diamond ring, which he wore on the little finger of his left hand. When the fight was over, he discovered he'd dislodged the stone from his ring and he put the word around that he'd appreciate it if anyone who found it brought it back. Now this was a time when people were so desperate for money that they'd pawn a suit for ten bob. But old Mrs Bevin, who came out of Chatham Avenue, found it and she took it back to him. He made a big fuss of her and gave her a £20 note to thank her. She'd never seen one of them in her life before and she fainted, and for a moment they were all worried that she'd had a heart attack and died, but fortunately she came round."

The story of the diamond ring, like the incident with Barclays Bank in Wardour Street, further contributed to Bill's Don Corleone aura, giving him a mystique most other bookies couldn't match. He had another skill too, employed deftly and behind the scenes when required. He fenced stolen goods. The journalist, broadcaster and former Labour MP Bryan Magee grew up in Hoxton, and in his childhood autobiography Clouds Of Glory, published in 2003, he recounted a story told to him by his grandfather and involving his neighbour 'a colourful character called Bill Chandler…an outstanding example of a villain who made good and went more or less straight eventually…'

It seems that one day in the early '20s, Bill had been tipped off by a local policeman that he knew he was in possession of stolen goods and was about to raid his house. At short notice, he knocked on Magee's grandfather's door and asked if he could look after some things for him temporarily. The older man felt he could hardly say no, suspecting jail awaited Bill if he declined. The goods were hidden and soon afterwards the law turned up at Bill's house as expected and were nonplussed not to find anything. Instantly they dispersed to all the homes and haunts of his criminal associates and found nothing in any of them either. Bill wanted to pay Magee's grandfather afterwards to thank him for his help, but the offer was declined, his neighbour not wanting to be a 'known receiver' of stolen property. But contrary to Bryan Magee's impression, The Guvnor never went entirely straight, and by the 1930s, he'd graduated to much richer pickings.

In the early hours of March 6th, 1935, three boxes of gold bullion worth in excess of £24,000 (more like £2million in the present day) were stolen from a concrete and steel strong room in the basement at Croydon Aerodrome. The still spankingly brand new Art Deco terminal on the London to Purley Road was the modish jumping off place for 1930s travellers. Biggles-type aviators could fly directly from there to Europe and then onwards by stages to all manner of exotic destinations, from Oran to Cairo and Cape Town to Dar Es Salaam, and in September 1938, Neville Chamberlain arrived back there from his meeting with Adolf Hitler in Munich, waving his infamous piece of paper and proclaiming 'peace in our time.'

Imperial Airways, who owned the airfield, flew almost as many freight runs as they did passenger flights, and at 9am on March 6th, they were due to ship £10,000 worth of gold bars from the National Westminster Bank bound for their Paris branch, and £10,000 of gold sovereigns and golden US coins bound for Brussels. The boxes were locked away in the Croydon strong room around 10.30pm on March 5th, but that night, there were just two men on duty at the terminal. A loader called Burtwell Peters, who 'absented himself' for several hours, and a night watchman called Francis Johnson, who left his post at 4.15am to go out onto the tarmac and greet the arrival of a German airliner. Johnson said later that he'd locked the strong room behind him, but at various times during the day he'd left it unlocked and with the key in the door. At some point, someone posing around in a pilot's uniform had got hold of the key and made an impression, and the thieves returned with their counterfeit key during the half hour that Johnson was away.

The three robbers had hired a taxi at King's Cross and told the driver, George Manson of Hornsey Rise, to take them to the terminal where they were so confident of success that they asked him to wait outside while they picked up 'a cargo.' Manson said later that two of the men wore bowler hats and overcoats and the third a trilby. A small touring car that had been parked at the airport earlier was used to transport the gold from the strong room to the black cab and then Manson was told to drive to Harringay – to Green Lanes, Harringay, to be precise – to the home of William George Chandler, bookmaker, businessman and fence. The passengers unloaded their cargo, returning with the empty wooden boxes, which the cabbie was then instructed to ferry half a mile away to a house in Pemberton Road where they were handed over to Cecil Swanland, described as a 47-year-old variety artist, painter and financier 'of no fixed abode.' The gullible Swanland's job was to destroy the evidence but, whether he realised it or not at the time, he had been set up, not just as an accessory to the crime, but as the fall guy.

The heist had been masterminded by Darby Sabini and his Italian confrère Bert Marsh, and the men who hired the cab were Silvio Mazzardo – also known as 'Schonk', a top Sabini gangster and getaway driver – the 74-year-old John O'Brien, described as 'a dealer', and a third man referred to as Little Harry. When reports of the robbery were published with banner headlines in the midday editions of the evening papers, George Manson went to the police and described the three men he'd driven to the airport and back to Harringay and took them to the address in Pemberton Road. When detectives searched Swanland's flat, they found wrappers, seals and the broken lids of the three boxes covered up with a raincoat. He was promptly arrested and made a first appearance at Croydon Police Court the following day. Over the course of the next fortnight, Silvio Mazzardo and John O'Brien were also arrested and charged, but then bailed, unlike Swanland who was remanded in custody until the trial got under way on April 29th.

Swanland appeared in the dock at the Old Bailey sporting a Homburg hat – which the judge ordered him to remove – a small black moustache and a spotted bow tie. The jury were told that he had previous convictions as a forger and jewel thief, and that on the afternoon of the robbery, he'd ordered £59 worth of new clothes from a tailor in Soho Square. Swanland's alibi was nothing if not imaginative. He said that on the night of March 6th, he'd been unable to sleep, so he'd got up and gone for an early morning walk. At around 6.30am, he'd spotted a taxi parked not far from his house, and inside it was a chap he knew, Harry, who was returning from a night out in the West End. The obliging chum told Swanland he happened to have some old boxes with him he'd like to get rid of. Swanland said he could use some more firewood and would be happy to help out. He took the boxes upstairs to his flat and later that morning the police arrived. Unfortunately for Swanland, the jury weren't impressed. He was found guilty, and with his expensively dressed young bride looking on and weeping from the public gallery, he was sentenced to seven years in prison.

Silvio Mazzardo and John O'Brien, who the taxi driver George Manson was 'unable to identify,' were both found not guilty. Significantly, there was no mention during the trial by Manson or any other of the witnesses of the stop off at Bill Chandler's house on the way to Pemberton Road, fuelling suspicions that Bill and the Sabinis had been assisted by crooked detectives who had probably been cut in for a share of the spoils.

Officers at Scotland Yard claimed they had been able to find 'no clue' as to the whereabouts of the gold, but there were intriguing hints as to what had happened in the testimony of SB Abelson, a London bullion broker, with an office in Charterhouse Buildings in Clerkenwell. "A businessman I know well, and about whom there can be no question, telephoned me and asked what I was prepared to give for a large quantity of sovereigns," he told the court. "I told him 35 shillings each. He came to my office with 50 and asked if I would arrange to have £2,000 in cash, as he was bringing a large parcel of sovereigns to me later in the day. He arrived in the afternoon, counted out a thousand sovereigns and I paid him £1,750 in notes." Further transactions, said Abelson, took place later that day and the following evening.

A week later, Scotland Yard called the bullion dealer, and after a conversation with him, they 'went to a certain address,' but no sovereigns were found there. That address was 313 Green Lanes, and the person interviewed – 'the businessman about who there can be no question' – was Bill Chandler.

The aftermath of the robbery became a long-running racecourse and underworld joke. The Sabinis set up a bookmaker in the south of England trading under the name of Nick Gold of Croydon, and when Bill was dying 11 years later, he told Frances and Ronnie Chandler that when the police came to see him in Green Lanes, they failed to notice that some of the gold sovereigns were still lying hidden at the bottom of the ornamental fish pond in the garden. Shortly afterwards, all of Bill's share had been successfully sold on and the profits invested in property and other businesses. Darby Sabini, meanwhile, was said to have taken two sacks of gold with him when he attempted to retire peacefully to Hove at the outbreak of WW2.

It had seemed like the perfect crime but, despite the success of their collaboration, Bill Chandler's relationship with the Italian Mob had one violent episode still to come.

Chapter Seven

The Team From The Nile

A lfie Solomons, the Jewish racketeer who had been involved in the Billy Kimber shooting in 1921, changed sides several times during the racecourse gang wars. But in the summer of 1936, it appeared that Solomons and the Sabinis were acting in tandem again and using force to install their own bookmakers in prime racecourse pitches in the south of England.

Bill Chandler, and the bookies who looked to him for patronage and protection, were concerned. If the Italian-Jewish alliance – otherwise an unlikely hybrid against the background of rising Fascism in 1930s Europe – took over the holiday and seaside tracks unopposed one year, what was to stop them controlling the ring at places like Epsom, Ascot and Northolt Park the next? Bill saw it as a decisive moment. He had hoped that fencing the gold from the Croydon robbery would be enough to keep the Sabinis at arms length. But now he accepted that his erstwhile partners could not be trusted and that a statement would have to be made. Lewes racecourse was chosen as the place to make it. It wasn't just a job for a minder either. It was time to bring in the Hoxton Mob.

THE TEAM FROM THE NILE

The Guvnor wasn't there in person on the afternoon of June 8th, 1936, but the men he sent down from London were very much "the team from the Nile," as Bobby Edwards described it. "There was Georgie Gardiner, George Edwards, Tiger Bennis, Jimmy Spinks and the rest of them." Spinks, uncle of the future British middleweight boxing champion Terry Spinks, was the leader on the day. A big man with a personality to match, he was regarded as a hero in and around Hoxton and Shoreditch, and as a formidable enemy by foes outside the neighbourhood.

Upwards of 30 members of the Hoxton Mob, along with Charlie 'The Hammer' Maskey, accompanied Spinks down to Lewes, which must have seemed an implausible setting for a gang fight. The Sussex county town by the Ouse, with its flint and weatherboard houses, its picturesque streets and narrow alleyways, was ostensibly a textbook Miss Marple community of tea rooms, second-hand bookshops and retired Majors. Eighty years on, Lewes has become a thriving and lively outpost of Brighton, but some things haven't changed. The lower town is still tinged with the aromatic scent of hops from the Harvey's Brewery by the river. The county court buildings are still there at the bottom of the high street, and further up the hill stands the Victorian prison, its high walls within sight and sound of the gallops that lead up to the old racetrack.

Lewes was a major training centre in the 1930s, '40s and '50s, but the racecourse, as Young Victor was to see for himself before it closed in 1964, was a distinctly third division venue. A Monday and Tuesday 'gaffe track' offering homespun cards for moderate horses. The programme that sunny June day featured the six-furlong Castle Selling Plate, the Seaford Selling Handicap and the mile-and-a-quarter Cooksbridge Plate, and among the fancied runners was a gelding called Le Touquet and a couple of three-year-old fillies named Bonnie Parker and Miss Goodsort.

The racing might have been mediocre but Lewes was still close enough to London and Brighton to draw a healthy crowd, and in fine, summer weather, the location was idyllic. The tussocky downland interspersed with thorn bushes and flowering gorse, and the rutted chalk tracks crammed with horseboxes, cars, coaches and charabancs weaving their way uphill from the town. As usual, touts were selling tips outside the entrance, competing with the paper boys working for the local Brighton and Evening Argus, whose correspondent had put up Charlie Smirke's mount, Patriot King, running in the Southdown Welter Plate at 3.30pm, as his bet of the day.

Away from the racing pages, the main stories in the Argus concerned rumours of more 'British dirty linen' about to appear in the US press (which was a coded reference to King Edward VIII's affair with his American mistress Wallis Simpson). But there were also reports of the kind of noirish criminality that so fascinated Graham Greene and his fellow 1930s novelist Patrick Hamilton. A well-to-do young couple had carried out a smash-and-grab raid in Newhaven; two racecourse pickpockets had gone on trial in Brighton; and a 37-year-old Exeter woman had been hanged for murdering her husband.

Jimmy Spinks and his fellow gang members may not literally have had murder in their hearts at Lewes races, but they meant to intimidate, and if the list of 'implements' found at the scene of the crime are any guide, they were extremely lucky no one was killed. Among the items recovered by the police were two hammers, four pieces of iron '18 inches to two feet in length,' a jemmy, a cosh or 'life preserver', a piece of steel tubing, the end of a billiard cue, a hatchet and a knuckle duster.

The targets of the Hoxton Mob were meant to be not just leading Sabini bookmakers and their minders. Spinky, Charlie The Hammer and the rest were after Darby and Harry Boy themselves, having been informed, wrongly as it turned out, that the brothers were going to be there in person. According to the memoirs of West End Central's Detective Superintendent Edward 'Ted' Greeno (who was a friend of Bill Chandler and who was invited to Victor senior's wedding in 1948), the Italians had been tipped off by some duplicitous North Londoner and then, in turn, the crafty Sabinis alerted the local police, who were out in force when the trouble began.

Superintendent Waghorn of the Sussex Constabulary testified later that he arrived at the racecourse at 12.45pm, just as thousands of spectators were streaming in from the town, and saw "a gang of men, about 20 or 30 in number, coming from the direction of an open space near the rear of the car park" and heading for the three-shilling ring. "Here they are boys," Waghorn's colleague, Inspector Stripp, allegedly heard Jimmy Spinks call out. "Get your tools ready." There may have been no Sabini family members present, but Spinks and the others had recognised the Italians' henchman Alfie Solomons and his entourage.

Solomons was just setting up his pitch, and with him was his clerk Mark Frater, who was wearing a curly brimmed black bowler hat. Spinky, reportedly flourishing his hatchet, struck Frater a blow on the head but, thanks to the bowler's reinforced crown, not quite sinking his chopper into the flesh and bone beneath. As Frater collapsed to the ground, Solomons, drawing a razor and wielding his bookie's stool like a cudgel, engaged Spinks and Charlie The Hammer in combat and simultaneously other Sabini cronies appeared and started fighting the Hoxton boys with razors, coshes and broken bottles. Solomons was injured too, and fearful for his own and Frater's life, the pair made a run for it, hanging on to their bookmaking satchel containing their cash float for the day's trade.

It was at this point that a large number of uniformed police officers suddenly closed in from the edges of the ring. "They're here boys," one of the Hoxton Mob called out. "Blow," shouted another. "There are too many top hats about."

Georgie Gardiner and four other men tried to get away in the open-topped sports car they'd driven down in from London, but a local constable jumped onto the running board and did his best to grab the wheel. Gardiner attempted to accelerate past the oncoming traffic and the police officer was thrown to the ground. Then a black police Wolseley blocked the road up ahead and Gardiner and his passengers were trapped. "I am sorry, Guvnor," he's alleged to have said to the arresting officer, "but we've all got wives and children. We've got to go to work this afternoon."

Charlie The Hammer slipped away into the crowd, but some of the others were not so lucky. Sixteen men were arrested in total, and after a night in the cells they were brought before Lewes magistrates the following morning, charged with numerous counts of assault and grievous bodily harm and remanded in custody until the next Lewes Assizes. No charges were pressed against Alfie Solomons, who gave his address as New Church Road, Hove, and who had been tended to by the St John's Ambulance Unit at the course, or Mark Frater, who had a serious head wound and was now being treated in the Royal Sussex County Hospital. A reporter for the Argus quoted the men as saying that neither of them had been concerned in the fight and had supposedly been 'attacked by mistake' as they were arriving at the course.

The trial took place seven weeks later, between July 26th and 31st, 1936, and was covered in detail by both the local and the London papers among their day-to-day reports spicing up the racing from Glorious Goodwood, the latest news of Edward and Mrs Simpson and descriptions of Wally Hammond's double century for Gloucestershire against Sussex at Hove. The presiding judge was Mr Justice Hilberry, and the accused were represented by two top-drawer London barristers, JD Cassels KC and GL Hardy. The briefs, while acknowledging that the weapons on display were "villainous looking things," pleaded self-defence on behalf of some of their clients while maintaining that the others "had nothing to do with the affray."

The judge noted sarcastically that the 34-year-old Mark Frater, who was meant to be the prosecution's star witness, had gone missing after being released from hospital. He was finally rounded up at a flat in Biddulph Mansions, Maida Vale, but in the witness box, with one eye on the defendants, he said that he "didn't know what happened. I got it and that is all I know." He added that he was unable to identify his attacker but that, yes, he had met Jimmy Spinks before in town for a drink and that they were "all good friends."

Such heartwarming assurances weren't enough to save the Hoxton Mob from guilty verdicts. The jury was absent and all the doors of the court bolted when the judge passed sentence. "Crimes of violence do not pay in this country," he warned the 16 prisoners as they formed up in three rows in the dock. "You were seen by no fewer than four officers to be leading or one of the leaders," he told Spinks. "You it was who urged the men on and struck the blow with the hatchet. Your record is that of a man of violence. I think you are undoubtedly desperate and dangerous." He sentenced him to five years penal servitude. By the time he came out, WW2 had begun, but Spinky was never called up, the military authorities recognising him as essentially unmanageable. Instead, he was allowed to combine superficial duties as an ARP warden with more profitable work on the black market, and after the war he became a respected boxing coach. The brothers Stephen and Timothy Bennis got three and two years hard labour respectively. Harry Wilkins got two years, George Gilder got three, Georgie Gardiner 18 months. Alfie Solomons' confrere, Albert Blitz, got four years, and the Sabini gangster Thomas Mack got three. In total, the sentences handed down by Mr Justice Hilberry added up to 53 and a half years.

In James Morton's 1994 gangland history *The Underworld in Britain and Ireland: Volume Two*, he tactfully observed that "it was said that the men's families were looked after during their time in prison by the founder of one of Britain's largest bookmaking firms."

The Battle of Lewes Racecourse, as it became known, may have ended in victory for the law, but a point had been made, albeit at a price. The Sabinis would continue to exert an influence on racecourse bookmaking and in things like the allocation of pitches at point to point tracks and on the hill at Epsom. But there would be no more incursions onto Bill Chandler's territory or threats to the pitches of his friends and allies enjoying similar Hoxton and King's Cross protection.

The case, and the events preceding it, was followed keenly by Graham Greene, and it was no coincidence that when Brighton Rock was published the following year, the central character, a psychopathic teenage hoodlum, was called 'Pinkie' (Spinky) Brown, while his race-course adversary, Mr Colleoni, was a prominent Italian gangster living comfortably in the Metropole Hotel.

The real Italian Mob didn't fare so well when Mussolini declared war on Britain in the summer of 1940. At 4pm on June 20th, Darby, Harry Boy and Bert Marsh – who had beaten a murder charge after a stabbing at Wandsworth dog stadium in September 1936 – were detained as 'persons of hostile origin' and interned, ironically, at Ascot racecourse before being moved to a camp outside Liverpool. "There is only one country for me and it is this country," protested Darby, who could barely speak a word of Italian. He and his brother were convinced that their detention was the Home Office's revenge for the Croydon Bullion Robbery. "The Sabini Gang was just a lot of chaps that used to go to get pitches on the racecourse," he pleaded. "And then there were some Birmingham chaps. But when you try to climb the ladder and you get on a little, you always have enemies to write about you and get you into trouble."

When Darby was released in 1943, he went back to his terraced house in Old Shoreham Road in Hove. At the time of his death in 1950, he was still officially working as a bookmaker, and the firm continued to be represented on British racecourses under the name of Joseph and Morry Levy right up until the 1980s. Alfie Solomons also retired to a house in Hove. His son Jack became a famous boxing promoter and his other son, Alfie junior, ended up as a director of William Hill.

In sharp contrast to his rivals' fate, Bill Chandler's wealth and power was at its height in the late 1930s and early years of WW2. All of the children, with the exception of Renie and Victor senior, had left home by then and Bill was spending more and more time in Central London at his office in Wardour Street and in the Victoria Sporting Club round the corner. Charlie Maskey remembers him having "a childish love of tricks. He liked to try and steal one grape from a barrow boy whose stall wasn't far from his office. The boy's attention would be diverted, the old man would take his grape, and then he'd leave a £1 note under an apple or orange to show he'd got away with it."

When the war broke out in 1939, Bill frequently stayed the night in a suite in either the Strand Palace or the Piccadilly Hotel rather than returning to Harringay. Sometimes he enjoyed the company of his mistress, Mrs Pearl, and sometimes he contributed to the wartime excitement by running an illicit casino in the Piccadilly Hotel basement during the blackout. Among the high rollers joining him there for the games of roulette, poker and Chemin de Fer, were Major Mackintosh – the impresario who ran the White City Stadium – the bookmakers Harry Parker and Hector McDonald – who was related to the leaders of the Elephant Boys Gang – and, after they joined the war in 1941, assorted wealthy Americans passing through London and looking to speculate on horses, cards or the black market.

One night, Bill left the game temporarily to go back up to his suite to get some more cash from his safe only to find there was an intruder in his bedroom. "It was a little Irish fellow, a well-known underworld character called Paddy the Burglar," explained Benno Miller. "Bill discovered him hiding in a cupboard, so he locked him in. He told him he wasn't bothered about him personally. He just wanted to know who'd sent him." The Guvnor left Paddy shut up in the wardrobe until breakfast the following morning. Then, when he'd got the information he was after, he let him go. Accounts of some sort were presumably settled while the Irishman "went off to do a penance," said Benno, "which usually involved lying in an ice-cold bath for an hour."

Bill might still have had a few predatory bookmaking rivals and demimonde figures to deal with, but he had no problems at all with the police who continued to be well looked after. "The Flying Squad used to drive around London in a Lagonda," added Benno, smiling. "Where do you think they got the money for that from? One of them, a detective who'd look into murder cases, was as crooked as a three dollar bill. He'd regularly have £200 or £300 on a horse. They all used to come round to Wardour Street or the Piccadilly to pay homage to the Old Man. They enjoyed his black market Scotch and food, and he'd usually give them a few tips to be going on with. They had their own pub, The Final in King William Street, not far from the Bank of England. It was run by an ex-Detective Sergeant, a fella called Phil Lee, and they'd have a lock-in there most nights of the week. They even ran their own book on the side too." (The Final, like the rest of King William Street, was totally destroyed during the Blitz).

Greyhound racing was halted at the start of WW2 – and up to 60 of the dogs at Walthamstow had to be put down – but when it resumed, it proved more popular than ever. Racing, which had been temporarily suspended in 1939, recommenced at selected courses the following year, and the wartime market, swollen by black market money, was a strong one. But petrol rationing meant that transport back and forth wasn't easy. Bill Chandler's on-course team acquired a removal van and had a table and chairs screwed to the floor in the back. It gave them somewhere to sit down and play cards during the delays and interruptions that were a regular feature of wartime journeys. The firm's float was carried round in a briefcase and entrusted to 'Nobby' Mack (Mcmahon), one of Bill's principal lieutenants and the father of Michael Mcmahon, who is one of Victor's oldest friends. Nobby always had a girl he was in a hurry to get back to. One day on the way back from Newmarket, the van stopped at a pub in Essex and Nobby used a coin-box to ring his lover of the moment and tell her what time he'd be home. But when they got back to the London office, he realised he'd left the float behind in the pub. He managed to commandeer a car, which was no simple matter at the time, and raced back to the roadhouse where the landlord was waiting for him. "I was tempted," said the landlord, as he handed over the briefcase. "But when I saw what was inside, I was too frightened to take it."

It was a similar story one spring day in 1942. Bill was counting out £800 in fivers at his desk in Wardour Street when a gust of wind blew half the notes out of the open office window. They landed at the feet of a couple of uniformed soldiers walking along below. Perhaps knowing the address and guessing the identity of the owner, the squaddies thought better than to pocket any of it for themselves. Instead, they picked up all the money and returned it.

Bill stood to win half a million pounds on the 1942 St Leger, which like all the classic races that year was run on Newmarket's July course. He'd placed bets totalling £30,000 (£1.5million today) on Lord Roseberry's filly Ribbon at 16-1, but unfortunately she was beaten a head by Lord Derby's colt Herringbone. Added piquancy was supplied by the fact that both Lords – Derby and Roseberry – were account holders with the Chandler firm, and Edward Stanley had backed his horse with Bill.

The Guvnor may have been characteristically stoical about his racing losses but "he hated the bombing," according to Benno and Frances, and was fearful that the war might claim his sons. He tried to safeguard them in his way, getting Charles and Jackie jobs as lighter men on the Thames. Ronnie had already been sent over to Northern Ireland in 1939 in the hope that he'd pursue a business career. One of Bill's sisters and her husband owned the Union Hotel on Donegall Square in Belfast and they were enthusiastic patrons of dog racing. There was also the little matter of Ronnie's lifestyle, in particular his gambling debts, which Bill had always paid to avoid embarrassment. While his son was away, he put him under the protection of a former Sabini bookmaker and gang member called Alessandro Tomassi who, partly to avoid being interned, had moved to Ireland and changed his name to the more prosaic Sandy 'Pickles' Rice. It was understood that if Ronnie got into any further trouble north or south of the Irish border, Pickles would take care of it and then contact Bill to be reimbursed.

The Guvnor wanted to set his youngest son up with a safe job in a factory, but Victor senior, who turned 18 in 1942, rebelled after a few months and went off to join the army.

Billy Chandler, who had long since broken away from his father's orbit, had joined the RAF, seeing action as a Pilot Officer. He was on leave, but still in uniform, when he went down to Salisbury races from Epsom with the trainer Staff Ingham (full name Stafford Walter Henry Ingham) on Saturday May 5th, 1945, only a few days before VE Day. He was going on to White City afterwards to keep an eye on the family pitches and he wanted to get away smartly before the last. In haste, he accepted a lift back to town with the journalist Roger Denton Cardew, 'Robin Goodfellow' of the *Daily Mail*, who had petrol coupons and a car. After crossing Salisbury Plain and approaching the village of Micheldever on the A303, they were hit head on by an army lorry. Billy, who was sitting in the front passenger seat, was thrown forwards against the dashboard and, freakishly, the button on the glove compartment penetrated his brain. He died instantly. Cardew and another passenger, Charles Stuart, a punter from London, were also killed.

The Golden Boy, so personable, vital and daring, was 35 years old, and hardly surprisingly, his father was shattered. Billy was buried in Manor Park Cemetery, two plots down from his mother Annie. The Chandler family never returned to call the odds at Salisbury, and from that day on, Victor senior and Young Victor were always chauffeured to and from the races by a professional driver.

The Guvnor never recovered from Billy's loss. His lung and bowel cancer set in the following winter and on March 25th, 1946, 10 days after Cheltenham and a week before the Grand National, he died in bed. The street bookmaker's son, who had built up a fortune for himself and his children, was 56 years old. Bill was buried at Manor Park too, reunited with his beloved Annie in the family vault. All in all, five members of the Chandler family lie there close together, their graves lovingly tended for years by Walthamstow Stadium.

Bill's obituary in the Greyhound Express praised his devotion to his wife and his large family, while the William Hickey column in the *Daily Express* commented on the impeccable Savile Row tailoring of a self-made man who 'could converse with equal facility with Dukes and Dustmen.'

Without their father to rule over them, the six remaining sons went their own way, and not always happily either. It had taken The Guvnor more than 25 years to build up an empire, but within months of his death, the brothers "were all at each other's throats," said Benno Miller. "Charles took the stadium, Albert the SP offices, Jackie had the garage up at Walthamstow and the Honeysuckle Milk Bar in Wardour Street, and he took over The Blower too, in partnership with Maxie Parker. Percy had the catering at the stadium. Charles took the boards pitches and the rails pitch at Cheltenham, and Victor's father worked for him for a while. But Charles was a failure at bookmaking and Victor senior ended up having to buy the pitches back at an inflated price. All of them were gamblers and Albert and Jackie were the worst. One day they each had £11,000 on a couple of 10-11 chances in a three-horse race at Ally Pally, and what happened? Up came Joe, the 33-1 outsider, and both the favourites got beat." It was a stitch-up, of course. The putter-on kept the money, bought a house and property and lived happily ever after, and with no Bill Chandler around to seek redress, the brothers never got their money back. "They were soon selling things to have cash to bet with," said Benno. "They sold Number One (Wardour Street) for £300,000. It would be worth tens of millions today."

Bill's legacy may have been dissipated at first, with various boys – Charles and Victor's father in particular – falling out with one another. But just as Victor senior would go on to perpetuate the racing and bookmaking tradition, inherited in turn by VC, so Charles and his son Charles junior would build up the stadium developing it, especially after White City closed in 1984, into the most atmospheric dog track in the country. Winston Churchill addressed an election meeting there in 1945, and eight years later the stadium was lit up with a loyal tribute to the newly crowned Queen Elizabeth II.

The distinctive neon greyhound continued to light up the sky three nights a week for the next 55 years. Jackie's son, Jack the Track, was the racecourse manager. Billy's son, William, was in charge of the catering. Young Victor's cousin, Annie, was in charge of publicity. Charles junior was the chief steward and week after week his mother Frances could be seen sitting up there in the family room in the stands. Defiantly glamorous with her glass of wine, her cigarettes and her 'sparklers' (diamond earrings, necklaces and bracelets).

Racegoers packed into the comfort of the glass-fronted restaurant or gathered in the bars where a youthful David Beckham was once a pot boy, or huddled outside on the terraces. Down below them, bookmakers like Dougie Tyler, who reckoned he barely missed a night at the 'Stow' from when he came out of the army in 1946 to when it closed, called the odds to a regular cast of fellow bookies and punters who went by such betting ring nicknames as the Maggot, the Dead Body and the Oily Rag.

The big Totalisator Board flashed its prices. The dogs paraded.

The 'one' dog nervous and neurotic. The 'four' dog wagging its tail excitedly. The lights dimmed, the hare was on its way and then the traps opened and the punters roared, and up above them, the moon and the stars looked down on Bill Chandler's London.

Chapter Eight

Young Victor

eaford is a quiet town. 'The lights shine less brightly than in LA,'
as David Hare described this stretch of Sussex coastline in his
1974 play, Knuckle. To the east, the chalk cliffs of Seaford Head
climb 500 feet above the English Channel before dropping down
again towards Cuckmere Haven and the Seven Sisters. The dowager
resort of Eastbourne lies eight miles further on. To the west, the light-
house that flashes outside Newhaven Harbour greets fishing boats and
cargo ferries from Dieppe rather than junks and sampans from the
South China Seas.

The town centre has its share of characteristic East Sussex shops
and houses: traditional weatherboard and flint, like Lewes, mingling
with mock Georgian. There's a popular tea room in Church Lane,
a fish and chip shop by the station arcade and a pub selling Harvey's
Bitter and shelves of second-hand books by authors like EF Benson
and Agatha Christie.

Away from the beach huts and the seafront, there are row upon
row of post-war bungalows mingling with bigger houses in respectable looking cul-de-sacs with names like Sandringham and Balmoral
Close. There are putting greens and tennis courts, with old balls from
summers past found lying beneath the hedges each spring, and there
are an extraordinarily large number of private schools. It's a Betjeman-

esque world of links golf and the Salts recreation ground. A world of dogs, gorse bushes and sea breeze.

It was in this safe, conventional and quintessentially English environment – a long way from Hoxton and the Nile – that Young Victor Chandler grew up. Victor William had been born in London on April 18th, 1951, and he spent his first 18 months at the house in Woodford Green on the southern edges of Epping Forest that his father and mother had bought shortly after their marriage in 1948. When Victor senior left Highgate School aged 18 in 1942, he joined the army, becoming a Sergeant and PT Instructor in the Royal Engineers. Not for him the evasion of his father Bill or some of his older brothers. "He was very patriotic," according to his close friend Charlie Maskey. "All his life he believed in King and Country."

Victor senior was a tall, handsome man: broad shouldered and narrow waisted with the family's distinctive curly hair and bright eyes. When they were demobbed, he and Benno Miller shared a flat in Carlton Court in Mayfair and drove around London in a Buick station wagon. Chandler was an early riser – "first up and best dressed," said Benno, but he was also shy like his son, and friends joked that, up until his marriage in 1948, he "couldn't find a broad in a bordello." His good looks masked the fact that he was in continual discomfort from a back injury he sustained during the war when he dived into a river to try and save someone's life. The pain was to plague him for the rest of his days and Young Victor remembers there were times when it was so bad "that he practically had to crawl upstairs to bed at night."

Fearing that he wasn't fit enough to stand up and call the odds on the racecourse day after day, Chandler was hoping to go to work as a director at Walthamstow Stadium instead. But it seemed that his older brother Charles didn't want him there, which was why, after a rancorous interlude, he was forced to buy back the family pitches. Initially he went into partnership with the bookmaker Albert Williams, described as "another immaculately dressed man of quiet demeanour," before taking Betty's brothers, the Morills, scions of another well-known bookmaking clan, in with him.

Victor and Betty's wedding was in April 1948 and they spent their honeymoon at the Carlton Hotel in Cannes. The Côte d'Azur – Cannes, Cap d'Antibes, Beaulieu sur Mer and Cap Ferrat – was, in Betty Chandler's eyes, "elegance personified" and the couple returned there many times. But neither their marriage nor Victor senior's career in the ring might have got far had it not been for the £40,000 he won (more like £1.5million today) from a bet on Sterope, the 20-1 winner of the 1948 Cambridgeshire at Newmarket. The four-year-old, who was not much bigger than a pony, was the son of a Derby winner and had never finished out of the first three in 14 races. He was trained in Yorkshire by Pat Beasley and owned by John Townley, a car dealer and Cambridge MA who had no fewer than 83 different bookmaking accounts. Townley's confidence had been boosted by news of an impressive gallop Sterope had done a week before the race with one of the respected Yorkshire trainer Charles Elsey's horses, and Victor's father had been alerted that Townley and Beasley were going for a touch.

There were 32 runners in the Cambridgeshire that year and the race was run in a howling gale. Sterope and his jockey Dennis Schofield, a 16-year-old apprentice from Leeds, only emerged from the ruck in the last hundred yards, getting up to beat Charlie Smirke's mount Royal Tara by half a length. The victorious punters then had an agonising wait as Smirke objected to the winner on the grounds of 'bumping and boring,' implying that Sterope had obstructed him in the closing stages. The racing correspondent Clive Graham reckoned that the news the objection had been overruled was greeted with "the loudest cheers ever heard outside the normally staid Newmarket weighing room." It's a safe bet that Victor senior was cheering too.

Young Victor arrived two and a half years later. His mother never forgot his first birthday party in April 1952 where he ended up sitting on the table, blowing a small trumpet and surrounded by strong, adoring women. Towards the end of the afternoon, Betty's husband and his bookmaking colleagues got back from Newmarket races in the firm's chauffeur-driven Buick. The same car that had once belonged to Bill.

There was Victor senior, Charlie The Hammer – who had continued to serve the Chandler family – the clerks Bill Sox and Percy Bendon, and the driver Lesley Ainsley, known as 'Fat Rollo.'

It was a chilly spring day, and as they came into the house, the men were still wearing their long overcoats and trilby hats and "they all looked like Chicago gangsters." The assembled infants greeted them with noisy excitement, with the exception of one tearful guest who took fright and crawled under the table to hide.

In October that year, the Chandlers sold their London home for £6,000 and bought a smaller house in Rottingdean, not far from Brighton, for £3,000. "We had nothing when we first went down to the coast," recalled Betty. Betting on horse and greyhound racing had been massively popular just after the war, boosted by returning servicemen and black market cash. It fell back a little in 1950, but a few years later, Victor senior was doing well enough to move six miles further east to a bigger house with land attached backing on to the golf course at Seaford Head. Chyngton Rise cost £18,000 and came with three acres of ground at the side. The style was comfortable, 1950s half timbering with tall chimneys and a patio, and the Chandlers had an open-air swimming pool built in the back garden.

The pool was a symbol of luxury at the end of the austerity era and would be much enjoyed by Young Victor and his sisters Liz, who had been born in 1952, and Debbie, who was born two years later. It may also have encouraged the neighbours to think that bookmakers really did all smoke cigars and drive around in a Rolls Royce, as the pundit Malcolm Muggeridge claimed in an article in the *Sunday Express*. Victor's father never owned a Roller, but by the end of the decade, he'd acquired a Bentley and an open-topped Lagonda, and later on he bought a Mercedes and a BMW too. He enjoyed a glass of champagne and he maintained his father's sartorial standards, whether he was working at the races or out on the town. "He was as smart as a whip," said Benno Miller, "and he had a wardrobe full of beautiful tailor-made suits and ties. By the mid-'60s he reckoned he had a different tie for every day of the year." One week alone in 1951, the bookmaker's tailoring bill with Lord and Stewart in Albermarle Street came to £1,853 and included 34 guinea suits, a dinner suit, a grey Cheviot Sports overcoat and a brown camel hair overcoat. His shirt maker was the legendary Frank Foster, an East Ender whose cutting rooms were in Clifford Street and who created shirts for many of the James Bond films as well as for stars like Marlon Brando, Frank Sinatra and Fred Astaire. He made gentlemen's underpants too.

The stylish aura that trailed Victor senior's world – the silver and gold cufflinks and cigarette lighters, the bespoke suits and coats, the Bentleys and BMWs – was a major formative influence on his son. "My father wasn't rich," said Young Victor, "but he worked hard and generated a good income, and in the good times we lived bloody well. There was always plenty of food and drink in the house and nice holidays and cars. But he didn't hoard things or count his possessions for their own sake. 'You can't take it with you,' was his view. So why not enjoy it while you've got the chance?"

In 1950, Victor senior had the distinction of becoming the first man to have his lunch served outside on the terrace of the Carlton Hotel, his former honeymoon destination, in Cannes. He had flown down there for a short break in the company of Benno Miller, his fellow book-makers Charlie Mendoza and Ted Sturman and the comedian and entertainer Bud Flanagan. It was a glorious spring day and the hotel restaurant was hot and stuffy. The French windows were open but, at the time, the management were not in the habit of serving meals outdoors. The Englishman's charm and courteous manner persuaded them to relent and they moved his table outside into the sunshine. He won fulsome praise and not a few free drinks from grateful fellow diners who were subsequently permitted to follow his example.

Sedate Seaford in the 1950s may not have offered quite as much in the way of hedonistic pleasures, but Brighton, only ten miles away, was Soho by Sea. Bohemians and actors, chancers and gangsters. Ozone, sex and sauce. You could have oysters and champagne in Wheelers or English's, dance to the big bands in Sherry's nightclub and then repair to a suite in the Metropole Hotel or the Grand. It also had its own larcenous but beloved racecourse up on Whitehawk Down where Victor senior called the odds throughout the flat racing season. But unlike Graham Greene's bookmaking Mr Big, the oily Colleoni, the town was never the base of Victor senior's operations. He opened a betting shop there near the station after they were legalised in 1961, but his main credit and SP office was on the top floor at number 81 Great Portland Street in London, and he kept a flat in nearby Weymouth Street in Marylebone.

The bookmaker travelled up and down each week, sometimes by car but often by train using the Brighton Belle Pullman service to Victoria. Smartly uniformed attendants would be waiting on Platform 5 at Brighton station and Platform 14 at Victoria, ready to escort passengers to their first-class seats where meals were served right up until the train's demise in 1972. One of Chandler's occasional companions on those Pullman journeys was Sir Laurence Olivier (as he was before his peerage in 1970), who had a house in Sussex Square in Brighton and also commuted regularly to London. Over kippers at breakfast or a glass of Pol Roger in the evening – Larry returning from the Old Vic, Victor senior from White City dogs – the two men got to know each other. All the best racecourse bookmakers are actors, and Olivier – the born showman who had just finished playing Archie Rice, the fading end of the pier comedian in John Osborne's play *The Entertainer* – relished the patter and style of the track. He even owned a so-called bookmaker's check suit in mustard yellow, which horrified the classically attired Chandler and was much louder than anything he would ever wear.

Victor senior was renowned for his generosity, and racing men down on their luck would sometimes hang around the concourse at Brighton or Victoria hoping to bump into him, strike up a chat for old time's sake and, like the punters in Jack's café in Hoxton in the 1930s, be loaned a few readies or offered a bit of work at 'Ally Pally' or Kempton Park. One of the supplicants was an outside man known as 'Puddin', who was married to one of Betty's cousins. One day he was accosted by an evangelist on Brighton seafront. "You there," said the man. "Do you love Jesus?" "I do," replied Puddin. "But I prefer the milder cheeses, like Cheddar."

Working life often took Chandler away from home, and not just up to London. Each June he was at Royal Ascot laying bets to wealthy racehorse owners like Jim Joel, the Duchess of Norfolk and Lord Carnarvon (the sixth Earl), who had been a client of his father's before the war. He hired a box to entertain in too, bookmakers and well-to-do punters mingling more freely at the races than was otherwise customary in 1950s and '60s Britain. There were also those points in the racing calendar when the circus would pitch up for days at a time in places like Cheltenham for the Festival – which grew rapidly in the 1950s – Liverpool, Lincoln and Doncaster. The top owners, trainers and bookies treated themselves well and all stayed in the same hotels, like the Midland in Manchester, the Majestic in Harrogate and Lincolnshire's Woodhall Spa. That was when the good times rolled, especially late at night in the restaurant or over games of poker and Chemin de Fer in the bar. But when the week's racing was over, Chandler would go back to Seaford and Betty always stressed that "win, lose or draw, he would never bring his work home with him."

Victor senior was no dilettante. His early life had been a tough one, losing his mother when he was barely 18 months old, and memories of adversity and how to cope with it had shaped his outlook. He also believed that peacetime prosperity should not be allowed to cushion his son from some of the character-building rigour he had been through. So, for Young Victor, who had been used to playing on the back lawn at Seaford in a Davy Crockett racoon skin cap and buckskin jacket complete with a toy pop gun, things were about to change. In September 1959, he was enrolled as a boarder at Hollingbury Court, a prep school formerly situated on the edges of Brighton but which had moved to Warninglid in rolling downland about six miles outside Haywards Heath. The easygoing bookmaker's son, who had been very happy living at home in the 1950s *Just William* world of the *Beano*, Tizer and ice cream soda, suddenly found himself transported into the equally 1950s but altogether less congenial ambience of aertex shirts, knee-length shorts and TCP behind the ears. The world of packed trunks, tearful goodbyes and regimented dormitory life. He hated it.

The Hollingbury Court headmaster, Ted Robertson, was an Anglo-Indian martinet who had moved to Britain after Indian independence in 1948. His regime, alas, was not a happy one, though Victor senior and Betty, who had been recommended the school by Young Victor's Uncle Albert, whose son Donald was still a pupil there, were not to know that.

Hollingbury Court was meant to prepare eight to 13-year-old Home Counties boys for the public school common entrance exam, and there were about 80 of them when VC first arrived. In 1983, the school closed down. The official reason was that numbers had fallen to unsustainable levels, while Robertson had received a good financial offer for the property that enabled him to dine regularly in Wheeler's in Brighton in his retirement – as Young Victor discovered to his horror when eating there himself a year later. But privately there had been increasing concern about the head's suitability as the custodian of vulnerable pre-pubescent boys.

The school was situated in a former private house, constructed in 1906, and the architectural style was black and white Tudorbethan half timbering with ivy climbing up the front walls. The buildings, long since converted into private accommodation, are still there and, outwardly, some of them have changed very little since the 1960s. The main hall, originally called Colwood House, was bought by a couple of wealthy Americans and used as a location for the last-ever episode of *Only Fools and Horses*, when the newly enriched Trotters were meant to have won the lottery and retired to a mansion in the country. There's a Gothic Revival gatehouse, a curving front drive and a separate service drive. The grass lawns are hidden from the road by high walls and there are a lot of tall pine trees, rhododendrons and rose bushes.

The school tennis courts are still in use, but the old cricket pitch has become part of somebody's back garden. The pavilion was moved into a corner by the hedge and now serves as a dilapidated garden shed. When it was being transported, old cricketing records were discovered among the musty pads and boxes of stumps. The deeds of once youthful openers and leg spinners etched in metal lettering on a wooden board. The inscriptions like archaeological records of childhoods long passed.

The dormitories and classrooms that were at the back and side of the main school were sold off separately and subdivided into smaller houses and weekend apartments. But no amount of brightly painted walls and cheerful family baggage can quite disguise their history. Sniff the air on a damp autumn afternoon and there's still the unmistakable scent of muddy rugger boots and closely supervised gloom.

The village pub, the Half Moon, may have been off-limits to Hollingbury pupils, but not to the staff who were clearly fond of carrying bottles back for further drinking sessions after closing time. "When the builders moved in after the school closed, they found literally dozens of old empties – beer, vodka, Scotch, gin – buried in the flower beds and beneath the hedge," said Jill, a one-time Hollingbury teacher who remained a Warninglid resident. "There was enough drink up there to stock an off-licence for years."

Some of the staff may have drunk to relieve the tedium of boarding school life, with its joint incarceration of teachers and pupils. There is no record of the headmaster joining in though, it sounds as if he had demons enough to seek solace from. "Oh, yes, Mr Robertson," said Jill, sighing. In common with other older villagers, she remembered how "abnormal and unhealthy" it seemed that the Hollingbury boys were allowed out so infrequently and were so strictly policed. There were tensions in the staffroom too. The head's daughter-in-law was employed briefly as a French assistant, but Jill and others went so far as to get her teaching qualification revoked after they saw her "losing it regularly" in front of her classes. "I think her neuroses always came back to the headmaster and his expectations, demands and general disappointment that she wasn't a boy."

Whatever Robertson's view of the general preferability of boys to girls, the eight-year-old Victor Chandler was one boy he didn't take to at all. The feeling was entirely mutual. Young Victor decided after only the briefest acquaintance that the headmaster was a sadistic tyrant, and absconded several times, once kicking Robertson in the shin in his study in the presence of his parents. On another occasion, he locked himself in his father's Mercedes after everyone had got out. It took Victor senior half an hour to persuade him to give up, and he only surrendered when his father told him that otherwise he was going to have to break the glass on the car window to get in.

Some of the older Chandler family retainers dubbed Young Victor "a scallywag," but as far as the delinquent was concerned, school sucked, and that was that. It wasn't simply a case of Moulsworth-style japery either. Plenty was the emotional as well as physical pain that could be inflicted from regular summonses to Robertson's study, where he could choose from a variety of canes, thick as well as thin, long or short, rather like a golfer surveying his bag of clubs. "You can say those were the days before the caring society," says Young Victor, looking back dolefully. Two masters were sacked for "touching up boys" while Victor was at Hollingbury Court but "nobody called the police back then." Children were expected to remain silent and whistleblowing was out of the question.

There were occasional respites. Victor's father's world, not so much the day-to-day minutiae of bookmaking, but the colourful larger-than-life people and places, was a constant source of fascination. "Epsom has always felt special to me. When we were children, my father used to take us to the funfair on the Downs on the Sunday before the Derby. You'd see people like Jabez Barker, the 'King of the Gypsies', who had a shock of white hair and was always immaculately dressed. When he was at the races, Jabez had a uniformed chauffeur in a peaked cap who used to follow him around with an umbrella in case it rained. My father had the number one boards pitch at Epsom. I remember one day there when he lost his temper with the pickpockets. 'Will you leave something for me,' he shouted. 'You're having it all.'"

As well as Epsom, there were father and son visits to Sussex gaffe tracks like Fontwell, Plumpton and Lewes. High up on the Downs, with sweeping views out towards Newhaven in one direction, Eastbourne in another and Brighton in another, Lewes was still one of the most attractive venues in the country, as long as the rain stayed away. It was still a training centre too, and home to respected figures like Tom Masson, Don Butchers – who saddled the 1961 Cheltenham Gold Cup winner Saffron Tartan – and Jack 'Towser' Gosden, father of John. But in 1963, the Betting Levy Board indicated that it was one of a dozen tracks from which it intended to withdraw financial support, a bit like Dr Beeching axing provincial railway lines. The prize money was poor and the facilities run down, and sadly it closed in 1964. "I seem to remember that we were there on the last day," recalls Victor. "Tom Masson, who had once trained horses in the circus, had his stable right by the course. He had a reputation for being brilliant with difficult animals and he trained a couple for the Queen. Unfortunately, they were taken away after Buckingham Palace discovered that he was 'living in sin' with Sylvia, his partner for over 25 years, rather than with his wife. He was always extremely well dressed, with a silk handkerchief overflowing from his top pocket, and he used to take a couple of bottles of sherry with him when he went up to the gallops in the morning. He knew my father well, and he had a fancied runner in the very last race. 'Don't worry,' he told us. 'They always run faster when they know they're going home.'"

The Eridge Park Maiden Plate was a two-year-old contest over five furlongs, and the 'good thing' – a 7-1 chance called Miss Rhondda, ridden by Bobby Elliott – won comfortably, well backed by Victor senior. There were celebrations with Masson in the bar afterwards, and Young Victor was thrilled by the chutzpah and sociability of it all, and by the assorted strange and colourful characters – owners, trainers, jockeys, touts and fellow bookmakers – who came up to pay homage to his father and share their company.

The 13-year-old boy went home to Seaford dreaming of the time when he too would be able to enjoy high life and fast times free from the oppressive constraints of school. Unfortunately, there was a further stretch of institutional confinement to endure first. Chandler junior may not have excelled at Hollingbury Court, but his father was still determined to make a gentleman out of him, and that meant following his own – and Ronnie's and Percy's – example, and going on to Highgate in September 1964. Victor senior had kept in touch with his old housemaster Theodore Mallinson, a kindly, literary man and keen racing lover who used to join Victor and Betty Chandler for a picnic lunch in the car park at Epsom on Derby Day each June. Mallinson, though, was not typical of the Highgate staffroom in the mid-1960s. Young Victor's housemaster was a bachelor called Norris Butcher, who had been a Highgate pupil in Victor senior's time and was regarded as "rather suspicious" by the boys and definitely not a racing man.

Butcher's strict approach was a reflection of the ethos and architecture of Highgate (motto: 'higher through prayer'), which remained a boarding school until the early 1990s and has only been co-educational since 2004. The mostly Victorian red brick buildings are redolent of cold showers and muscular Christianity. There's a chapel and cloisters with stained glass and standard motifs of crusaders with swords and shields and Latin mottos. Three and four-storey classrooms with high windows make it hard for the pupils to peer out, and black wrought iron Memorial Gates guard the entrance on Highgate West Hill where a notice continues to inform all visitors that they 'must report' to the porter's lodge. Not 'please' would they report, or they are 'requested' to report, but they *must* report. Schools never lose their distinctive tone. "They still had fagging when I first went there," recalled Young Victor. They still had corporal punishment too, and VC was thrashed by Norris Butcher for loyally refusing to grass up a fellow pupil to the authorities.

There was one other sympathetic master as well as Theodore Mallinson. "When I was about 14, my history teacher, Mr Rowlandson, was fascinated by racehorses and bookmaking, and he taught me mathematical fractions. 'This will be useful to you if you ever go into the family business,' he said." Mr Rowlandson was a far-sighted man, and years later, Victor would send both him and Mr Mallinson tickets to the races at places like Ascot and Epsom.

The bookmaker's son passed one O Level at Highgate – woodwork at the age of 14 – but otherwise failed to distinguish himself. Looking back, he honourably admits that he "may have fallen into bad company." But bad company was so much more enjoyable than good, and part of the problem for restless adolescents cooped up in the Highgate dorms was that, for all its rules and stern edicts, the school was within sight and easy reach of all manner of metropolitan temptations and delights.

The teenage Chandler's favourite band was The Rolling Stones. "I think at that time you were either a Stones fan or a Beatles fan, and I preferred the Stones." But it was that trip down to the Flamingo Club in Wardour Street to see Big Dee Irwin, who had posted a top ten hit with 'Swinging On A Star', that brought about his downfall. As well as the music and the aura of forbidden pleasure, the other big attraction was the opportunity to mix with girls, a prohibited species at Highgate but available in large numbers at Channing School for girls, a 10-minute walk away.

Sadly, Victor's absence was noted and an investigation launched. Nemesis followed with all the usual trappings. The headmasterly summons. The solemn interviews. The disappointed parents and Norris Butcher invoking the subversive influence of 007. Young Victor couldn't just be thrown out (as the future Middlesex and England cricketer Phil Tuffnell was from Highgate in 1978) as his father was an old boy. The ritual required that he be 'asked to leave.' And asked he duly was.

Those were not good times for Young Victor Chandler, his spirits soured by five years at Hollingbury Court and three more at Highgate. He succumbed to lethargy and depression, which his mother Betty felt may have been caused by glandular fever or may have been a kind of ME, which was not officially recognised or treated at the time. On a family holiday to the Bahamas the previous year, he had felt so low that he'd attempted to drink a bottle of gin and walk into the sea. Something was clearly awry. But what now? Another school? A move abroad? Work? But doing what? At the time, Young Victor had no desire to follow in his father's footsteps. He loved the glamour of racing but wanted to rebel against the older generation, just like his Uncle Billy had set up in opposition to Bill.

Fortunately, salvation was at hand. It just needed to wait for a chance encounter later that summer to manifest itself.

Chapter Nine

Boss Meyer

I n March 1966, Harold Wilson's Labour Government introduced a new betting tax at 2.5 per cent, which went up to 5 per cent by the end of 1967. The new duty, along with other aspects of Labour's high taxation policies, alarmed Victor senior, who foresaw hard times ahead for the bookmakers. But there was one other sector of the British gambling industry that was thriving.

The collapse of the 1958 case against John Aspinall, who had been charged with holding illegal Chemin de Fer parties in private houses in London, presaged the broader changes that resulted in the 1960 Betting and Gaming Act. The new law not only legalised off-course betting shops, ending over a century of hypocrisy, it also contained a loophole which became known as 'the Vicars' Charter.' Designed to permit whist drives in church halls, it was exploited to allow the opening of new casinos and members clubs, offering gambling as well as food, drink and late-night entertainment. The Conservative Prime Minister Harold Macmillan, an Old Etonian ex-guards officer married to one of the Duke of Devonshire's daughters, was uncomfortable with the pace of change. But the British public, finally emerging from the post-war austerity age with all its stiff upper lip inhibitions, were hungry for materialistic pleasures, and within six months of legalisation, there were an estimated 10,000 off-course betting shops in Britain. There were also over 1,000 casino licences successfully applied for within five years.

The new betting offices were obliged by law to be inhospitable affairs with creature comforts kept to a minimum to discourage punters from hanging around in them all day. But the new casinos ranged from flash local niteries in northern cities, like the racehorse owner Joe Lisle's Sixty Nine Club in Newcastle, to the exclusive Clermont Club in London's Berkeley Square. The Clermont's owner, John Aspinall, specifically targeted moneyed members of the aristocracy with the intention of parting upper-class fools from their money. But on the cusp of the Swinging Sixties, clubs like the Astor, the Playboy and the Nightingale, catered to a more gregarious demimonde, with a mixture of toffs and villains, starlets and MPs, passing through their doors every night.

London's gambling scene attracted the interest of the Mafia, who had been looking for new locations since Castro's revolution drove them out of Cuba in 1959. Meyer Lansky, the Mob's financial master-mind, and his right-hand man, Dino Cellini, set up a croupier's school in Hanover Square, and in February 1966, the Philadelphia crime boss Angelo Bruno, who ran the hotel and casino business in Atlantic City, flew over to London and stayed for a week at the Hilton Hotel on Park Lane. Meetings took place between Bruno and Albert Dimes, the homegrown gangster whose Italian father ran a café/restaurant called La Veneziana in Saffron Hill in the 1930s. Dimes had inherited a number of the old Sabini family interests, including their involvement in horse racing, and had his own bookmaking business with an office in Frith Street, next door to the Bar Italia. The Americans proposed a partnership to Dimes, with them taking shares in the Colony Club in Berkeley Square (not to be confused with Muriel Belcher's Colony Room drinking club in Soho). A substantial sum was spent on doing the place up, and the old Hollywood star George Raft was brought over from California to act as frontman and greeter. A lifelong Mob associate, Raft had made his name in 1930s Warner Brothers gangster movies like *Scarface* and *Each Dawn I Die*, but is best remembered today for his entertaining self-parody as 'Spats Colombo' in *Some Like It Hot*.

The first junket, or Pan American plane-load of high rollers, arrived within months, accompanied by Raft, who told reporters that he was delighted to be in England and, no, he'd never heard of the Mafia and had no idea what it was. A few nights later, he was photographed, dapper as ever in black tie, spinning the roulette wheel at the Colony's grand opening. Las Vegas glamour, it seemed, had come to London.

In fact, the Mafia's involvement was to be short lived, and Raft and Dino Cellini were among eight Americans denied re-entry to the UK by the Labour Home Secretary Roy Jenkins the following year. But confidence in the market remained high, and in the same year as the Colony launched, Victor Chandler senior, no doubt mindful of his father's illicit Piccadilly Hotel casino during the war, decided he'd get on board. In partnership with the racehorse owner Charles St George and Sam Norman, a self-made Cockney who had made a fortune in jukeboxes and married Billy Chandler's widow Elsa, he opened the New Casanova Club in Chesterfield Street, a short walk away from Berkeley Square.

The club had formerly belonged to an exotic Polish gambler called Ricky Dayjur, one of three émigré brothers who had come over to London before the war. There was a smart restaurant and bar downstairs and a gaming salon upstairs along with special rooms for private gatherings. The manageress, Pauline Wallis, was an exuberant character who was born in Ireland and had previously run The Pair Of Shoes in Hertford Street. Her brother, Colonel Tommy Wallis, was the managing director of the Jockey Club subsidiary Racehorse Holdings Trust, and her nephew, Stephen, would one day become manager of Epsom and Newmarket racecourses and is currently group director of international racing and racing relations at the JC. Pauline's passion was greyhound racing – she used to walk around London with one until it ran away one day on Marylebone High Street – and, after her nightclub days were over, she married a multi-millionaire Irish dog-racing fanatic and became a successful trainer of greyhounds in both Ireland and the US.

It was Wallis who dressed and trained the Casanova Club hostesses, who had to be smart and glamorous, not bunny girls or hookers, and the tactile mix of hot women, bouffant hair, thick pile carpets and clinking glasses was intended to persuade customers who came for drinks and dinner to go upstairs to the gaming tables afterwards and then to stay long enough to spend a fair measure of their winnings, if they had any, on the premises.

Richard Burton and Elizabeth Taylor, the megawatt celebrities of the age, were guests at the 1966 opening-night party. Old money and new rubbing shoulders amid the soft lighting and the cigarette smoke. Princess Margaret and her set came regularly too, and she even had her own chair with her initials on the back. Another celebrity guest was the Maharajah of Baroda, who used to wear a shot silk pink or lime green Nehru jacket with diamond buttons. One night he was drunk, and losing heavily, so he ripped the buttons off his jacket and threw them down on the table. "There," he said. "You've had everything else. You might as well have them too."

In London in that era, there were sometimes less welcome visitors. Gangsters like the Kray Twins, who tried to shake down West End clubs and demand money in return for 'protection.' Victor senior had a minder, a tough character called Johnny Kelly who had worked for Owney Madden, the owner of the Cotton Club in New York, who 'looked out for him' and ensured the New Casanova was safe from predatory incursions. But as the bookmaker surveyed his clientele one warm July evening, he noticed the same solitary male punter who seemed to have been there on the same stool every night for the past week. He had no idea who he was and initially wondered if he was there on a hostile mission. But as befits a good host, he went over to engage the gentleman in conversation, ordering them both a large drink as he went. It transpired that the solitary gambler – tall, moustachioed, wearing a dinner jacket and resembling a cross between John Cleese and Ronald Coleman – was Rollo John Oliver Meyer, better known as Jack or 'Boss' Meyer, founder and headmaster of Millfield School in Somerset.

The 61-year-old Meyer, a distinguished school and Varsity cricketer with a Cambridge Blue along with a double first in Classics, had been a private tutor in India. He started Millfield when he returned to England in 1935 and his first seven pupils were Indian boys, six of whom were sons of Princes. By the 1960s, he had gradually established Millfield as one of the more unusual – and expensive – public schools in the country. In particular, Meyer's policy of admitting naturally talented pupils, especially athletes, whatever their background, and then making the parents of his richer students pay for their education, was creating a less conventional mix than the typical 1960s intake at more traditional establishments like Charterhouse or Rugby.

Meyer was frequently described as eccentric, and his willingness to challenge conformity was typified by his passion for gambling in general, and horse racing in particular. Victor senior found him good company and unfailingly charming to the club staff. He had been on a losing run at the tables, but it was when he started asking searching questions about racing odds and tips that the bookmaker appreciated just how different he was to the Highgate-Hollingbury mould of schoolmaster. As they shared a bottle of champagne together, the clock moving on beyond 1am, he explained to the sympathetic listener the problems he was having with his delinquent 15-year-old. Boss had an obvious answer. "Why don't you send him down to me?" he said, "we'll see what we can do."

In late August, while Victor senior was away at York races, Betty Chandler drove their son down to the West Country. The interview with Meyer was, as expected, an unorthodox one. He began by asking Young Victor what his ambitions were. The teenager replied that he wanted to leave school and go to Europe and work in a casino. "Well, why don't you come here first and finish your education and then you can go and work in a casino," suggested Meyer. No doubt conscious of his mother's presence, and that there didn't seem to be an awful lot of alternatives, Young Victor agreed.

Boss asked VC how much money he'd got in his pockets? The boy investigated. The answer appeared to be in the region of £4-10 shillings. "Very well then," said Meyer. "We'll play two holes of golf

for that this morning. If you win, I'll double it. If you lose, I keep it."
Young Victor had negligible golfing experience, but Meyer was as good
as his word, winning the two-hole contest with ease and pocketing his
new pupil's funds. He didn't expect him to plea to be reimbursed either.
A lesson of sorts was being learned. If you want to play... you've got
to pay.

The game of golf was a rare instance of financial dealings between
Meyer and the Chandler family going in the headmaster's favour. "He
was a big punter on racing with my father," recalled Young Victor,
"and invariably a losing one too. He was also losing money at the club,
and I think that in the whole time I was there, we never had to pay very
much in the way of a bill. The school fees (which were about £1,100
a term in 1969, and more like £12,000 a term today) were always just
deducted from Boss's gambling losses."

Hardly surprisingly after Highgate and Norris Butcher, Young Victor
settled down quickly to Millfield life. "The whole three years there were
nothing but a pleasure," he remembers. There was no official uniform
– the boys wore sports jackets rather than blazers – and although they
did have prefects and punishments, they didn't seem to bother the new
boy who found himself free to follow his own interests most days of the
week. The academic side of things was stimulating – with English his
favourite A Level subject, and Graham Greene, Somerset Maugham,
Scott Fitzgerald and Henry James his favourite authors – but never
too pressing, and excursions to the races were seen as no less character
building than team games. How could they not be when the headmaster took two days off each year to go to Royal Ascot, and attendance
at Bath and Salisbury, as well as at West Country point to points, was
not discouraged.

The school is situated on a hill on the edges of Street, a rather run
down Somerset town famous for the Clark's shoe factory that closed
in 1993. The rows of modest post-war houses that line the road up
to the campus give little clue to the breathtaking facilities, especially
sporting facilities, that lie beyond the gates. There are innumerable
floodlit rugby, football and hockey pitches, grass and hard tennis courts,

riding stables, an Olympic-size swimming pool, a mini Crystal Palace athletics track with a cinder surface, and a county-standard first eleven cricket ground with a pavilion – which faces out towards Glastonbury Tor – festooned with the details of past winning teams. To arrest any impression of sport-obsessed philistinism, the last 30 years have also seen the construction of a lavishly equipped theatre and English and History blocks as well as a range of Business and Technology, Craft and Design Centres.

The golf course is in front of Millfield House, the oldest remaining building where Meyer had his study and once part of the Clark family estate. There's a striking bronze bust of Boss on the lawn outside, but almost every other school classroom and office now dates from after Victor's time and was built in the late Seventies at the earliest.

Current staff members seem anxious to distance themselves from the public perception of Millfield in Boss's era. "We're not really liberal anymore," insisted one house parent, a PhD graduate and son of a comprehensive school headmaster from South Wales. "Millfield's changed a lot since Meyer's day." Not according to a long-serving cab driver in Street, a self-proclaimed 'cider drinker and working man' who reckons the pupils have hardly changed at all. "They've always been 20 per cent rich and friendly and 80 per cent spoiled and vile," in his view. "They're always ringing up for a taxi to take them into the town at lunchtime. Most of them won't walk anywhere."

Young Victor's background, if not rich, was certainly comfortable, but contemporaries remember him as friendly and generous rather than spoiled and vile, though he didn't favour walking. "Victor's clothes were always impressively well tailored," recalls his old school friend Adam Cole, who had also been taken on by Boss after being expelled from Harrow. The two boys met on the train on their way down to Taunton at the start of their first term. Adam lived in Winchester and his father owned a company which manufactured garage forecourts. The older Cole had stern views about gambling and didn't approve of either Victor or his father. That didn't bother the teenagers who, although they weren't in the same house at Millfield, quickly became friends, staying with each other during the school holidays and sharing the same mildly rebellious tastes. "Victor used to take us all to a café in Street for egg and chips, and he always paid," remembers Cole. "He also had his own taxi driver pretty much on permanent call." The cabbie in question was a Mr Durston, better known as 'Dirty Durston,' who owned a grocery shop and drove a Vauxhall Victor, which he kept permanently supplied with boxes of condoms he was prepared to sell to Millfield pupils at a discount. Dirty Durston was the chauffeur of choice in daylight and when the authorities might be watching, but Victor and Adam Cole also had another driver, a sixth former like themselves, who ferried them around after dark.

Victor's Millfield lifestyle was subsidised not so much by his parents as by a windfall from a tip he was given by one of his father's Brighton connections. Harry Pearlberg was a punter and financier who threw famous Christmas parties in a house decorated with a lot of new money "but not a lot of taste." Pearlberg was something in the City, even if the City didn't approve of him, and when Young Victor was 16, he told him to buy a stake in a soon-to-be coveted stock called Brayhead, trading at the time at one shilling and sixpence a share. Victor cashed in his post office savings book and bought "about £700 worth of shares. Mr Hawker, who taught commerce at Millfield, found me a broker, and within six months, the stock had gone up to ten bob and I ended up with a profit of over £6,000."

Victor had shared Harry Pearlberg's tip with some of his friends in the same house, and between them they clubbed together and bought an old Austin A40, which they gave to their fellow sixth former Mokato Assai, who was a year older than them and already had a driver's licence. The son of a diplomat at the Japanese Embassy in London, 'Sid' was happy to conduct his friends on nocturnal jaunts around Somerset village pubs where they all "drank that revolting cloudy cider and played skittles."

One night, Victor and Adam went further afield using the cover of a school 'hop' or dance to skive off to Bristol where they hoped to get into an appearance by the Maharishi Mahesh Yogi, the transcendental meditation guru who had become a spiritual advisor to The Beatles. But when the boys got to Colston Hall, they found that the show was sold out. On another occasion, Victor went off to the local point to point at Kingston St Mary, where a boy called Nigel Wrighton was due to ride his father's horse, which was considered a good thing. "We all piled into the horse box, loaded up with readies. The odds were 6-4 and it was a fence in front with only one left to jump. We were all screaming our heads off, but just at that moment, Nigel looked up to see what the noise was and the horse hit the top of the fence and came down." The horse was fine but the readies were lost.

The day at the races had been officially sanctioned but, strictly speaking, some of the other escapades were in breach of school rules. Fortunately, teachers like Mr Hawker "were very relaxed about things like smoking and drinking." As well as teaching business studies, he also ran the go-karting team, of which Victor was a member. But he did draw the line at skipping his lessons. "One day I was meant to be at a double period, but I fell asleep outside reading a book in the sunshine. He (Hawker) found me there and remonstrated that, of all the classes in the school, his were the ones I should be attending." Victor did his best, but there were still days when the bookmaker's son and keen student of form felt his commercial interests compelled him to visit the nearest betting office, which was not in Street, but in Glastonbury, a few miles away.

Racing and bookmaking are hardly the dominant themes of Glaston-bury circa 2021. But before the town's reincarnation as the spiritual home of new-age travellers, healers, street musicians and mystical incense salesmen, it had a betting shop down a side street just off the marketplace. It was owned by the West Country bookie David Pipe, father of the future champion trainer Martin and grandfather of David junior. In 1973, Pipe sold his chain to William Hill, using part of the money to buy Martin a stable, but when Young Victor spent long hours there 50 years ago, the shop was still all Somerset. Dave Pipe knew Victor senior and kept a friendly lookout for his son, inviting him to "a very cordial Sunday lunch." The friendship lasted, and more than 20 years later, one of Martin Pipe's owners put VC, by then a bookmaking high roller, on their novice hurdler Sondrio, who landed a gamble in the 1989 Supreme Novices' Hurdle at Cheltenham at odds of 25-1.

Racing matters seemed to offer the schoolboy an acceptable excuse for his absences, though there was one occasion when a non-racing and non-drinking and smoking Millfield member of staff followed him to the Glastonbury shop, waited for him to come out and then trailed him back to school again. Colin Atkinson, a former Somerset county cricketer who was chairman of the club when Ian Botham, Viv Richards and Joel Garner left acrimoniously in 1979, was a more traditional authority figure than Mr Hawker. He confronted Young Victor with the evidence of his truancy and then marched him off to the headmaster's study. But to his frustration, Boss was unmoved, merely observing that given the nature of his father's occupation, it was understandable that his son would want to "pop round" to a betting office from time to time "to see how he was getting on."

Meyer's tolerance was no doubt also prompted by awareness of his betting arrears with Victor's father, which gave him little scope for punishing his son. On one occasion, he even recruited the pupil to get his money on for him, frustrating school business preventing him from being at the races himself. It was June 1968, and Young Victor was called to the head's study and told "You're going to Ascot." Meyer wanted to back three horses at the royal meeting, all of them trained by Major Peter Nelson, whose sons John and Charlie were also Millfield pupils. The bets, which were spread over several days, were to be £200 to win on the first one, three £100 doubles and one £100 treble, and Young Victor was under strict instructions to get the best possible odds and ring the headmaster each evening to tell him how he'd got on. He travelled up to London on the train from Taunton, Boss having purchased him a ticket, stayed with his father and mother in their flat in Marylebone, and accompanied them to the races, enjoying the hospitality in Victor senior's box each day. It was a memorable week. "The first one won and the second one won, but the third got beat. When I got back to school with

Boss's winnings, he gave me a £20 tip and said 'I hope you backed them too.'"

What with pub crawls, visits to the races and the café in Street, Young Victor's sixth-form career was rarely a strenuous one, but he didn't get off so lightly during the school holidays. His regular vacation job was working for his father in the London credit and telephone office, which by then included a betting shop on the ground floor, at 81 Great Portland Street, not far from Oxford Circus. The older Chandler didn't hold with liberal nostrums where timekeeping and application were concerned. "I was sacked at least twice when I was working for my father. On one occasion, he came in and caught me using an upturned umbrella to putt golf balls into a cup on the office carpet. He didn't really feel that was what he was paying me for. Then there was another day when he came back from lunch and found me asleep in a chair. Racing had already started and I was meant to be answering the phone." Young Victor was sleeping off the effects of a good night out. There were a lot of good times by his 17th year, and one of his best and most inspirationally wayward companions was his Anglo-Irish cousin.

Victor's Uncle Ronnie was the most handsome of all the Chandler brothers, and he retained his good looks right up until his death in 2008, aged 88. When they were teenagers, Percy, Ronnie and Victor senior were nicknamed The Three Musketeers, and they all learned to ride together, competing in point to points and hunting with the Enfield Chace. Victor senior had a palomino called Pink Gin, and all the horses were named after cocktails. But as befits a son of the founder of Walthamstow Stadium, Ronnie's special skill was his almost God-given talent at training a champion greyhound like Dillie's Pigalle, one of his hat-trick of winners of the Irish Derby at Clonmel between 1964 and 1966. Away from the coursing fields and the greyhound tracks, Ronnie remained an enthusiastic, if not always successful, punter, and a world-class bon viveur and ladies' man. At one point, it seemed to his envious English-based siblings that he spent much of his time in the bar of the Shelbourne Hotel in Dublin, where he was always surrounded by beautiful women.

In 1948, Ronnie married Iris Todd, the dark-haired, dark-eyed daughter of a drapery and shoe shop owner from Belfast. She was a Protestant and regular churchgoer and, as Victor recalls, she "had to do a lot of forgiving. Ronnie would come over to London periodically to go wild, and one year he went missing. My father had to go looking for him and eventually he tracked him down in a hotel in the West End." Ronnie explained that he'd been with the fabulously slinky American actress and singer Eartha Kitt and that they hadn't come out of her bedroom for three days. There was also a possibly apocryphal family story that Ronnie once slept with a bride on her wedding night after the groom was unable to perform his conjugal duties.

Back in Northern Ireland, Ronnie and Iris owned a beautiful house overlooking Strangford Lough at Killyleagh in County Down, which was where Ronnie had his first training kennels, and they had four children. The eldest, Ronnie junior, who was a year older than Young Victor, was determined to maintain some of the family traditions, and his English cousin was only too happy to help him.

As a schoolboy in Ireland, Cousin Ronnie had excelled at fencing, and his renown came to the attention of Boss Meyer, who reckoned Millfield's sabres champion of the same age was unbeatable. A challenge was issued and Cousin Ronnie was flown over to take on the Millfield standard bearer. Meyer had a thick bet on his boy with Victor's father, and the result went his way, enabling him to reduce his arrears with the Chandler firm.

Cousin Ronnie made periodic visits to London and sometimes worked with Young Victor at the Great Portland Street office during the school holidays. One lunchtime, he arranged an assignation with two girls in a friend's flat near Abbey Road in St John's Wood. The boys drove round there in Ronnie's open-topped sports car and after a while Ronnie and his date disappeared into the bedroom, leaving the other couple to get down to things on the sofa. "All of a sudden, the bedroom door flew open," said Victor, "and Ronnie came charging out in his underpants. He raced off down the stairs with me in pursuit asking what on earth had happened."

It transpired that the cousins had been entrusted with £40,000 worth of cash that they were meant to pay into Victor senior's bank before the racing started that afternoon. Consumed with lust, Cousin Ronnie had forgotten all about it and had left the float in a bag on the back seat of the open-topped car. When he and Young Victor got out onto the street, they found that Ronnie had left the handbrake off too and the MG had rolled gently down the hill, coming to a halt beside a phone box. Mercifully, little damage had been done to the car, but the real lifesaving discovery was that the money bag was still sitting untouched on the back seat. They never told Victor's father.

It seemed that temptations of one kind or another – sexual, sporting, financial – were never far away during Young Victor's adolescence. Alan Mills sometimes worked downstairs in the Great Portland Street shop, which was in the Rag Trade district and would be packed most afternoons with gambling-mad Yiddisher punters. One busy midweek day, Mills remembers Young Victor "approaching the counter and asking rather sheepishly if he could cash a cheque with the firm. For £10. Of course, his father was away at the races. We weren't sure if he would have approved, but we gave him the money anyway." That wasn't the end of the story. As you might have expected of a leading racecourse bookmaker used to calling the odds, Victor senior had "a very deep and powerful voice" and the next day Mills heard him summoning his errant son. "'Victor,' he was calling. 'Where are you Victor? I need to speak with you at once.' Shortly afterwards, Young Victor appeared looking just like a naughty schoolboy. They disappeared upstairs into his father's office and we could all hear him getting a dressing down."

If Chandler was sometimes the stern parent regarding his son's out-of-school peccadilloes, he took a much more hands-off attitude to what happened in term time. "I don't think he ever came to a single parents' evening or read a report all the years I was at school. But he did sometimes make appearances at Millfield if he'd been racing not far away at places like Taunton or Bath or Cheltenham. Then he'd take me out to supper somewhere special and we'd talk a bit about me and how I was getting on, and a bit about the past. It was the same when I was in London. He used to arrive back at the Weymouth Street flat after work and he'd say to me 'what are you doing this evening then?'" However casual the inquiry, it came with a father's earnest, if unspoken, hope that his much-loved profligate son would say 'nothing in particular, Dad,' and then Victor senior would say, 'well how about a spot of dinner?'

Those were memorable evenings. "He'd reminisce about his life and tell me stories about all kinds of people, and we wouldn't get back until really late." There were so many good stories too, most of them cautionary ones. The racecourse betting ring had never been a place for the naive or the unwary, but when Victor senior was starting out in the post-war era, there were some notorious sharks and snakes – owners, trainers, jockeys and fellow bookmakers all trying to double-cross each other. In 1947, the year before the Sterope gamble, Chandler had gone for a touch on a horse called Arbar in the St Leger at Doncaster. The French colt was owned by the all-conquering textile millionaire Marcel Boussac, and the bookie stood to win £84,000 (more like two and a half million today) if it triumphed. What Victor senior didn't know was that Arbar's rider Charlie Elliott, a top jockey but also an incorrigible punter, had backed the Derby winner Pearl Diver instead. As a result, he delayed his challenge up the long Doncaster straight, only kicking on when he was satisfied Pearl Diver wasn't going to win. Arbar finished strongly, but too late, and was beaten a head by Sayajirao, owned by the Maharajah of Baroda.

Another crafty jockey-punter was Elliott's rival, Charlie Smirke, who rode Royal Tara, runner-up to Sterope in the 1948 Cambridgeshire. One summer evening a year later, 'Smirkey' was riding in a two-year-old race at Alexandra Park. In the weighing room beforehand, the young apprentice riding the favourite boasted that his mount was unbeatable. But as they went out to saddle up, Smirke leaned over to him and said "Son, you've got no chance. I'm riding a three-year-old."

One of the biggest casualties of that period was Chandler's friend and fellow bookmaker Percy Thompson, who used to lay and place enormous bets. At one point, he drove the same car as the royal family and gave his wife a diamond ring similar to the one Edward VIII gave Mrs Simpson before the abdication. But in 1951, his biggest client died in a light plane crash on his way back to the south of France. He owed Percy over £300,000 at the time and the bookie never got paid. There were other defaulters too, and as Thompson's situation worsened, he started drowning his sorrows in Scotch whisky. He ended up selling his racecourse business and his Mayfair office and working anonymously for Victor's father in his Brighton betting shop.

A happier story was Victor senior's participation in the famous coup landed by Frankincense in the 1968 Lincoln at Doncaster. The four-year-old was trained at Newmarket by John Oxley, who's travelling head lad Barry Hills had watched the colt beating his stable companions out of sight on the gallops and couldn't envisage defeat on Town Moor. Victor's father helped Hills to get his money on ante-post, taking a raft of prices from 66-1 downwards. Starting 100-8 favourite on the day, Frankincense won by half a length, securing Hills enough money to set up on his own as a trainer and also leaving Victor's father handsomely in profit. Barry Hills, he advised his son, was a very shrewd man who "liked to lay horses as well as back them, and knew what he was doing all the time."

Young Victor was fascinated by all the exotic tales of big winners and losers. But perhaps as a result of his earlier experiences, his father's anecdotes didn't include any encouragement to his son to follow in his footsteps. "I think by the late Sixties he was really worried that bookmaking, especially traditional racecourse bookmaking, was on the way out. The betting tax had been introduced both on course and off. The Arabs had yet to come in and high taxes had wiped out a lot of the old post-war punters. He didn't see any future for me and him working together. I think he just hoped I'd make a good life in some world away from the racecourse."

University in the UK may not have been an option, but Boss Meyer felt Victor was just the type to benefit from a less formal college education in the US and "twisted my arm" to take the multiple-choice American SAT, or Selective Attainment Test, at the English Speaking

Union in London. After the exam was over, Young Victor set off on the archetypal 18-year old's Greyhound bus trip across the States in the spring of his final school year. Mike Kearns, an American friend at Highgate, whose father was the CBS correspondent in Europe, had been awarded a scholarship at the University of West Virginia in Morgantown, and VC stopped off there to check it out. "It was a really weird place. I was watching TV in my hotel room and they were reporting on a shooting, and I realised from the pictures it had taken place right outside where I was staying."

The English boy got back on the bus and carried on to the infinitely more seductive surroundings of Southern California. In Los Angeles, he was looked after by a couple of old racing friends of his father's: "Anne Stirling, an incredibly sexy woman who lived in Beverley Hills, and her mother Mrs Lazarus, who lived next door to Paul Newman and was racing mad. She used to get me to drive her out to Santa Anita in the afternoons." Victor fell in love with the whole laid-back Californian ambience and applied to read English at UCLA "but it was a long way away and, to my regret, I decided to go to catering college in Switzerland instead as a stepping-stone to casino and hotel management. I'd applied to the Glion Academy in Montreux at the same time, and Dad said, 'well, if you're going to go there, you'd better go to Paris first and learn French.'"

And so it was, that in the summer of 1969, Young Victor's scholastic education came to an end. He left Millfield, saying goodbye to Boss Meyer and Mr Hawker, and to friends like Adam Cole – who went on to start the 'adult film company' Electric Blue – Japanese Sid and Tony Connell – who had been at Highgate and "at one time owned five or six wine bars in the City and the West End, and whose father was one of the original Mad Men in the advertising world." There was one final jamboree in the Millfield school grounds, where Betty Chandler and Elsa Norman ran the champagne tent, and then Young Victor headed off for London, Paris, Zurich and beyond. Destined to work briefly, though memorably, in all kinds of different jobs, but absolutely determined to enjoy every experience along the way.

Chapter Ten

Adventures of a
Prodigal Son

I n the autumn of 1969, Young Victor Chandler was in love. The
object of his affection was Gisèle Cesar, whose mother was from
Madagascar and whose father was a General in the French army.
Five-foot five-inches tall, dark and gamine, Gisèle had come over to
England to work as an au pair girl and then had gone on to be the re-
ceptionist at the Casanova Club, which was where she and Victor met.

Come September, Victor was meant to be setting off to Paris to begin
his rite of passage and the first stage of his apprenticeship in the hotel
and catering trade, and he managed to persuade Gisèle to follow him.
The couple rented a modest second-floor room in a hotel on the Left
Bank Rue de l'Université, which ran parallel to the Boulevard Saint-
Germain and was only a block away from the Seine.

Young Victor, now long haired and wearing an Afghan jacket, a black
polo-necked jersey and shades, took to life in Paris with all the enthusiasm you would expect of an imaginative 18-year-old newly released
from school. He loved French wine, tobacco and the coffee that was so
much stronger than the insipid cups of instant served in Britain. He
loved the atmosphere in the cafés and the opening hours, so much less

restrictive than at home. He loved the delicious taste of steak tartare and steak frites, and the big displays of shellfish – oysters, langoustines and crab – all boxed around with ice and on display outside the grand old brasseries like Lipp and La Coupole.

But Victor was on a budget and had promised his father he'd contribute to his upkeep while he was away. On his own initiative, he managed to get a job as a trainee skivvy in the kitchens of the Plaza Athénée, the sumptuously smart five-star hotel on the Avenue Montaigne, a short walk from the Place de la Concorde and the Champs-Élysées.

The Plaza Athénée restaurant, complete with red velvet curtains and marble floors, served food of exceptional quality and dizzying expense, like their trademark Mille Feuille de Homard, which even back in 1969 retailed at roughly £50 a plate. Young Victor's task, hidden away in the bowels of the subterranean kitchen, was to peel and prepare vegetables and throw away the rubbish. He lasted four months before the head chef – a strict disciplinarian who would deal severely with even so much as one incorrectly prepared courgette or haricot vert – sacked him for failing to turn up to work for two days running.

VC had been getting a small allowance from his father, but without the additional stipend from the Plaza Athénée, his situation living with Gisèle in the hotel on the Rue de l'Université was untenable. There was also an awkward moment when Gisèle went over to London for a few days 'on business' and Victor called her early one morning, only for his cousin Ronnie to answer the phone.

With the romance under strain and funds running low, Victor senior decided that things should be reorganised on more economical lines and consulted his great Parisian friend Patrice des Moutis, who was the biggest illegal bookmaker in France, about alternative accommodation. "Dad came over and got me to move out of the hotel and move in with an old friend of Patrice's called the Comtesse de Damas, who lived in this great big house in Saint-Germain-des-Prés. Her family was very aristocratic, but a bit Nouveau Pauvre. Her great grandfather had been the French ambassador to the court of Catherine the Great. It was his job to send back reports on her love life. I only really saw the Comtesse at mealtimes. I think she thought I was completely insane."

By this point, Gisèle had moved on in search of another job and perhaps sensing that life with her young English boyfriend might not be so much fun now that he was corralled under somebody else's roof. Victor's status at the Comtesse's house was that of a paying guest, and he was under orders from home to behave himself. He was expected to show up at breakfast in the mornings and then again at dinner in the evening, and to begin with, he had no difficulty keeping the appointments. "I was completely skint at the time and I couldn't have afforded to eat anywhere else, even if I'd wanted to."

The young man's scope for adventure was further curtailed by his father's insistence that he enrol in a language school, so as to properly learn French if he wanted to go on to Glion afterwards. The majority of Victor's fellow students in the Lycée Catholique on the Rue Raspail were "women from all over the world, and we had to speak French all the time." With time on his hands each afternoon, Victor spent it on long walks around the city, gazing longingly through the windows of the best (and most expensive) galleries, restaurants and shops.

In the summer, when the Lycée was closed for the holidays, his new-found linguistic skills enabled him to get a night-time job as a barman at Le Chat Noir (a play on the French word for pussy), a strip joint not far from the Champs-Élysées. "All the Parisians left town in August, but the dives remained open for the tourists, and the club was packed every evening. It took me a while to realise that most of the girls were actually boys in drag, but the foreign punters never seemed to catch on." The 18-year-old fell for one of the hostesses at the club – "who was definitely not a boy" – and she became his new girlfriend. When the couple weren't working, they and their friends used to go to the Piscine Deligny, the floating swimming pool on the Seine, which was moored in the 7th arrondissement, right in front of the National Assembly.

When his job at the Black Cat Club came to an end, Victor progressed to the rather more chi-chi role of menswear salesman at the

Boulevard Saint-Germain shop of the designer Jean Bouquin, who had one branch in Paris and another in Saint Tropez. In the late Sixties and early Seventies, Bouquin had a reputation as an ultra-stylish purveyor of hippie chic to actresses like Brigitte Bardot and Jane Birkin, but he also dressed men and "was looking for someone bi-lingual and moderately sensible to help look after his American customers." Victor performed the role very capably, enjoying the Bohemian ambience and was rewarded with several shirts and pairs of crushed velvet Bouquin trousers at reduced rates.

Finances were improving and, from spring to autumn, Victor started making solitary Sunday afternoon trips out to Longchamp racecourse on the edges of the Bois de Boulogne. More than 30 years later, he would make the same journey in a chauffeur-driven Mercedes provided by the Hotel George V, but back then it meant finding his way there in the white Mini Cooper with the black roof he'd driven over in from England. Longchamp is one of the most beautiful racecourse settings in the world, especially during the Prix de l'Arc de Triomphe meeting in October. When Young Victor first went there, it was dominated by two vast modern grandstands that were put up in the 1960s (and demolished in 2015), but then, as now, outside of the biggest days, the crowds were sparse.

In Victor's eyes, the most conspicuous absentees were the bookmakers who had been banned from French racecourses since 1891. With no rival odds-makers competing for custom, punters were officially hostages of the notoriously inefficient PMU, or Pari-Mutuel Urbain Tote-based system with its restrictive prices and wondrously unsmiling cashiers. Not surprisingly, VC found his first taste of the PMU monopoly a soulless affair, a bit like drinking thin consommé when you could have been enjoying a hearty onion soup. He wasn't the first member of the Chandler family to think he could have livened things up. His father had already been down that route.

On Arc day in October 1969, Victor senior was arrested in the Brasserie Gladiateur at Longchamp and accused of illegal bookmaking. He had to spend several hours locked up in the racecourse police station until the combined efforts of Patrice des Moutis – who was himself banned from going racing but was reachable by phone – and the racehorse owner Charles St George persuaded the French racing supremo Jean Romanet to let him go. He was given a stern talking to first, and warned never to do it again. His son found the whole story highly amusing. "He had three clerks with him, and they were sitting there at a table in broad daylight taking fortunes."

One day, Young Victor would take on the PMU himself, playing a cat and mouse game with the French gambling police, like an outlaw with a posse and ending up at the top of their most wanted list. That first Sunday, though, he contented himself with bluffing the official at the entrance to the Salle Privée area behind the paddock into thinking he was an English trainer's representative or a jockey's agent. Then, once safely inside, he sidled up to Lester Piggott as the great jockey made his way back from the unsaddling enclosure to the weighing room. Victor knew Lester, or to be more precise, his parents did. The Long Fellow was a lifelong friend of Victor senior, and Victor and Betty Chandler and Lester and Susan Piggott had holidayed together in the Bahamas, Lester renting the Chandlers his beach bungalow in Nassau and moving into the house of his patron, the financier Sir Victor Sassoon, for the duration of their stay.

By 1970, Lester was going over to France every Sunday to ride at the big meetings at Longchamp, Chantilly and Saint-Cloud. Sometimes he was employed by visiting English and Irish trainers, sometimes by the locals. Expressionless as ever, he recognised Young Victor, and where frustrated journalists may have been straining unsuccessfully for a word, he rewarded the teenager with a few terse but priceless observations about his upcoming rides. VC, respectful but also excited at having made contact with an icon, fell away afterwards and went off to back the jockey's tips at the PMU windows. Then, at the end of the afternoon, his pockets frequently bulging with francs, he'd watch from a distance as Lester was ushered into a taxi to be whisked away to the airport for his flight back to Britain. More than 30 years later, the selfsame Lester, now long retired but still a family friend, would be one of Victor's regular guests for the whole Prix de l'Arc de Triomphe weekend.

Instead of long walks, VC began driving around the Left Bank in his Mini Cooper hoping to make an impression. At home in Seaford, he'd owned a Beach Buggy but found it "incredibly troublesome and difficult to manoeuvre. I managed to persuade my father to let me swap it for the Mini, which we got from the car dealer David Salamone, who had been one of the stunt drivers in The Italian Job." On one occasion, the young man with the British car tried to convince a sceptical Parisienne that he was a freelance photographer, like David Bailey, or the David Hemmings character in the film *Blow Up*, which was very fashionable at the time. "I did have a camera on the back seat, but unbeknown to her, there was no film in it. We were heading down the Boulevard Saint-Michel when we suddenly found ourselves caught up in the middle of a big demonstration. We could see the riot police up ahead banging their shields with their batons and we could see some of the students up on the rooftops armed with chunks of paving stone."

Victor decided it would be a good idea to get out fast, bewildering his companion who couldn't understand why a professional photographer was fleeing from the scene of a news story. They didn't see each other again.

A few months later, Victor was driving along the Rue de l'Université early one Sunday morning when a lorry suddenly shot out and hit the Mini Cooper side-on. "I went straight over the top of another car and into the window of a chemist's shop. I was very lucky. I could have hit the concrete wall and been dead. I was unconscious. The police came and were going to arrest me, but fortunately the couple who lived opposite were sitting on their balcony having breakfast and had witnessed everything, and they testified that I was the victim of the accident and not the architect."

Miraculously, Young Victor escaped with just cuts and bruises, but he was temporarily admitted to a hospital near Port Royal from where he telephoned an alarming message to his mother. "I've had a crash... and I'm in hospital...and the car's a write-off...but other than that, tell

Dad I'm fine." Not exactly reassured, an anxious Victor senior came over to Paris again and decided it was time for his son to move on. He had completed his course at the Alliance Française and was at least notionally competent in French, if not wholly fluent. His father felt it was time for him to embrace a more structured lifestyle in Switzerland, and thanks to his generosity, Young Victor was enrolled at the Glion Academy in time for the start of the next term.

There was just enough time before the course began for Victor to go and stay for a month with his father's great friend Gerry Albertini at his beautiful house, Can Sa Roca in Ibiza. Albertini was a tall, handsome and charming gentleman gambler whose American father had inherited a fortune from Reynolds Tobacco and the Union Pacific Railroad. Gerry had come into his first million at the age of 21 and had proceeded to redistribute it generously among the casino and bookmaking fraternity. He was one of "the mugs," as his wife Laurel called them, who incurred huge losses playing Chemin de Fer at John Aspinall's Clermont Club. He was equally enthusiastic about racing and on one occasion nearly pulled off a famous Yankee, having backed the same combinations with both Ladbrokes and William Hill. The first three legs all won, and if the last had gone in too, Gerry would have scooped over £3million. But the Ladbrokes and Hills representatives on course, both staring down the barrel, combined to stitch up the last race, paying the jockey of Gerry's selection to stop his horse.

At home in Ibiza, Gerry was in his hippie phase, "wearing kaftans and smoking dope. There were a lot of parties and a lot of eccentric characters there, like the actor Terry Thomas, the singers Nina and Frederik, and the author Clifford Irving, who had written the fake biography of Howard Hughes. My cousin Robert, who was Uncle Percy's son, came to stay for a few days. He'd been at Hollingbury and Highgate too, and he virtually lived with us when we were young. One morning, he told me that the Albertini children's' nanny, who was very pretty, had come into his bedroom at about half past one in the morning, but that he'd sent her away. 'I didn't send her away,' I said."

At one party, Victor found himself cornered by the Hungarian artist and forger Elmyr de Hory, who claimed that 90 per cent of the world's top museums had been fooled into buying one of his Picasso, Matisse and Modigliani pastiches. De Hory was amusing, but when his attentions began to become a little more pressing than Victor was comfortable with, the young Englishman wandered off upstairs and shut himself in a bedroom. "By then I'd smoked several joints and they'd made me feel really drowsy, so I lay down on the floor and went to sleep." When he woke up about 40 minutes later, he found that he'd rolled right under the bed. The next moment he heard the sound of two people coming into the room and flinging themselves down on the mattress. Clothes were rapidly being discarded – a shirt, a bra, trousers – and Victor realised he couldn't possibly remain there much longer. So he sat up and said very politely, "Excuse me. I've got to go now." The lustful couple were understandably surprised by his sudden appearance beneath the bed, but before they could say anything, he scrambled out of the door and back down the stairs.

When the summer holidays were over, it was time to head to Glion, which was an international finishing school for aspiring hoteliers, chefs and sommeliers. Situated in a former Grand Hotel outside Montreux, on the shores of Lake Geneva in French-speaking Switzerland, it offered three and four-year BA and Master's degree courses, and its graduates have included subsequent managers of some of the world's great hotels, from Claridges and the Savoy, to the Adlon in Berlin, the Carlton in Cannes and the Palace in St Moritz.

When Young Victor arrived at Glion it was mid-September 1970, and there was that all-too familiar new-term feeling in the air. Montreux and the neighbouring town of Vevey, full of neat, prosperous houses all cradling their privacy and their stunning views of the lake and the castle of Chillon, seemed to be the epitome of discipline and order. But then, as Young Victor was to discover "there was another side to Switzerland too, a wild side with nightclubs and skiing in the winter, and all kinds of unusual people."

The regime at Glion was a strict one, with a timetable not unlike school. Students combined their residential studies with three months practical experience in a hotel or restaurant, and Victor's course – which focused on both the preparation of food and the economics of the catering industry – included a stint in the kitchens of the Schweizerhof in Zurich. A traditional station hotel which opened for business in 1857, the Schweizerhof catered predominantly for wealthy businessmen and Swiss-German burghers and their wives passing through on their way back to Munich or Berne. Sober, respectable and used to dining well, they would have been shocked if they knew about some of the antics going on in the high-ceilinged kitchen below.

According to Victor, the head chef, a bearded German with a fondness for red wine and schnapps, was "completely mad. He used to wander up and down in his chef's hat and apron with the checked trousers, and he always had a bottle of wine in his hand. He'd keep these vast pots of Bolognese sauce bubbling away on the stove. You had to walk up several steps to reach them. He'd tip wine into the sauce throughout the day and every time he poured a glass or two into the pot, he'd drink one himself, so that by lunchtime he was always completely pissed. He kept shouting about what shits he thought the customers were. 'Why don't they ever complain?' he'd yell. 'Nobody ever complains.' One day, he unzipped his trousers and relieved himself ceremonially into the sauce. 'Let's see if they complain now,' he cried. But nobody ever did."

Young Victor's fellow students, most of them sons and daughters from well-heeled backgrounds, were more refined. Some of them did indeed go on to storm the commanding heights of European hospitality and cuisine, and maybe Victor too could have been a future Anton Mosimann, Joël Robuchon or Rick Stein had fate and his susceptibility to good times and gambling not taken a hand. "My crime was going missing," he explained, with what can only be described 50 years later as an unrepentant grin.

Every young man or woman studiously doing their best needs to battle with and yield to temptation from time to time. Who needs too much sobriety when you're 20 years old and living abroad in an exotic and unfamiliar environment? Victor's downfall resulted from his friendship with "a fellow student called Fernando Ponce-Torré. He was a small Mexican and possibly the most sexually athletic man I've ever met." Ponce-Torré received regular parcels from home, which sometimes included pots of cold cream and Johnson's Baby Powder lovingly despatched by his mother, so Victor believed, to protect the baby-faced charms of her boy. Then, one day, Fernando revealed the true contents of the cold-cream packages. They were bundles of cash, US dollars mostly, all ready to be changed into Swiss francs and sent by Mama Ponce-Torré to ensure that her diminutive offspring wouldn't want for any of life's essentials. And underneath the cash, neatly wrapped in tinfoil, there were stashes of dope. "We used to roll up joints and then play cards," recalls Victor. "There was a Jordanian student, a Japanese, all kinds of people. We were the Wild Boys. Everyone got so stoned, but Fernando had the strongest head and he used to win every time."

At one point, the young Mexican borrowed Victor's Mini Cooper, which had been miraculously patched up since the Paris episode, without asking. "Then he had an accident and smashed it up. It ended up being rebuilt in two countries. He lent me a Volkswagen he was renting to make up for it. We were living in a flat in the village at the time, and one night I took a girl student out to dinner. She was a Thai Princess who had allegedly never been out with a man before. It was midwinter, and on our way back I'd just managed to get my hand on her knee when we hit a patch of black ice. We ended up going the wrong way down a dual-carriageway on the roof. I was arrested at the scene of the accident. Then the police looked through the papers for the Volkswagen and found that, contrary to what Fernando had told me, I wasn't insured to drive the car. So they went off and arrested him too, and he got a huge bill and a fine. We spent a day and a night in prison before they let us go. The film *Borsalino* had just come out (a French gangster movie set in the 1930s and starring Jean-Paul Belmondo and Alain Delon) and Fernando insisted on wearing his *Borsalino* hat in jail." It wasn't to be their last escapade.

Returning from a trip to Geneva in June 1971, Fernando found a two-franc casino chip down the back seat of a taxi, and without further

132

ado, he and Victor took a ferry across the lake from Lausanne to France and went to the casino at Évian-les-Bains. Playing roulette until the early hours, Fernando won "an awful lot of money," and they returned to Montreux the next morning, hungry for more excitement. In that moment, the prospect of another day of classes at Glion – double Pheasant, hotel staff plans and a Patisserie Practical – seemed impossibly dull. "I've never been to Rome," said Fernando. "Neither have I," said Victor. "I think we should go, don't you?" "Why not?" said his accomplice.

Italian-bound express trains passed through Montreux every hour, and by lunchtime they were settling down in the restaurant car and hurtling towards the Simplon Tunnel. When they reached Rome, Fernando was in no mood to economise on either their accommodation or transport. "We took a suite in the Hassler Hotel near the Spanish Steps. Fernando paid cash in advance. They wouldn't let us in otherwise. Then he went off to a car showroom and bought an old Alfa Romeo that wasn't quite what it was meant to be. But we had a great time driving it around, showing off to Italian girls and inviting them back to the hotel."

The friends were busy spending their casino winnings "unwisely," as Victor puts it, with Ponce-Torré ringing up tailors and getting them to bring suits and shirts up to the room. Then the Mexican had a prang in the Alfa Romeo and panic set in. "The car ended up in the garage in the hotel basement and we ended up effectively barricaded in our suite. We were there for about a week until the money ran out." An uncomfortable visit from the hotel manager, who was threatening to return with the Carabinieri, left Victor with only one option. "We had nothing left to get home. I had to ring my father and tell him what had happened. It was the worst phone call of my life."

The full extent of Victor senior's wrath, which could be impressive, was delayed in the short term. The hotel bill was settled by telephone by Fernando's mother, who also paid for her son to return to Montreux by train, travelling second-class this time. Young Victor, meanwhile, was instructed to take a plane to Nice and then proceed onwards to Beaulieu-sur-Mer, where his mother and father were on holiday nearby. On arrival at Nice airport, he was met by Betty, who warned him that he was in the biggest trouble of his life. "'At some point, your father will probably kill you', she said. I was petrified." They took a taxi to Beaulieu, then on to his parents' hotel, the Voile d'Or in Cap Ferrat. "They went there every year between Epsom and Ascot. No children. It was their private break. The hotel manager knew Dad well and he thought it was all very amusing. 'Your father tells me that I have to give you the worst room in the house,' he said, grinning. He was as good as his word. It was a sort of chauffeur's or butler's room at the back. Not so much a room as a cupboard. It was only a single bed and there was no window and no bathroom either, not even a basin."

Victor was told that his father wanted to see him as soon as he'd unpacked. It wasn't a pleasant encounter. "He finally lost his temper with me and it lasted quite a while. The first thing he did was tell me to walk into the village, find a barber and 'get a decent haircut. You look like some bloody hippie.'" The exasperated parent had received a call from the college supervisor at Glion telling him his son was missing and that, as result of the Rome escapade, both Victor and Fernando Ponce-Torré had been expelled. It felt like Highgate all over again, and he rounded on the culprit, going through a full list of his misdeeds.

Young Victor was reminded of how much money had been spent on his education from Hollingbury Court to Highgate and Millfield, and then in Paris and Switzerland. How could he have behaved so irresponsibly? What would his grandfather have thought of him? And what kind of person did he expect to turn into? Without his father's help, he could have been thrown in jail in Rome. What on earth had he been thinking of and where would it all end? Well, Victor senior knew where it was going to end. It was time for the 20-year-old to pay something back. It was time for him to do a proper job.

Later that month, Young Victor was packed off to Lloret de Mar on the Costa Brava to be one of four Englishmen working for Panorama Holidays. "I did a whole season at a hotel there. I was meant to be the receptionist, but sometimes I did everything from the cooking and serving in the restaurant to unloading the luggage and organising the beauty contests around the pool." It was "bloody hard work" and not especially well paid, but there were compensations in the shape of plane-loads of eager, bikini-clad girls arriving by the week. Victor wasn't entirely without family support either, despite the row with his father. His sister Elizabeth came out for three or four days and ended up staying a month. "Liz would always help me out when I was in trouble. My other sister, Debbie, is quite a bit younger than me, but there's only a year between Liz and myself and she was more motherly." She was also able to act as a conduit of good reports of the reformed Victor between Spain and Seaford.

At the end of that summer, VC was employed by his Uncle Albert, the second oldest of his father's five surviving brothers and the one whose teenage drinking had incurred Bill Chandler's ire at Green Lanes before the war. Albert owned a pub in Southgate in North London and had just moved out to Menorca to open a club called the San Jamie. "He owned a lot of land and property there too, and he'd made money since he'd given up gambling." Victor's job was "to help get it started" and he was meant to be a sort of barman-cum-odd-job-man and chef too, if required. But Uncle Albert, who was still "partial to large amounts of vodka," had his 25-year-old workaholic son, Donald, who came out to take charge, making Victor's role more peripheral. So, over the winter, he went to work for an engagingly raffish management consultant called John Douglas instead.

"Suave, sophisticated and probably gay," Douglas had been a shareholder in the Lygon Arms in England. In Majorca, he was retained by a big Spanish company called Servicio del Sol, and did a lot of work for Clarksons, the travel business, going around hotels from the Balearics to the Costa del Sol advising them on refurbishing and refitting. "He was looking for someone younger to help him out. He was absolutely charming. I think he fancied me, actually." The pair teamed up for what turned out to be six very entertaining months, beginning in Douglas's office in Majorca and then travelling around Spain. Young Victor discovered hotels "where balconies were falling off and bedrooms sliding into the sea," and learned about all the cowboy cons and rackets of the package holiday trade.

It was fun while it lasted, but almost inevitably where Victor was concerned, it didn't last long. "There was a lot of black economy working going on among the various hotel and restaurant staff, and they didn't like these outsiders coming in and upsetting things." Then Clarksons, the UK-based company who were giving John Douglas most of his commissions, went bankrupt and the work dried up. At least Douglas had savings to fall back on. "He bought a house in the hills up above Palma, and for a while I had an apartment there too. John was a wheeler-dealer and he always landed on his feet."

In April 1972, Victor went home briefly to England for his 21st birthday. "Dad threw me a big bash in a house belonging to a friend of his in Regent's Park. I wasn't very grateful. I remember saying to him, 'I don't want any of your old people there.'" As it happened, a select group of Victor senior's old people, including Charlie Maskey, Benno Miller and the not-so-old Alan Mills, who was surprised and flattered to be asked, did come to the party. They had been friends and colleagues of Victor's father all his working life and several of them had known his grandfather too, and they would extend the same loyalty to Young Victor when the time came. This, sadly, was to be sooner than any of them could have imagined.

At the end of the evening, the birthday boy took a bunch of friends on to Tramp to continue the festivities. Before departing, his father gave him an envelope which Young Victor took out and opened when he got to the nightclub. He was expecting to find a cheque in there for a generous sum but instead it was a statement of the balance of his account with his father over the past three years. "He was effectively saying that it was the last time that he was going to bail me out. 'You're a man. Now you can start paying like a man.'"

In the summer of 1973, Victor went home again for his sister Elizabeth's birthday, and this time he decided to stay. He'd been abroad for almost four years, the last of them in gainful employment, and felt he'd pretty much atoned for the Rome debacle and his expulsion from

Glion. But he still had no clearly defined idea of what he wanted to do. Back in Sussex, he was Jack the Lad, aspiring to earn a bob or two from a variety of dodgy ventures. He lived temporarily in a flat over the top of his parents' house at Chyngton Rise. He had black sheets on his bed. He smoked French cigarettes. He still had long curly hair and shades, and he still wore his Afghan jacket.

As befitted a young Chandler, he went often to Brighton races and Hove dogs. He met the redoubtable old Jewish bookmaker Jackie Cohen, who lived on the south coast. One day, Jackie's Rolls-Royce was left parked on a road facing downhill near the greyhound stadium. The "pissed bookie" had left the brake off and the car started rolling down the slope. Mindful of the day he and Cousin Ronnie had rescued the MG in St John's Wood, Victor sped after it, jumped inside and slammed the brake on. Jackie Cohen was impressed. He nicknamed Young Victor 'Superman,' tipped him £50 and paid him to work on his pitch a few times at the dogs.

Cohen owned greyhounds. Young Victor thought he'd like to own them too. His grandfather Bill Chandler had, after all, been a famous breeder of dogs, his Uncle Ronnie trained them and his father had once owned the favourite for the Greyhound Derby. Young Victor thought he might become a breeder himself. But then very briefly he ran a mail-order business from a PO Box in Brighton. "A friend of my father's had started it. He bought the stock, things like car coats, in Hong Kong and advertised it in the papers in England." Only that clearly wasn't a full-time career option, so Victor decided he would sell it and speculate to accumulate…with a little more help from his father, that is. "A friend and I bought this old estate agent's office at Fiveways, on the Lewes Road. It belonged to a Dickensian character called JR Cracknell, who was a real Uriah Heep. I borrowed some money from Dad and we sort of took over the business."

It proved to be a brilliantly ill-timed and unpropitious foray into the commercial world. The Slater-Walker boom was just about to end, and a property crash – and Ted Heath's three-day week – were not far around the corner. For a few months, though, Victor enjoyed, in an unashamedly amateur way, the trappings of business life. He was the first to admit that he knew nothing about selling property, but he had found a way to make the job more diverting. Since Gisèle in Paris in 1969, there had been numerous girlfriends in Victor's life – French, English, Spanish and North African – but they had all been brief encounters. Then, at a party in London in September 1973, he met the woman with whom he would share his life for the next 29 years.

Carole Masters knew all about the Chandler family. She had grown up in a very similar background. Her maiden name was Mendoza, and her father Israel, or Izzy, was one of three brothers almost as renowned in the bookmaking fraternity as the Chandlers were. In 1915, the East Ender Benjamin Mendoza, known as Benny The Swanker, married Florence Craze, who was Frances Chandler's aunt. They had six children and the three boys all became bookies. Carole's father worked for the Ladbrokes owner Maxie Parker and was very friendly with his nephew Cyril Stein. Her Uncle Louis (pronounced Lewis, but better known on the racecourse as 'Lulu') was a boards and rails bookmaker in the south of England, and her other Uncle, Charlie Mendoza, was both a bookie and an antique dealer and one of Victor senior's closest friends. Charlie was on the Cannes trip with Benno Miller and Bud Flanagan in 1949, and since the late 1960s, he'd been working on the Chandler pitch.

In September 1973, it was Charlie's son Mark Mendoza's bar mitzvah in London. Victor was planning to go with Jane Davidson, who was "the daughter of our next-door neighbour when we lived in Rotting-dean. She was lovely and went on to become a famous model." Unfortunately, Jane couldn't make it that night as she was away working in Europe, but Victor's sister Liz and her boyfriend went, and he agreed to pick them up afterwards and drive them back to Brighton. It was when he got to the party that he met Mark's cousin, Carole, who was unaccompanied, and she asked him if he could give her a lift back too. Liz and her boyfriend sat in the back. Carole sat in the front seat next to Victor. She was blonde haired, slim and extremely attractive, with a warm relaxed manner and an inclination to regard

138

Young Victor with a permanently amused smile. Recently divorced, she had two children, Danny and Paula, at school in Sussex, and she was living in Hove not much more than 20 miles from Seaford. By the end of the 90-minute drive back, Victor realised he'd met the older woman of his dreams.

Carole, though, was sceptical and admits she was attracted to the father before the son. "Victor's dad was so charismatic. Tall and curly haired with these bright eyes and always beautifully dressed. When he stood up on his pitch at the races, I remember looking up at him and thinking…ooh…it quite made me tremble. You didn't cross him, though. He was a very strong character, whereas to begin with I could tell that Young Victor was a lazy bugger. He was 22 when we first met. I thought it might last six weeks if we were lucky. Instead, it lasted 30 years. He invited me to be his 'unpaid secretary' at the Cracknell's office on the Lewes Road. I used to be typing out front and he'd be asleep in the back. Then he'd come through and pretend to be doing something for five or ten minutes, but it was no good. He can't be bothered with paperwork. So he'd suggest we went out for a good lunch. The first time he asked me out properly in the evening, we went to see a play at the Theatre Royal. Victor was late, of course, so we missed the first act. We ended up having supper in a little Italian restaurant in Kemptown. The bill was about £5. I thought 'well, he's never going to make anything of himself, he's too lazy.' The awful thing is… if his father hadn't died…he wouldn't have become the man he is now. It freed Victor up to be himself."

One of the great ironies about Victor senior was that for all his height, charm and commanding good looks, he had never really been a well man. That back injury he sustained during the war had prevented him going straight into the racecourse bookmaking business when he was demobbed. He simply wasn't fit enough at first to spend so much time standing on a pitch in all weathers, and his doctors concluded that the back trouble was indirectly responsible for the other problems that surfaced later on. "I remember when I was about nine years old, he couldn't walk for six months and, the following year, he had a collapsed lung. John Sutcliffe senior, who was a good friend, was going to finance him to buy about 70 or 80 betting shops in London. If that had gone through, he might have spent less time on the racecourse and it might have prolonged his life. But then John's son applied for his trainer's licence and his father felt he couldn't be seen investing in a bookmaking firm. So he pulled out of the deal at the last minute."

In February 1973, Victor senior and Betty were returning from one of their winter holidays in the Bahamas when he came down with what he thought was a chill on the plane home. A month later, he was diagnosed with liver cancer and it subsequently spread to the bowel and colon. He underwent a five-hour operation in the King Edward VII Hospital in Knightsbridge, and at first he thought it had gone really well. Friends tried not to disabuse him, but Betty had been told that he might have a year to live at most and gradually the whole family found themselves drawn into the collective ordeal of treatment, hope, recovery, relapse, deterioration and decline.

Once fully aware of the situation, the bookmaker confronted his fate with equanimity. He had been closely monitoring the progress of Charlie Maskey's wife, who also had liver cancer, and had no illusions about what was in store for him. "Book me a front-row pitch, Charlie," he said, alluding to a grave.

In the last six months of his life, Chandler seemed to sense that, sooner or later, and despite his earlier reservations, his son was bound to be drawn, after all, into the family business. He even tried to warn him after a fashion. "Dad was being nursed at home. He was dying really, but there was that strange atmosphere where no-one wants to admit what's happening. When I was in Switzerland, he'd sent me to see an old friend of his called Philip Martyn, who was a professional backgammon player. He was also seriously ill and in a sanatorium in Lausanne."

Young Victor couldn't resist showing off a little in Martyn's company and talking boldly of how he would price up various horses and races if he were a bookmaker. The boasts found their way back to Chyngton Rise. "Dad used to have the *Sporting Life* on his bed but sometimes he was too weak to read it, and you'd just see it lying there the wrong way up. There was one day, though, not long after I'd got back, when he reached up and took me by the arm. 'You can't lay 6-4 on and 6-4 against in a two-horse race and hope to make a profit,' he said. I'm not sure he held out much hope for me."

There was a brief remission in February 1974 when father and son went to the cinema in Brighton to see *The Sting* and then on to Wheeler's for supper. It was the last time they ever went out together. Victor senior loved the film, especially Paul Newman's performance as the handsome, charming and quick-witted bookmaker Henry Gondorff. That was his kind of man. Only now there was no more life left for him to live. "The year before, my father had taken my sisters to the south of France. It was the last holiday they had together and I should've gone too. But I'd stayed behind trying to be an estate agent. I still feel guilty about it to this day."

The end came on April 8th, only a few days before Young Victor's 23rd birthday. "He died early that morning. We were all at home and my Uncle Ronnie had come over from Ireland, he was the one who closed Dad's eyes. You could see that he was in terrible pain. He cried out when the nurse tried to turn him over onto his side. I was just leaning over him and saying 'go on, Dad...just go.'"

The funeral took place at St Peter's in Brighton, and the 'cathedral' on the Old Steine was packed. "Young Victor was my rock," said Betty Chandler.

Her husband, the seventh and last of Bill Chandler's sons, was buried in Brighton Cemetery high up near the chapel and facing out across the valley towards the racecourse on Whitehawk Down. 'To live in hearts we leave behind is not to die,' says the inscription on his tombstone. Seagulls hover daily on the flint and red brick chapel roof, and in summer a gentle breeze drifts in from the sea, ruffling the grasses and the wild flowers.

"I remember wandering around in a daze afterwards," says Victor. "And that's when I sort of half realised that I was going to have to go into the business. My elder sister Liz had left school by then, but my younger one, Debbie, was still boarding, and then there was my mother too…and it suddenly dawned on me that someone was going to have to look after them."

Young Victor Chandler was about to grow up.

Chapter Eleven

The Greenhorn

W ednesday June 5th, 1974, was a perfect English summer's day
with blue skies, sunshine and more than half a million people
gathered on Epsom Downs to watch the 196th running of the
Derby. Around 30,000 of them were squeezed into Epsom's
ageing grandstand. The rest – the usual Derby Day mixture of gypsies,
fortune-tellers, touts, and away-daying Londoners determined to enjoy
their annual outing – were camped out on the hill opposite.

For weeks, the betting on the race had been dominated by the two
horses who had finished first and second in the 2000 Guineas at
Newmarket a month before. Nonoalco, trained at Chantilly by the
soigné Francois Boutin and ridden by the French champion jockey
Yves Saint-Martin, had displayed an impressive turn of foot to beat
the odds-on favourite Apalachee in the Guineas. But, on breeding, he
was by no means certain to stay the extra half mile at Epsom. The case
for the Newmarket runner-up Giacometti getting the trip was stronger,
but not watertight, encouraging shrewd punters to look elsewhere for
value. Two guaranteed to stay were the improving Imperial Prince, representing the great Newmarket trainer Noel Murless, and the Lingfield
Derby Trial winner Bustino, who was owned by Lady Beaverbrook and
trained by Major Dick Hern. Then there was Snow Knight, a 50-1
outsider from Peter Nelson's stable in Lambourn who had finished

143

third behind Bustino at Lingfield and had shown promising form as a two-year-old.

Snow Knight was a quirky colt, but a talented one with just the right mixture of speed and stamina in his pedigree, and his final piece of work before the Derby suggested he'd come on appreciably since the Lingfield race. Nelson communicated his enthusiasm to his son John, who passed on the tip to his old Millfield contemporary Victor Chandler. "John's father's only worry was that the horse might get upset by the crowd and sweat up and lose the race in the paddock." The economic situation in Britain was so bad that there were only about half a dozen rails bookies at Epsom that year, many of the old firms fearing that high-rolling punters were on the verge of extinction. "We had one of the pitches and Charlie Mendoza was standing on it. I was lurking around waiting for John to come and find me after they'd given the jockey the leg-up. He was going to tell me whether we should go ahead and back it or not. But then his father told him to walk the horse down to the start and try and calm his nerves. What I didn't realise was that he'd unseated his jockey Brian Taylor just after they came out of the paddock."

There were no mobile phones in 1974, and no big viewing screens either, and when Victor saw John Nelson and Snow Knight walk by him in the parade, everything seemed to be okay. "I had £250 on me, so I gave it to old Charlie Maskey – Charlie The Hammer – who was still working for us, and he dashed up to one of the boards and stuck the lot on. If I could, I'd have had more on it, on credit. 66-1 had been freely available early on, but by the time of the off, the price was 50-1."

Brian Taylor gave Snow Knight a brilliant ride. He broke well from the stalls, was in a good position with a mile to run, and took up the running coming down the hill. At Tattenham Corner, he kicked clear and stayed on strongly up the straight, beating Imperial Prince by two lengths, with Giacometti not quite getting the trip back in third. Bustino, who would go on to win the St Leger and be involved in the race of the century against Grundy at Ascot the following year, finished

'C at Cheltenham in the 1990s. 'He wanted to back
very winner and lay every losing favourite too.'

Victor's grandfather Bill Chandler, 1930s. Rogueish,
visionary and daring, he was a natural leader of men.

Dinner at the Dormy House Hotel, March 1998. Victor is second left. Alan Mills is at
the end on the right standing next to Charlie Maskey and Mike Carlton. It was the night
efore the Gold Cup and the Cheltenham management were touring the trophy around
ome of the local hotels. Roger Jenkins and Paul Mendoza are holding the Gold Cup,
which was won the next day by The Fellow.

Hoxton, 1940s. Now an impossibly fashionable manor but once a place of poverty, rickets and rank bad housing.

Victor senior, dressed as Christopher Robin, cuddles a winning greyhound. All of the Chandler brothers grew up to be punters.

A presentation at Walthamstow Stadium, 1930s. Bill Chandler, bare-headed, stands at the back. In front of him is his third son, Charles. 'To begin with there was no prize-money, just a trophy. He believed there'd be less crookedness that way.'

rackwork at Harringay Stadium, 1920s. Bill Chandler sits in the back row on the left. Bill took is money out of Harringay and Hackney Wick to invest in Walthamstow.

he Morill Sisters (from left to ght): Mickey, Frances and Betty. ll three of them married a handler boy.

Annie Jones, Bill Chandler's wife and Victor's grandmother, 1919. 'It was obvious that Bill worshipped her.'

Victor senior on horseback in a London street in the 1940s. He had a palomino called Pink Gin.

Some of the Chandler children on the beach at Bournemouth with Miss Grover in the 1920s. Charles in black swimming costume and (left to right) young Ronnie, Victor senior (in Charles's lap), Renie and Percy. In July, Bill moved his family down to the south coast for six weeks.

The actor and life-long Mob associate George Raft with Frances and Betty Chandler at Walthamstow, 1950s.

Ronnie Chandler. A stud portrait, late 1930s. Ronnie wa Victor's favourite uncle and th most handsome of all th Chandler brother

Benno Miller, Victor
senior and Charlie
Mendoza, Brighton,
1950. Brighton
was Soho-by-Sea.
Bohemians and
actors, chancers and
gangsters.

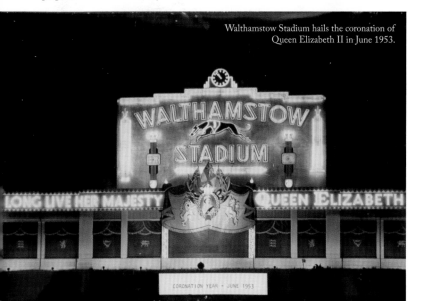

Walthamstow Stadium hails the coronation of
Queen Elizabeth II in June 1953.

Victor senior (bottom row, right) in the army water polo team, WW2. 'All his life he believed in king and country.'

Billy Chandler in his RAF uniform, 1945. The picture was taken a few weeks before his death.

Victor senior and Betty stepping out at the Carlton Hotel, Cannes, 1948. To Betty the Cote d'Azur was forever 'elegance personified.'

Chandler family holiday, early 1960s. (From right to left) Victor senior, Young Victor, Betty and VC's sisters iz and Debbie. 'There was always plenty of food and drink in the house and nice holidays and cars.'

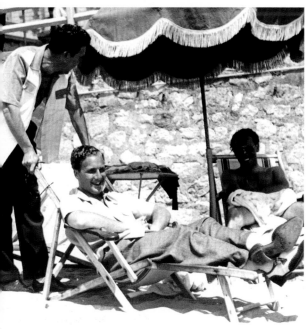

Victor Senior in a deck chair on the beach at Cannes in 1950.

Victor senior's tailoring bill, July 1951. He had a wardrobe full of beautiful tailor-made suits and ties.

LORD & STEWART
LIMITED

CIVIL & MILITARY TAILORS

DIRECTORS
J. STEWART
E.S. STEWART

19, ALBEMARLE STREET,
LONDON, W.1.

REGENT
3301/2

24th July 1951.

V. Chandler, Esq.,
4, Woodland Way,
Woodford. Essex.

To balance of account 1945/1946	68	–	–
1 Suit – 40gns – 1946	42	–	–
1 Suit – 40gns	42	–	–
1 Suit – no vest – 39gns	40	19	–
1 Dinner Suit – 44gns	46	4	–
100% Purchase Tax – 31gns	32	11	–
3 prs Trousers – 12gns	37	16	–
1 Brown Camel Hair Overcoat 50gns	52	10	–
1 Gaberdine Sports Overcoat 45gns	47	5	–
4 Suits – no vests – 50gns	210	–	–
1 Suit – no vest – 50gns	52	10	–
3 Suits – no vests – 50gns	157	10	–
1 Suit – no vests – 50gns	52	10	–
1 Jacket – 35gns	36	15	–
1 Grey Cheviot Sports Overcoat	52	10	–
1 Brown Sports Suit – 50gns	52	10	–
1 Blue Suit – 50gns	52	10	–
4 Suits – 50gns	210	–	–
1 Dinner Suit – Shawl Collar	73	10	–
1 White Jacket – 35gns	36	15	–
1 Blue Suit – 50gns	52	10	–
1 doz prs Socks – 15/6d	9	6	–
1 pr Slacks – 14gns Mrs.Chandler	14	14	–
account rendered	60	4	–
pressing Suit		10	6
3 Suits – no vests – 50gns			
Blue, Grey, Brown Basket Weave	157	10	–
3 Model Buttons – 12/6d	1	17	6
1 Beige Gaberdine Suit – 50gns	52	10	–
1 Blue Grey Sports Jacket &			
1 pr Blue Gaberdine Trousers	52	10	–
1 Gaberdine Raincoat – 50gns	52	10	–
invisible repair to Gab: Suit	2	2	–
clean & press White Jacket		12	6
	£1853	1	6
	NETT CASH:		

A tanned Victor senior and Betty are reunited with the greyhound Hi Joe in 196

fourth and the non-staying Nonoalco was seventh. Victor Chandler had won over £12,000. He needed every penny.

Victor's mother Betty had been afflicted by a severe post-natal depression after her daughter Debbie was born, and her husband's death brought on a similar condition. She went from being a virtual recluse in the house in Sussex one week, to being out every night the next, until Victor's Uncle Percy Chandler paid for her to go into a clinic. When she came out, she bought a house in Hove with Victor senior's old friend Charlie Mendoza, but then he died a year later, leaving Young Victor feeling acutely responsible for her welfare. He might reasonably have expected to come into some kind of financial inheritance that would have taken care of things. Not on the Great Expectations scale maybe, but at least a legacy of sorts. Not a bit of it. "I'd imagined there was a lot of money in the bank, but I was swiftly disabused."

At the time of Victor senior's death, "the business was absolutely on the floor," said Carole. "They had a six-figure debt, and there's no way Victor started out with any kind of silver spoon in his mouth. He inherited his father's name and reputation, and a lot of the old customers, some of whom went back to his grandfather's time, but that was it."

Given the audacity of Victor senior's wagering, and the general impression of wealth and style that followed him around, his son wasn't the only one to be surprised he didn't die a millionaire. But as Victor gradually understood, his father was always a bookmaker rather than a Turf Accountant, and commerce, in the narrowly acquisitive sense, was not his strong suit. "He wasn't overly ambitious, and he had such a huge love of racing and being there on the racecourse. I think that towards the end of his life, he regretted, from a financial point of view, that he hadn't got more involved with betting shops. He had about 40, some of them in London, the others down in Sussex, though when the offices first started, they never really got anywhere. It was only when the public companies got involved that they took off. He'd also invested heavily in property in Brighton and London, and the crash in 1973 affected everything. I had to sell most of them at a loss."

In the late 1960s, Victor's father was one of a deputation of senior bookies who went along with the Betting Levy Board Chairman George Wigg to meet a group of crossbench MPs at the Dorchester Hotel. They were there to try and lobby for a reduction in on-course betting tax. One of the honourable members present was the West Midlands Labour MP Brian Walden, who professed to love racing and went on to enjoy a prominent second career in broadcasting. Walden was an acclaimed orator and parliamentarian who made a famous speech against the restoration of capital punishment. But not for nothing was he also known as 'the bookies' runner.' At that meeting in the Dorchester, "Victor's father started to explain their position, very politely," recalls Charlie Maskey, "but Walden didn't want to hear it." He summoned Victor senior and his colleague John Pegley into a private room and "all he wanted to know was how much money he was going to get to press their case, and he wanted hard cash in a brown manila envelope. Victor's father was shocked. He always had this slightly naive side to him, and he never imagined that members of parliament behaved like that."

Old friends like Charlie Maskey and Betty's cousin Benno Miller felt that this naivety and willingness to see the best in everyone made the bookmaker a soft touch for less scrupulous colleagues, including one or two who spent a lot of the firm's money buying him luxurious hampers when he was dying. Food that he was much too ill to eat. Some of those involved initially carried on working in the same jobs after his death, but at the end of 1974, Young Victor made a few big decisions of his own. He had instinctively realised that if the Chandler name was to survive and anything be saved for his mother and sisters from the ruin, he needed to follow his grandfather's example and become a leader of men. "To begin with, my cousin Michael, another of Uncle Albert's sons, was running the credit and SP office, which had moved to Osnaburgh Street, with me as his assistant. The betting shop had already gone. It lasted about eight months, by which time we were nearly bankrupt. I remember our accountant Joe Jayson saying to me, 'the company's insolvent.' 'What does that mean?' I asked. 'It means you owe more than you've got,' he said. So I sacked Michael and took over managing the business myself. He'd been given a 25 per cent share but, with tremendous help from Joe, his son Bernard and a wonderfully sympathetic manager at the Allied Irish Bank, I was able to buy him out over a period of time."

Charlie Mendoza and Victor's father's clerk, Val Powell, had been running the on-course book in the first few months after the older Chandler's death. Now Young Victor, reluctantly reconciled to the fact that bookmaking, not hotel or casino management, was to be his career, applied to take over the family's boards pitches. But as he hadn't already worked for his father for the required minimum two-year period, the BPA (Bookmakers Protection Association) – applying rules that dated back to Darby Sabini's time – turned him down. It was a fateful moment, and as a result, Young Victor, like Bill Chandler before him, became a rails bookmaker instead. "The best thing that happened to Victor, in a way, was that he lost the boards pitches," reckoned Bobby Edwards. "Otherwise he wouldn't have been able to do the things that he did. I don't think there were any really wealthy bookmakers left on the boards in 1975. They could only make what they could take with their own hands. Victor was lucky. He didn't have to go to the races every day. He could become more of an entrepreneur, like his grandfather."

Young Victor's first working day on the racecourse – the real beginning of his adult life – came at Kempton Park on May Bank Holiday Monday in 1975. "They let me bet there without applying for a pitch first, but I was so nervous that the first time I stood up to shout the odds, nothing came out. It was scary to start with and I hadn't the slightest idea what was going on. I felt a real fish out of water."

There may not have been a lot of money in boards bookmaking by 1975, but there were some very big hitters – bookmakers and punters – along the rails, and if he was to hold his own in this company, the young pretender with the curly hair needed to wise up fast. Bookmaking, as he was to discover, was not just a game of chance, but a skill that had to be learned. Making a book was about balancing a book and understanding how to lay the favourite and the second favourite to the right amounts so that the bookie would win on the race whatever the result. Chancers trying to get by on a bit of inside information were just guessing. Fortunately, the fourth generation member of the Chandler family to lay the odds had some good people to help him. "Victor had this mentor called Joe Dunbar," explained Benno Miller. "This fellow was a very sharp cookie and he effectively taught Victor the fundamentals of the business. Like when to bet, when to lay off and, basically, how to survive."

Dunbar wasn't his real name. "He had some kind of Jewish Mittel-European background," remembers Victor. "Austria, Hungary or wherever. I'm not sure exactly when he'd first come to Britain, but he was the best trade bookmaker [meaning a bookmaker hedging bets with and for other bookies rather than just laying bets to the public] in the game. He ran our trade office and had a 50 per cent share in the business. He had a staff of 20 and he made them stand up all the time. He claimed that you weren't really working if you were sitting down. He had hundreds of accounts with other firms, including Ladbrokes. He and Cyril Stein, the Ladbrokes Chairman, had always been close, and there was a kind of friendly rivalry between them.

Then there was my father's old clerk, Val Powell. He was a character too, and jovial in a theatrical sort of way. He could tap dance, despite being rather portly, and he used to do a dance every year on his birthday. Whatever I know about odds and percentages, I learned it all from them. I was meant to do homework, and there were regular tests up in the office. Fortunately I'd had a bit of a grounding in fractions from Mr Rowlandson at Highgate, but Joe was still highly critical of my mathematical abilities." Chandler grins disarmingly at the memory, underlying again his apparent gift for not taking things too seriously. All his life, he's seen no point in struggling to master a skill he's no aptitude for – typing, tic-tac, computers, paperwork – preferring to make use of somebody else's knowledge and trust them to get on with it.

Victor had inherited 25 betting shops, his father having disposed of the others before his death. He sold the London offices to Ladbrokes but kept half a dozen down in Sussex. One August day in 1975, his father's friend Charlie Maskey – Charlie The Hammer's son – accompanied him on a train ride from London to Brighton for the races. On their way up to Whitehawk Down, they dropped into the Surrey Street betting shop that VC had been left by his father near the station. It was the summer holidays, with three or four low-grade meetings taking place, but the shop was full of punters. Charlie spotted the office manager working up at the front and for a minute or two the pair of them communicated in tic-tac signals rather than talking out loud in front of the customers. The messages were all about how business was going that day, what kind of bets they were taking, a favourite to back or lay at the course later, and so on.

All the while, Young Victor, the official shop owner, stood by Charlie's side grinning and nodding towards the manager. When they finally left, Victor turned to Charlie. "What was all that about?" he asked. "You mean you don't know?" responded Charlie, shocked. "Of course not," said Victor mischievously. "That's what I employ people like you for."

Surrounded by these few trusted friends and retainers, and initially dependent on their knowledge, VC ventured further into the still Dickensian world of betting and racing, with its age-old word-of-mouth mechanisms, its faces, frauds and crooks, its irresistible characters and its humour and panache. His first visit to Cheltenham was in March 1975, the year the first day had to be abandoned after heavy rain and Comedy Of Errors regained the Champion Hurdle the following afternoon. Irish stables landed a series of big gambles led by Ten Up in the Gold Cup, Padge Berry's Bannow Rambler in the Lloyds Bank Champion Novices' Hurdle (Supreme Novices'), and Davy Lad, trained by the immortal Mick O'Toole, in the Sun Alliance Hurdle. But just as many plunges went astray on the heavy ground, including a massive punt on Edward O'Grady's Kilmakillogue, who started favourite for the Champion Novices' Hurdle but, shades of Youlnever-walkalone, could only finish third.

Cheltenham in that era was all about rain, sleet and snow. Trench coats and trilbies, flat caps and camel hair, champagne bubbles,

Guinness and great wads of pounds and punts. Trying to take it all in, Victor was struck by the manic nature of the gambling as well as the realisation that a bookmaker "could do a small fortune there if he wasn't careful." But the still not 24-year-old was also bewildered by some of the people and their jargon and style. Shy and diffident, it seemed to him as if "everyone was about 30 years older than me. I wanted to run away and be a beach boy. I just stood around and attempted not to feel totally useless." It was just as bad when Royal Ascot came around that summer. It felt to Victor as if most of the rails bookmakers were still behaving like an advert for upmarket car dealers in the 1920s. "'Purveyors of motor vehicles and fine horseless carriages to the nobility and gentry.' There was still a huge class difference between various parts of the racecourse then, boundaries that had continued long after they had begun to come down elsewhere." Royal Enclosure punters didn't come up to him with a fistful of readies. It was all about whispered enquiries in the ear. The bookmaker was supposed to respond equally discretely and he was mindful of Charlie Maskey's story about the two bookies who had been warned off not so long before for being caught running in the Members Enclosure at Newmarket.

Over the course of that first year, the newcomer also seemed to continually brush up against old memories and associates of his father, and sometimes it felt as if Victor senior had forever been the good man fallen among thieves. "Towards the end of his life, my father owned a very smart two-year-old called Fortuitous, who was one of the ante-post favourites for the 2000 Guineas in 1974. But then it was beaten at odds of around 4-7 in a race up at York at their late-season meeting. Dad and Ben Hanbury, who trained it, always suspected something had been going on. Nothing was ever proved at the time, but when the following summer came around, it was never really the same.

Well, about a year after my father's death, I went to the funeral of Henry Cohen, the money-lender who helped a lot of bookmakers get started. It was at the Jewish cemetery in North London and I was coming out of the Gents afterwards when this gangster-type comes up and puts a hand on my shoulder. 'You're Young Victor, aren't you?' he says. 'I want to apologise to you. I did Fortuitous…but I'd never have done it if I'd known it was your Dad's horse and I'd known he was so ill.'"

A more benign, if gloriously eccentric, acquaintance from the old days was 'Colonel' Ted Oxley, a 'form man' and occasional journalist whose newspaper byline was 'The Owl.' A big man with bushy eyebrows, a plummy voice and half-moon glasses, Oxley "was a proper Evelyn Waugh character and something of a black sheep in a family that included a General and a Bishop. His brother used to teach riding at Millfield. Ted had been an officer in the Pioneer Corps in WW2, and he was mad about racing. He was Gerry Albertini's main tipster and they used to meet up at Gerry's house in Belgravia in the mornings. 'Give me the Life, Albertini,' he'd say, meaning the Sporting Life. 'I'm going to have a pony on the favourite. I'll see you anon.' Then he'd disappear to the lavatory for about half an hour to work out his selections. He made himself useful to my father too, because he seemed to be able to verify the credentials of people who'd ring up calling themselves Lord This and Lady That and wanting to open a credit account. Ted could always find out if they really had any money. 'Do you want to know the full SP?' he'd say to Dad.'"

Charlie Maskey had a number of priceless encounters with the Colonel in Hyde Park, which was his favourite rendezvous when he wanted to get somebody to place a bet for him. "He used to step out suddenly from behind a tree, holding a walking stick. 'A pony ($£25$) would do it, Maskey,' he'd say, giving me the details. You see he hadn't got the money to get it on in person. Then there were the trips to the races. Ascot was his favourite. The phone would ring around 7am and you'd hear his voice. 'What time are you bringing the horse and cart round?' he'd say, meaning the car. We'd have to meet him in the bar of Langford's Hotel around 10am, and he'd usually be drinking Bollinger. 'When we get to Ascot, Maskey,' he'd say to me, 'you'll see thousands of c…. drinking champagne after midday. Promise me, Maskey, promise me you'll never touch it after twelve.' He believed an officer should have moved on to whisky by then."

At the racecourse, the by now well-lubricated Colonel would saunter up to the Cavalry Club tent complete with his umbrella, shooting stick and overcoat. "'Have you got a badge sir?' a gateman would ask. Of course, he never did have a badge, but he'd greet the gateman with a snort of derision. 'Maskey, speak to the man,' he'd say to me. 'Yes Colonel,' I'd be expected to reply while he strolled on in."

The Colonel married a barmaid "when he was about 73" and ended up living in a room over a pub in Brighton. He died there of cancer a few years later. Young Victor, like his father before him, used to look after him in little ways, sending him pots of caviar and bottles of champagne. Oxley, who enjoyed the refreshments, didn't appreciate the more godly attentions of the local health service. "You'll never believe what the bastards did to me today," he said to Victor and Charlie in one of their final conversations. "I looked up and standing there beside the bed was one of those blasted sky pilots (a clergyman). Ugh!"

When the Colonel passed on, a simple notice appeared at the bottom of one of the inside pages in the *Sporting Life*: 'The Owl is Dead.'

Wise Owls like Ted Oxley didn't just enlighten bookmakers like Victor and his father about potentially fraudulent customers wanting to bet on credit. They also acted in their more sober moments as a conduit of information about the latest moves of the sharpest owners, trainers, jockeys and their connections. It was vital intelligence, foretelling moves that might represent a bullet heading in a bookmaker's direction, and when Young Victor started out, he was dependent on it. He was the greenhorn walking into a frontier saloon without really knowing the medium, the game or the etiquette and, to keep his shirt, he was badly in need of advice about who were the mugs who could be taken on and who, for whatever reason, he should avoid.

In Victor's father's day, one of the trainers the bookies were most wary of was the Sussex-based Captain Ryan Price, who was equally successful both over jumps and on the flat. The piratical Captain, who had been a Commando during WW2, was no stranger to controversy, notably over the running of his 1967 Schweppes Gold Trophy winner Hill House, who romped home at Newbury despite having finished well down the field in his previous race at Kempton Park. The aftermath of the Schweppes was equally dramatic, with the winner failing a dope test and then the trainer being exonerated on the grounds that Hill House was a self-doper who naturally manufactured his own cortisone.

The bookmakers weren't having it and remained convinced that the Captain, or a couple of nefarious characters associated with him, pepped up some of his horses with narcotic stimulants several times a year. Suspicion revolved around two mysterious backers of Price's stable, with names and personalities right out of a Sherlock Holmes story. "They were called Baron Hatvany and Dr Reuter," said Benno Miller. "The Baron was landed gentry of old Austro-Hungarian stock. He was a hawk-faced fellow with a hunched back. The doctor was a chemist, and they were both big punters. In the 1960s and '70s, the jumping season used to begin quietly down in the West Country in August, and the Captain and the rest of them used to stay at the Imperial Hotel in Torquay. It was while they were there that they used to plot up which horses they were going to give a little assistance to over the coming months. Fred Winter, who was Price's stable jockey until he retired in 1964, was never privy to the discussions, but he knew all about them. 'They'll never find the gear he uses,' he said to me once about the doctor. Then when their plotting was finished, they'd all have drinks together and smash up the bar. They'd pay maybe £200 in breakages every year."

Ryan Price progressed from pulling strokes over jumps to conditioning blue-blooded thoroughbreds to win classic races. Ken Payne, who at one point had stables in Lambourn and Middleham, operated at the other end of the scale. A former window cleaner, Payne became known as the selling race king, landing gambles in the lowest grade of contest. 'Window Payne' later admitted that a lot of his winners were administered steroids to improve their performance, but it wasn't always the stable number one that triumphed, requiring extreme caution on behalf of bookmakers pricing up his runners. His other trick was to sell shares in the same horse to different people several times over. Gullible owners who thought they'd bought the horse outright would be unaware that somebody else thought they owned 50 per cent and two others had been sold 10 per cent, and so on. Payne, meanwhile, was collecting all the fees and issuing three or four different sets of training bills for the same horse.

Victor sometimes encountered Ken Payne during "riotous nights" in the Dover Castle, a semi-racing pub near Great Portland Street where the restaurant owner Peter Langan, the actor David Warner and the journalist Jeffrey Bernard, were all regulars and where Payne liked to entertain potential owners when he was in the West End. "One evening, he was in there lording it up as usual, and he had this beautiful French girl with him. I got talking to her and she said that she had left her husband for Ken and that she was paying for them to stay in a five-star hotel because Ken's London flat wasn't free as his tenant hadn't moved out yet. I told her it was highly unlikely that Ken had either a flat or a tenant and warned her not to give him any more money. I ended up giving her some cash and putting her in a cab back to Heathrow."

It wasn't just crafty trainers like Ken Payne and the Captain that the bookmakers were convinced were 'at it.' There were gambling jockeys too, who had their punters just like Charlie Elliott and Charlie Smirke in the 1940s. The riders were still officially prohibited from betting and were also banned from passing on information for profit, and from time to time a jockey and a bookmaker, or a professional gambler, would be the subject of a ritual clampdown. In 1978, John Francome was fined £750 and suspended for six weeks for allegedly passing information to John Banks. The Glaswegian was one of the boldest and most flamboyant bookmakers of the era, famous for his catchphrase 'There's only one bank in Scotland...John Banks.' He had a lifelong feud with the Ladbrokes Chairman Cyril Stein, who he used to taunt mercilessly. When he was refused permission to name a racehorse Greenwich Mean Stein, he called it Adorable Cyril instead. Banks warned punters that they shouldn't be 'disheartened' when Ladbrokes refused to lay them a bet. They should be 'perturbed' when they did. He vigorously denied that any money had changed hands between him and John Francome but, according to the amateur rider turned journalist John Oaksey, reactionary Jockey Club members had decided that Banks "had become excessively visible and needed to be slapped down." To his indignation, he was fined £2,500 and warned off for three years. Victor was on the bookmaker's side. John Banks had liked and respected his father and he initially helped his son out at the races too. Young Victor could see that he was "smart, funny and daring, and never afraid to take a view. He had a coterie of big punters in the Ascot and Sunningdale area, and when he came back from his suspension in 1981, we remained good friends."

Banks brought a touch of native Scots grit to the betting ring, whereas another of the most colourful gamblers of that era was all-velvet collar coats, Mayfair and the City. The silver-haired Charles St George was Lester Piggott's great patron, and had been a good friend of Victor's father and a shareholder in the New Casanova Club. His brother, Edward, had been married to William Hill's daughter, Kathleen, who committed suicide in 1961. Edward made a fortune in the Bahamas when Meyer Lansky and Dino Cellini were building casinos there on Paradise Island in the 1960s, and both the brothers were ardent racing lovers and punters. Charles had numerous horses in training, some with Henry Cecil and some with Ryan Price, including a flighty filly called Ginevra. "Will it win the Oaks?" he asked the Captain one day at Lingfield in 1972. "It did yesterday on the gallops," replied Price. Thick bets were placed on behalf of both the owner and trainer, some of them with Victor senior, and Ginevra duly landed the odds at Epsom at 8-1.

St George owned a house in Newmarket as well as a London townhouse not far from Berkeley Square. His official business was the Lloyds Insurance Market, and during working hours he could sometimes be found in an old Victorian office near Leadenhall Market. It was there that Benno Miller would track him down when the suave gambler owed him money. "I was working as a commission agent at the time, which meant trying to get your clients' bets on with various bookies, Victor included, at the best possible odds, and I had an office in Bond Street. I got a commission on the wager if the horse won, and I'd give them a discount on the tax too, say 7 per cent instead of 9 per cent.

Well, Charlie was another sharp cookie and he had a gambling friend in America called Dr RB Chesne. They named a horse after him, and Henry Cecil trained it. Dr Chesne was a heart surgeon and he used to go to the sales with St George and check the horses' heart rates before he'd buy them. He would frequently phone up from California and ask me or Victor for a string of £100 Yankees, but then if the horses lost, he'd generally pay Charlie, who was meant to pay us. I think St George often kept some of his winnings too, without him realising it. So a situation would invariably arise where you had to go round to Leadenhall Street to try and get the debt settled. 'Charles,' I'd call up – he'd never answer the door, even when we knew he was there – 'you've got to give us the money.' Then his head would appear out of the top-floor window. 'Don't worry, old fruit,' he'd say, grinning cheerfully. 'Everything is going to be just fine.' And that's when you'd know that you were really f....d."

St George, a charmer on and off the course, wasn't the only 1970s gambler who was reluctant to pay up. One of the most notorious was the commission agent Chummy Gaventa, who owned horses with names like Chummy's Pet and used to back them on credit on the rails. "He was possibly the most horrible man I ever met," and considering how willing Victor is to see a positive side to everyone, that's a pretty damning judgement. "His parents were a very wealthy Jewish family, and he used to regularly go to his brother, who was a legitimate businessman, and ask him to bail him out when he got into trouble with his betting. One day, he went to the brother's house in Surrey, pleading for help to settle a debt, and his brother took him into his office and opened his safe, which was stuffed with cash. Chummy had arranged for a distraction so that his brother briefly left the room, and while he was out, Chummy cleared out all the money and ran off with it. As far as I know, he never went back."

Gambling debts would not be legally enforceable for another 30 years and, as the young bookie was discovering, there were plenty of other 'knockers' like Chummy, and often the biggest and most outrageous defaulters were the ones who put on the most impressive facade. Like Ronnie Cornwell, for example. The father of the novelist David Cornwell – better known as John le Carré – was an outrageous and totally unscrupulous con artist who posed variously as a financier, speculator and businessman. Memorably depicted as Rick by his son in the novel A Perfect Spy, and later in Le Carré's autobiography The Pigeon Tunnel, the seemingly indestructible Ronnie loved racing and Royal Ascot and the company of jockeys, and used to have an account with Victor's father. Only he rarely bothered to settle up, and when Young Victor examined the books in the autumn of 1974 and discovered the scale of the arrears and tried to contact him, he never replied or answered the telephone either. So VC decided to pay him a call.

Despite several bankruptcies and terms of imprisonment, Ronnie's offices at the time were a splendiferous set-up in Jermyn Street, rejoicing under the name of Global Enterprises Ltd. A pair of uniformed flunkeys showed Victor up into the great man's presence where Ronnie greeted him with a 'Hello, old son,' putting an arm around his shoulder, offering him a cigar from the box on his desk, commiserating with him over the death of his father and assuring him that, where money was concerned, there was absolutely nothing to worry about. Victor left the office half an hour later with an IOU, and the following year Ronnie died. Needless to say, the debt was never cleared.

Victor had "found all the people who couldn't pay," as Benno put it, "and was getting screwed every week." All in all, 400 people owed the firm over £250,000. So in October 1975, Victor decided to try a different strategy and go over to Paris for the Prix de l'Arc de Triomphe, where he believed, with good reason, a number of the firm's oldest clients and debtors would be present. If he found them all together in holiday mood, glasses in hand, perhaps they might feel shamed, for the sake of honour and decency, into repaying some of the losses they'd incurred with him and his father before him. "One of the names on our list was this 35-year-old lawyer called Roger Barby. I saw he had an actual address in Paris, so I thought I'd drop by the day before the Arc – they only had a routine meeting on the Saturday back then – and pay him a visit."

Victor arrived at a block of flats in the swanky 16th arrondissement, pressed a bell and explained who he was. When he came out of the lift, the apartment door was opened by a butler and he could see there was a party in full swing. "There were pots of caviar on the sideboard and glasses and bottles of champagne all over the place. Looking around, I thought, 'well, he shouldn't have a problem settling up.' But the first thing Roger did when he came up and introduced himself was usher me into the kitchen, shut the door so that it was just the two of us, and then announce dramatically, 'the thing you've got to realise is that I've got no money.' 'Well I can see that for myself,' I said. 'I'm serious,' said Roger, 'I've got a Rolls Royce Corniche downstairs and I can't even afford to put petrol in it to get to the races. I'll have to get a lift.'"

Roger Barby didn't settle his debt there and then. There was a strike on the French stock exchange which, he said, was impairing his affairs, but a fortnight later he came over to London and gave Victor a call. The two of them went out to supper, and over the course of the evening, listening to extracts of Barby's life story, VC warmed to his company. "Roger's been a constant in my life ever since. He started out at the bar when there were other racing-mad characters like Patrick Milmo and John Kelsey-Fry, and Roger's pupil master was the criminal barrister John Mathew, QC." In 1954, Mathew had been the junior counsel for the crown in the Francasal case which involved the running of a ringer at Bath races. He went on to defend the Great Train Robber, Charlie Wilson, and prosecute the Kray Twins, and in 1978 he appeared for David Holmes, one of the co-accused in the Jeremy Thorpe trial. "But Roger got bored by the law and had bigger ambitions, so he went into the stock market instead. He's made and lost a fortune several times, but whenever he's been cleaned out, he's gone back, worked bloody hard and paid off his debts. He returned to the bar for a while, then went into computers, then he went off to trade on his own in the derivative markets. I remember him saying to me one Friday in 1991, 'I'll either be a very wealthy man in the morning or completely skint.' When I went to see him the following afternoon, I found him lying on the floor of his London flat. 'I'm afraid the worst has happened,' he said. 'I'm completely wiped out.' What fascinated me about him is that he was a bit like the descriptions of my grandfather, in that generally you'd never know from his demeanour whether he'd just won ten million or lost it."

Barby was a passionate racing lover (one of his horses was the great French staying hurdler Baracouda, which he sold to JP McManus for £350,000 in 2000), and as Victor discovered, he was a daring high-stakes punter. The first big flutter the pair had together was on a greyhound called Victorious Star, which Victor – emulating his grand-father – bred himself, selling a share to the Sussex builder Jimmy Charman. "It was November 1975, and Roger and I had both pretty much hit the wall at the same time. The trainer Derek Knight said this dog was a certainty one night at White City, so Roger and I backed it on credit to win about £40,000 between us."

Not £400 or even £4,000, but a five-figure pay-out that would have returned £20,000 to VC. A landmark of sorts in his progress as a gambler, and a reminder that 'shy Victor' was also still the tearaway he'd been in Fernando Ponce-Torré's company and naturally tempted by high stakes.

As expected, Victorious Star went to make her run down the far side, but on the penultimate bend she got a bump and she and another dog crossed the line together in a photo finish. The track bookies were convinced Victorious Star had won and offered 10-1 the other dog. "'Shall we have some insurance?' asked Roger. 'Don't be silly,' I said. 'That's just throwing money away.' Then came the result of the pho-tograph and, of course, the other dog had won it. Roger could hardly bear to look at me."

The losers managed to scrape enough money together to pay their bookmaking bill. Then, come the next Saturday, Victorious Star was due to run again in a higher grade.

Once again the trainer said she couldn't lose. "'Last week was just a practice,' he said. So I issued a few cheques I wasn't quite sure would go through, and we backed her to win a bit more than we had the first time. She was four lengths down at the final bend….but she got up to win by half a length."

A visceral and unforgettable moment, but not, alas, a case of solvency at last. Victor may have been enjoying himself as a punter in Barby's company, but as a bookmaker he was still predominantly ending up on the wrong end of things. Either his clients were all winning or they were losing and not paying their bills, and the firm was still getting screwed.

By this time the firm had moved offices again, to 151 Great Portland Street, the rent at Osnaburgh Street having become too expensive. One wet Monday afternoon in April 1977, Chandler and a few of his staff were sitting in the pokey top-floor room reflecting on a ruinous day's trading at Sandown the previous Saturday. The well-backed Whitbread Gold Cup winner Andy Pandy had looked like winning the Grand National until he fell at Becher's second time round. Victor reckoned his Aintree exertions would have left a mark, and took him on. Now he was counting the cost. "We were looking back over the results in silence and feeling like shit when a new secretary came in with a tray of tea. 'Oh look,' she said, gazing out of the window at the London sky. 'What a lovely sunset.' 'Fuck the sunset,' said Victor in a small voice. The secretary was frightfully upset and left the room in tears. I had to go and find her and apologise. You could say she didn't realise quite how bad things were."

So bad, in fact, that the newly 26-year-old Victor was seriously considering selling up and walking away from bookmaking and racing all together. It seemed that he would never really understand it, never win at it and that he just wasn't cut out to follow in his father's and his grandfather's footsteps. A few weeks after the Sandown debacle, he went to pay an early evening call on Alan Kinghorn who, at the time, represented Playboy Bookmakers on the rails and would go on to become a close friend as well as a colleague. At the time, the Playboy Club Casino was the most prosperous in London, annual profits of up to £16million dwarfing the take at the Clermont (which Playboy bought in 1972) and Crockfords, and the head of Playboy Europe, Victor Lownes, had set up a bookmaking arm to enhance the company's reach. Lownes and his partners were looking to acquire existing bookmaking firms and betting shops and intimated that they might be interested in buying the Chandler business.

Victor was considering his options. He'd already turned down an offer from Pat Densham at Sunderlands who had wanted to buy him out when his father died, promising him 'a job for life.' By coincidence, Densham's son Martin had been a contemporary of Victor's at Millfield, and since leaving school, he too had gone into the family business. VC had said 'no' in 1974, but maybe if he sold out now he could still at least salvage something for his mother and his sisters, and then take his chances in the casino or catering trade. Before his father's death, he'd gone so far as to approach the racing lover Bernard Walsh, an old friend of the family and boss of Wheeler's Restaurants, to see if there might be a role for him in their set-up. Perhaps the Glion graduate could manage their Brighton branch or, better still, their celebrated Old Compton Street restaurant in Soho, a favourite haunt of many past and future Chandler customers, including Jeffrey Bernard and 'Freud Eggs and Bacon,' as Walsh called the artists Francis Bacon and Lucian Freud. But Alan Kinghorn dissuaded him.

"Alan was up in his office over the Playboy Club on Park Lane. It was the end of the afternoon, and when I arrived, I'd decided to sell, but by the end of the meeting Alan had talked me out of it." The then 30-year-old Kinghorn, who died of cancer in 2004, was a bright, droll man with a mischievous sense of humour, and although he never worked directly for Victor, the two stood side by side together on the rails for years afterwards. "Alan's father had been a postman and he always remembered walking through the ring with him at Epsom when he was a boy in the 1950s and seeing all the people in smart suits and ties and thinking, 'one day I want to look like that.' So he became a bookie." Kinghorn started out as a board man, chalking up the odds in the London office of Heathorns, another old independent firm. "Michael Simmonds represented them on the rails. His brother Ernest Hunter Simmonds ran the office and he was totally eccentric. 'Do you have any more chalk for the board?' Alan asked him one afternoon. 'No.' replied Ernie, 'but I have a sister in the navy.'"

Over the years, Victor and Kinghorn often shared a car to the races, "though he never seemed particularly interested in studying the form. He'd leave that to me while he did the Telegraph crossword. He was a genius at kidding people without them realising it. One day we gave Benno Miller a lift down to Fontwell. Now Benno was a bit of what you might call an old misery, and Alan loved winding him up. 'Tell me, Benno,' he began one day with the straightest of straight faces, 'how are you coping with the break-up of Take That?' Benno's response was unprintable."

Kinghorn had a penchant for off-colour stories, like the year at Cheltenham when he told the other bookies about the night he supposedly met the murderer Fred West in a Gloucestershire pub. Kinghorn said he was standing at the bar when the fellow next to him started chatting. "When the pub closes, why don't you come back to my place and we can have a party," the man said. "That's great," said Kinghorn. "I'll bring a few beers." "That's great," said the man. "I'll dig up a few women."

The jokes may have been tasteless, but Kinghorn's advice to Victor that night back in 1977 was sincere and carefully considered. He might have been expected to use all his powers to persuade his rival to sell to Playboy, but instead he encouraged him to stick with it. "The margin between success and failure in bookmaking is incredibly narrow," he told Victor. "When the going gets tough…you have to get tougher." Or to repeat what became the Chandler mantra, "it's a combination of luck and good friends that enables you to survive."

VC didn't toughen up overnight, but he did get lucky, and his change of fortune began at Royal Ascot that summer. "It was the year of the Queen's Silver Jubilee. I didn't have a pitch on the rails back then. We were betting upstairs at a desk in the old stand and, for a change, the results were terrific. We were extremely busy and found some very big punters betting in cash. It wasn't just one race. I realised that I could attract clients away from the big firms by offering them a point or two over the odds and giving them a more personal service with a human face. I used to go and see them every day in their boxes. Of course, Ascot is always Ascot. I remember one very pretty but slightly tipsy girl coming up to me and wanting £50 each way on a horse called Roger Bacon. 'You know why it's called Roger Bacon, don't you?' she said, practically falling off her high heels. 'No darling, why's that?' I replied politely. 'It's because it fucks pigs,' she said giggling. 'Right,' I said. The horse lost."

The only drawback to the week was that, with the demand for staff at a premium, Victor had to employ the 80-year-old retired clerk Bill Sox, who had worked for his father. "He smoked Villiger cigars all day and I reeked of them. On the Monday morning after the meeting, I was getting ready to send out the bills to the credit customers when I realised that Bill had got nearly every settlement wrong. The firm's financial director, Roger Jenkins, who was one of the nicest, most genuine and steady people I've ever known, and I had to stay up three nights running with about three hours sleep rewriting them all. But, at the end of it, we found that we'd won over £150,000, which in those days was an absolute fortune. We'd taken a chance...and everything had gone well."

The template had been struck and there could be no going back now. No Wheelers. No sell-out. The young man was hooked and his future had been decided. He would become the fourth generation of his family to lay the odds. He would look back to his father's example for inspiration and even more so to his grandfather, but whatever happened, he would be his own man.

He would become Victor Chandler.

Chapter Twelve

It's A Good Life

One person was not in the least bit surprised by the way Victor had dealt with adversity. Throughout the first few years of their relationship, Carole had seen him ride his luck many times. "Not long after his father died, we were living together in my house in Hove Park Way in Brighton and we were absolutely on our uppers. But I remember Victor going off to this big local card game one Christmas Eve, and he was just like when he went off to Cheltenham once he'd got the hang of it. All Jack The Lad with his long curly hair and shades. Among the other players, there was an accountant known as 'Evil' Bruce Atkins, and Max Cox, a wealthy antique dealer. I half wondered if I'd ever see Victor again."

The game was seven-card rummy, and Carole – who was a skilful bridge player – was there at the beginning of the evening but she walked out thinking Victor was losing too much money. He reckons his losses sobered him up and the next morning he walked back into the house, his pockets bulging and grinning from ear to ear. "I remember I threw the money on the bed and said 'Happy Christmas.'"

Max Cox and Evil Bruce weren't the only ripe characters in Brighton in that era. The town was still home to numerous other spivs and scoundrels left over from the tail end of WW2. There was the chain-smoking Sadie Major, who ran a club on the seafront and hosted all night card parties. There was Victor's Millfield benefactor, Harry Pearlberg, and there was the incorrigible 'Harry Boy' Rogers and his confederates 'Fat Norman' and 'Dapper Thwaites.' Norman's speciality was cooking a big Sunday lunch of roast beef or lamb and then eating the entire meal himself while watching TV. Harry's father owned the rock shops selling the distinctive sticks of pink candy, and Harry Boy was a tipster before encountering a few problems with the law and ending up in prison in Monte Carlo. But for about 10 years, he used to bet with Young Victor and, as with so many other chancers, the bookie's biggest problem was getting paid. "One time he told me he was going to put an envelope through my door on a Saturday. Well, when I got back from the races that evening, the envelope was there alright, but it hadn't been sealed and there was nothing in it. When I called him up on the phone, he was horrified. 'Somebody must have stolen the cheque,' he said. Of course, there'd never been a cheque in there in the first place."

Harry Boy and Fat Norman, who was a solicitor, ran a set-up on the beach at Cannes pretending to be a private bookmaker and his high-rolling client. They fooled another man into joining their 'syndicate' and he started laying Norman's bets himself. What he didn't realise is that Harry had a tic-tac man up on the balcony of a room at the Carlton Hotel. The tic-tac was getting the racing results by telephone and then relaying them down to Harry Boy and Fat Norman so that they could place bets with the mark after the races had been run.

One year, another associate of Harry Boy's called Little Freddie tried it on with Victor at Cheltenham. "He turned up with a bag of gold coins which he said were Krugerrands. There was no internet you could look things up on back then so I said we'd call them sovereigns. But there was no way you could give him credit."

From time to time, Harry Boy landed a touch, and one or two profes-sional gamblers used him to put their money on. He earned enough to drive a mauve Mercedes and own a couple of sex shops in Soho, but not long after that, he went to jail. In his later years, he was a reformed character and, apparently, as straight as the Rowley Mile until Corona-virus claimed him in April 2020.

As far as Victor was concerned, the Runyon-esque crooks and conmen were the salt and pepper flavouring of the racing and book-making life, and he was never judgemental about their activities. There were a lot of colourful actors and entertainers who liked going racing back then too, and who wanted to have a companionable bookmaker on call whenever they felt like a wager. One of the most engaging was the veteran American film star Mickey Rooney, who co-starred with Elizabeth Taylor in *National Velvet*, and with Judy Garland in numerous old Hollywood musicals. When his movie fortunes dimmed, he revived his career by appearing on stage in *Sugar Babies*, a musical revue and tribute to the Burlesque era of the 1920s. The show played on Broadway for five years and then transferred to London's West End. The impresario Bernard Delfont, who himself was a big punter, rang Victor up before the London opening and said, "Would you look after Mickey Rooney? He's staying at the Ritz and he loves racing and wants to know how to have a bet in England."

Delfont arranged seats for the first night for Victor and Carole, as well as tickets for the party afterwards. After the curtain call, an announcer came on stage and asked if the bookmaker Victor Chandler was in the audience and could he put his hand up.

Victor did as requested and was advised that 'Mr Rooney' would like to see him in his dressing room. "There was a big queue of people trying to get in but we could hear him calling out 'I only want Vic the Bookie in here. I don't want anyone else.' While he was taking his make-up off and changing, he told me his days off and wanted to know my number and when the racing was on. At the party, we were on the same table as Mickey and his wife, and the placement said 'Vic the Bookie' and 'Vic the Bookie's wife'. I got the betting shop racing coverage set up in his room at the Ritz and he used to bet every day, though never more than £20 or £50 a time. We took him flat racing at Ascot one afternoon and marked his card, and Carole and I used to see him and his wife for dinner about once a fortnight. He told loads of jokes but one of his favourite stories was about a typical handicapper (as Americans call a punter) who went off into a cave with all his form books, determined to work out the winner of a big race that was coming up. He concluded there was a 40-1 shot that had been overlooked by everyone else and should be near enough the market leader. But then when he got to the track and walked up to the window, he reverted to type and put all his money on the favourite…and, of course, the 40-1 shot won."

One of the British thespians with a penchant for racing at the time was Oliver Reed, whose powerful performance as Gerald Crich in Ken Russell's 1969 film *Women In Love* had not yet been eclipsed by his descent into alcoholism. Reed used to bet with Victor until he moved away to Guernsey at the end of the 1970s. "He was good friends with another customer of mine called John Plackett, who was a loony and a punter and did fittings for betting shops. John introduced me to Ollie, and I went to a few parties at his house near Cranleigh in Surrey, and they were pretty wild. Ollie was a great practical joker. One day, he was on his way to the Derby at Epsom. The car was going through the town when they passed a butcher's shop. Ollie saw the name of the owner over the door, a Mr Blackwood. So he got out of the car, went into the shop and said to the man behind the counter, 'Are you the Mr Blackwood?' The man nodded. 'Were you in the army during the war?' Ollie asks. 'Yes,' says the man. 'I thought so,' says Ollie. 'I believe you were in the same regiment as my father. I just saw your name and it reminded me that he often used to mention you.' The butcher was thrilled, especially when Ollie invited him to join him at the races. He entertained him with champagne all day, introduced him to other people as his father's old comrade, and the butcher never realised it was all a joke. Ollie acted like he couldn't give a damn about anything, but he had his serious side. A few years after my father died, I was betting on the rails at Epsom for the first time when he came up and took me by the arm. 'How are you managing?' he asked. I said it was tough. He nodded. 'It's very hard to follow in those footsteps,' he said, 'but you've just got to get on with it. That's the way it has to be.' I liked him."

Since that week at Royal Ascot in 1977, Victor had been getting on with it, purposefully and in style. He was prepared to take risks to prosper and to embrace his father's maxim and enjoy life anyway he could while also attempting to grow the business in the ways his father hadn't managed to. And as the late 1970s gave way to the 1980s, and Britain's economy began to look up again after the near 25 per cent inflation of the Wilson-Callaghan years, VC was on the cusp of the good life. "Between 1978 and 1990, I had the most wonderful time," he recalls. "There weren't huge fortunes involved, but everything was still fun and we were holidaying three times a year. The Caribbean in winter, somewhere quiet like Nevis where the racing crowd didn't go. Greece maybe in May. Deauville in August. Then Paris in October for the Arc, and sometimes New York too. I always remember when I had my first pair of shoes made by Mr Cleverley, who had made shoes for my father and grandfather. His shop was in the Royal Arcade in Piccadilly and he carried on working there until he was 93 years old."

Mr Cleverley's death in 1991 didn't mean the end of George Cleverley, bespoke shoemakers. The family business, described as 'making the most beautiful shoes in the world' by the former Vanity Fair editor Graydon Carter, continues to prosper under the management of George Glasgow senior, who worked for Mr Cleverley for over 20 years, and Victor is still a regular customer. "He absolutely loved those shoes," said Carole, "and the little box of brushes that came with them. Whenever we went out from then on, his shoes always had to be immaculately brushed and his trousers pressed."

Not just the new shoes, but Victor's general sartorial progress from Afghan Jacket to Savile Row amused the Hoxton old boy Bobby Edwards, who had joined the racecourse team. The young bookmaker had been smartened up by John Kent, who started out aged 15 with Bernard's of Bethnal Green and then progressed to the Duke of Edinburgh's tailor, Hawes and Curtis. Since 2014, Mr Kent has had his own business, Kent, Haste and Lachter in Sackville Street in Mayfair, and VC continues to be a client. "It was half the secret of the game back then to have a different suit on every day," said Edwards, laughing. "Victor senior had always been impeccably dressed with excellent manners, and you could suddenly see that Young Victor wanted to be the same. I think, as a young man, he was possibly a little naive, but he was never a fool. He learned fast and sometimes knowledge comes through the actions of other people."

Despite his reputation as primarily a high-stakes rails layer, Victor didn't make his father's mistake and neglect opportunities in the off-course sector. Between the late '70s and the early '80s, he sold two chains of betting shops to Ladbrokes and then he and a friend, David Knowles – better known as 'The Little Fellow'– built up another chain of shops, which they eventually sold to E. Coomes Ltd. By then the old South East London-based bookmaking firm was being run by Vera Coomes, the formidable widow of Wally, who had been one of Bill Tye's first employers when he left school in 1972.

As the new decade progressed, Victor used to spend the weekdays in London living in his father's old Weymouth Street flat and the weekends with Carole in Brighton and Hove. "There were no mobile phones or emails to bother you back then and, in some ways, I wish we could all go back to that. Before was a better world, gentler and more considerate. Racing and bookmaking still had a sort of camaraderie too, which I loved. If you were staying away from home, there were always entertaining conversations and people to have supper with." He won't quite go so far to say that, in the modern era outside of occasions like Cheltenham, Royal Ascot and Arc weekend in Paris, that colour has all but drained away, but Carole has no such reservations. "There were so many wonderful personalities back then but now there are hardly any left."

One of the biggest characters was John Banks, and when the Scotsman returned from his suspension in 1981, Victor, his mother and his sisters, took him out to a celebratory dinner at L'Etoile in Charlotte Street. It was Victor's way of thanking him for the help he'd given him in those first few years after his father's death, and Banks had already noticed a change in his younger rival. "His first day back was at the Ebor meeting at York and about halfway through the afternoon he came over to me and said, 'Well, well. Somebody's improved by about three stone.'" The analogy was to a racehorse's improvement in form, not an increase in Victor's weight.

In the early Eighties, bookmakers like Victor and John Banks could count on a nucleus of maybe 150 punters they would see regularly at the same race meetings in the south of England every week. Ascot, Kempton, Sandown, Epsom, Lingfield Park. They'd always be there. "A lot of them were Jewish people who were in the clothing business," remembered Bobby Edwards. "They might put anything from £15 to £20,000 into the ring, even on an ordinary weekday at Plumpton, so the bookies would always have something to chase." One of Victor's biggest clients in that era was Sam Bartak, who bought dresses for British department stores ranging from Debenhams to Selfridges. "He used to go racing two or three times a week and dine regularly in Les Ambassadeurs on Saturday nights. He lost a lot of money in the recession in the 1990s but, until his fortunes changed, he was a good customer who always paid his dues."

David Kozack, better known as 'Dave the Jeweller' from Brighton, had both a wholesale and upmarket jewellery business and was at the races almost every day. Kozack was a Dutch Jew and his father had been a jeweller in Amsterdam before the war. "When the Nazis invaded, they were taken in by a Christian family who kept them safe for several months. The couple had a daughter and Dave became very friendly with her. A photograph was taken of them walking together, but when he saw it, he cut it in half so that she wasn't in the picture. He was worried that if he was caught one day, she and her parents would be arrested too. In the end, Dave walked all the way from Holland to Gibraltar and escaped from there to Britain. He was a lunatic punter and he sold jewellery to all the jockeys. What he called his cheap stuff, or paste, for 'weekend partners' and the better stuff for wives."

As well as the Yiddisher element, there were those marginal chancers and optimists, small timers mostly, who trundled along in the wake of the racing caravan. "We had one punter who had credit with us called Jack The Ghost," said Victor. "He had this extraordinary white hair and white face. In all the years he came racing, we never did know his proper name. There was Blackie, a former tipster in the Fifties, who used to appear in our office with great wads of cash but always wearing the same disgusting looking raincoat that must have been at least 30 years old. Then there was Natey. He used to come up to the bookies and tell them what he'd heard the jockeys saying as they left the parade ring. He had sweets in his pocket that he'd give to the jockeys and the bookmakers. He was always hoping you'd stick him a few quid. Sometimes we just gave him half a crown for a cup of coffee."

More than a few of the regulars inhabited a twilit world in which scams and rackets took the place of gainful employment. A Scotsman called Jock, for example, who went missing for three years and then suddenly turned up again one Friday at Sandown. "'Hello, Jock,' I said. 'Where have you been?' 'Oh, well,' he said. 'I got caught. In my business you get caught from time to time and I had to go away.' 'Oh,' I said, realising that further enquiries might be tactless. 'Well…it's good to have you back again.'"

One particularly roguish individual, who eventually had to go away voluntarily, was a charming bookmaker called Terry Kirk. "He was trading in the Leeds area as Henry Hallam and he was the first man to introduce me to computer speed figures making allowances for different tracks and distances. I remember him telling me that when Old Vic won the Chester Vase in 1989, it was the fastest time he'd ever recorded. I had a big bet on it next time out in the French Derby at Chantilly and it won by seven lengths. Terry was doing very well at one point, driving around in a blue Rolls Royce with a personalised number plate, TK1. But about three months after the 1979 General Election, he was in difficulties. Then, one day, he got a phone call out of the blue from this character who said he wanted to back himself to be the next Prime Minister. 'I want to invest £25,000,' he says. 'Oh really?' says Terry, thinking there is a God after all. 'Yes,' says the man. 'What odds will you offer me?' 'Well,' says Terry. 'I'll have to have a think about it.' He waits for ten minutes then rings the man back. 'Well, sir,' he says. 'I've done a bit of research into your chances,' which of course was nonsense, 'and it seems you're a 100-1 shot. But you do understand that the bet will have to be in cash?'

"The punter agreed, and so a few days later, Terry drove down to this little town in the Welsh valleys. The bloke was living in a two up, two down in a row of terraced houses. As Terry walked up to the front door, he looked in through the window and saw a Securicor man in the front room with an easel and a map of Britain. 'What's the map for?' he asked the punter when he got inside. 'We are planning the route from Leeds to here to bring the money back when I'm elected,' said the man. Terry, trying desperately hard not to laugh, left about half an hour later with a briefcase containing £25,000.

Then, a few weeks later, he got another call. 'I want to make a further investment,' said the punter. 'Oh, really?' says Terry. 'Well, I'm afraid I can't lay you 100-1 anymore… because there's been a lot of money for you since your first wager.' Of course, there hadn't been a penny but Terry couldn't resist hamming it up. 'How about fifties?' 'That'll do,' said the punter. 'In cash?' says Terry. 'In cash,' says the punter. Terry was practically in tears when he put the phone down."

Needless to say, the investor – who wasn't called John Major or Tony Blair – never made it to 10 Downing Street. "It turned out he was some eccentric Welsh Nationalist who had recently come into an inheritance and thought he was going to be the next Lloyd George."

It was the easiest £50,00 Terry Kirk had ever come by and it encouraged him to go in search of similarly flush but deluded souls who needed parting from their funds. A few years later, he was working as the 'betting advisor' to a very wealthy but ignorant Leeds man who was a big gambler. "Terry would tip him these 20-1 chances, telling him they were all overpriced. The punter would have anything from £500 to £5,000 on but, unbeknown to him, Terry was putting the bets on with some local bookmaking friends who were in on the scam. Of course, the horses never won and they all shared the profits.

"From time to time, Terry would stick in a 6-4 winner, just to keep the punter happy. What the bloke didn't realise was that Terry and his mates were in cahoots with the regional betting shop commentator who worked for Extel (the Exchange Telegraph Company), and he was in on it too. Terry would take his client into the shop to listen to a race and the commentator – just a voice over the tannoy in those days before satellite TV – would have been told to give plenty of mentions to the 20-1 shots to make it sound like they were running a big race.

"Well, this went on for over a year, and then, one day, Terry tipped him a 50-1 chance. The punter has £1,000 on and they go into the shop to listen to the commentary together. And, of course, this is the day when the 50-1 outsider really does win. Terry realised he was in trouble when he heard the commentator yelling 'and this is for real. I'm not making this up.' The punter was ecstatic, totally unaware that Terry hadn't put one pound on him, let alone £1,000. Terry had to do a disappearing act. But he was a real character and he was in racing all his life."

Taking down suckers had been Terry Kirk's speciality. Taking on the favourites, especially rotten value odds-on chances, became Victor Chandler's. He had the nerve and, thanks to the old family retainers, he had the expertise. On race days, the firm would meet up in the mornings at Great Portland Street or in The Castle round the corner in Portland Place. "There were four or five us," said Bobby Edwards, "and we were a decent team. Joe Dunbar still used to be the first into the office, even well into his eighties, and Val Powell's ability to clerk was terrific. He'd take one look at the expected odds and say to Victor, 'this is a good race to bet on because the percentages are all in our favour.'"

A set of odds on a race are calculated according to a percentage chance table of nought to 100. If a horse is trading at, say, 5-2, that means it has a 29 per cent chance of winning. If it's trading at 7-2, it would have a 22 per cent chance; or at 4-1, a 20 per cent chance; and so on. If all the odds were fair, the total of these percentages would always add up to a hundred but, in practice, the total nearly always exceeds that number. This excess is called the over-round, and the greater the over-round, the bigger the margin of potential profit for the bookmaker. Shrewd, numerate clerks like Val Powell and Bill Tye would work out what they thought a proper set of odds should be on a race – factoring in the going, information and form – and if they spotted rival firms appreciably out of step for no good reason, they would recommend this as a race to attack. In that era, it was still possible to say that you could meet all sections of British society – from toffs and swells, to barrowboys, spivs and chancers – rubbing shoulders on a race course. Monday was the day for the costermongers at Wye. The street traders and Kentish fruit dealers flush with funds from a good morning's business at Ashford market and ready to play. When Wye closed down in 1975, some of their Monday fixtures moved to Folkestone, and the bookies and the market traders went with them.

Then, the following day, Victor might be attending to the requests of one of his grandest and most loyal clients, Lady Lonsdale, first wife of the 7th Earl, a Jockey Club Steward, and someone who left a specific instruction in her will that her bookmaker – VC – should be paid any debts outstanding from her estate.

Her Ladyship was a spiritual relation of the eccentric Mrs Collins, who was related to the Joel family and "lived just off Hyde Park in a mansion flat with staff. Her husband, Fred, was the former Master of a City livery company and one of the first people to import goods from Russia to the UK. Racing was her life and she used to bet by phone on practically every race, every day of the week, and she settled every quarter. Sometimes she'd forget what day it was. 'But, Mrs Collins,' you'd have to say. 'That's yesterday's card.' Now and again she'd ring me up and try to enlist my help with some errand or other. 'Victor,' she'd say. 'Have you got a good run around?' meaning a member of staff with a small car to run errands. 'I've got four people coming to lunch today but Fred's away. I want the best crackers from Fortnum's and I need someone to fetch them for me.' The job would usually be entrusted to Garry Melsom, who'd joined the firm at the age of 17 and was very charming."

Not all well-to-do punters were honourable ones, some of them seeming to feel that regular payment of their bookmaking bills was something that only common people bothered with. Some of the worst offenders were members of the Turf Club in Carlton House Terrace, where the concierge Mr Grace ran a private bookmaking service from his cubbyhole near the entrance. "He used to put money on for all the toffs, and sometimes he'd ring up and lay off with me. 'My book is too full, Victor,' he'd say, 'and the problem is these bastards don't pay.'"

One of the worst offenders was the *Daily Express* racing correspondent Charles Benson, who was court jester to Robert Sangster and his circle and as bibulously entertaining as he was profligate. The Old Etonian Benson, who entitled his autobiography '*No Regard For Money*', was once entrusted with a credit bet by his friend Bobby McAlpine, who wanted him to place a Yankee on his behalf. "Charles put the list of horses in his pocket and forgot about them and then, of course, they all won. He came up to me afterwards and asked if I would put the bets through the book all the same. I said 'certainly not. It was your mistake and now you're expecting me to pay for it.' He had to make a speech at Bobby's birthday party that evening. 'You know that Yankee you gave me,' he began. 'Well, I forgot to put it on.'"

Despite letting his friend down, and being memorably described by Sir Peter O'Sullevan as "unlikely to ever expire from overwork," Benson continued to be invited to the best homes and parties, singing for his supper, which was always free. By 1983, Young Victor was becoming something of a champagne and caviar man himself, though more to look after the high rollers than to supplement his own lunch breaks. Among his best clients were Max Kingsley and Phil Isaacs, who ran the company London Clubs, which owned casinos in London and elsewhere in the UK, and their friend Henry Gold, who was a big punter. "They went to Ascot every year and they were all mad. Henry Gold was the same age as me. He had a patent for selling a type of anti-rust paint for cars to the Japanese, and he travelled a lot. One trip, he got back to London earlier than expected and thought he'd spend the night with his mistress and then go home the next day. He phoned the Barracuda Club in Baker Street from the airport and told them that he wanted the best champagne, the best claret and food, and said that he'd be round to pick them up in about half an hour. But when he got there, they told him, very helpfully, that they'd already had the food and drink sent to his house. He rushed home in a blind panic, coming in through the door and saying 'Surprise, darling. I'm back,' but his wife wasn't fooled. 'How stupid do you think I am?' she said, surveying the feast. Henry said the club's mistake ended up costing him a £15 million divorce settlement."

Gold's confederate, Phil Isaacs, was an equally faithless husband, but his wife also had her revenge in the end. When Isaacs was seriously ill in hospital in London, she walked into his private room one day smartly dressed and carrying an array of expensive shopping bags. "Now you're effing dying," she said, "I'm going to spend every last effing penny on myself."

An even bigger punter than Isaacs and Gold, albeit a more discreet one, was a rich businessman called Dr Menon who "had a big house in Wentworth in Surrey but had started out as an untouchable and a bus driver in India. He'd made money in all kinds of ways, including beer, and he adored racing. He used to come to Royal Ascot every day and it would be nothing for him to bet a million in a week. We took an extra box there, just so that we could entertain him, and Carole hosted the lunches." The box was in the Royal Enclosure too, just like Victor senior's 20 years before.

It wouldn't be long before the firm's position improved, moving from that desk on the mezzanine floor, down to the rails. Bill Tye remembers the transaction that brought it about. "Victor was originally number 21 or 22 on the list to get a rails pitch at Ascot, and there was only room for 20. Terry Barfoot was number 20 so, one year, Victor bunged him a couple of grand to drop out, and we were moved up."

Royal Ascot "was business, and bloody hard work with all the entertaining." But whereas Victor had found the royal meeting intimidating when he first went there as a bookmaker in 1975, now he embraced it as a money-making opportunity almost on the same scale as Cheltenham. Immaculately dressed every day in the full Royal Enclosure gear, complete with black top hat, button-hole and a pair of Mr Cleverley's shoes, brushed up gleamingly for the occasion. Carole watched him going out of the door each morning "looking like a band box." The sartorial effort was worth making. Doctor Menon, who always settled his accounts promptly, wasn't the only big fish on the royal heath as

Mrs Thatcher's second term Premiership kicked in. "There's been a huge change culturally, and there's a different kind of person going racing there nowadays, but when I started out, the great majority of those boxes at Ascot were all still privately owned by hugely wealthy individuals." Thirty years later, they are nearly all corporate owned or rented out to corporate parties by the day.

Some of the old-school racing families were having difficulty adjusting to the 1980s zeitgeist as the Big Bang meritocracy unleashed a new breed of trader on the Square Mile. But the extraordinary thing about Royal Ascot, at least from the bookies' point of view, was that the combination of champagne, racing and dressing up continued to exert an almost narcotic influence on successive generations of otherwise smart individuals, be they old money or new. As Michael Simmonds of Heathorns put it: "as soon as they set foot in the Royal Enclosure, some of my biggest customers, clever men with hugely successful business careers, seem to put their brains in their back pocket."

A lot of people didn't survive and Victor saw "loads of punters come and go." In June 1983, the Australian entrepreneur Alan Bond – a national hero Down Under after financing Australia's historic America's Cup victory that January (but due to be jailed for fraud there 14 years later) – came to Royal Ascot kitted out in full morning dress. Before the racing began, he sought out Victor on the rails and, in the best gun-slinger tradition, informed him that he'd heard he wasn't afraid to lay a proper bet. Bond wanted to open a credit account there and then, and he wasn't talking about a £100 limit. Victor used the blower to call a friend working at Aspinall's Club in Curzon Street. They'd already seen Bond at the tables the night before and confirmed that he was good for whatever sum he wanted to bet up to. "He proceeded to have between £30,000 and £50,000 with us on each of the first five races. All the bets lost. None of them were particularly shrewd selections and he couldn't have known the first thing about the form. After the fifth race, he came up and looked me in the eye and said, 'You're no good to me. You're bringing me bad luck.' So he went down the rails and promptly had £20,000 on a big-priced winner with Heathorns in the last. As far as we were concerned, he'd have been welcome back any time."

The next night, Victor and Carole were having dinner with friends in Annabel's in Berkeley Square, and Alan Bond was at the next table. "He couldn't have been more friendly," and when Victor went to get the bill, he found that Bond had already paid it.

Bond wasn't the only Australian punter to look up Victor when he was in town. Neither was he the biggest. Kerry Packer, the plutocratic media magnate and founder of World Series Cricket, used to bet with the firm too. Packer loved polo and had founded his own team and bought a house and estate in West Sussex so that he'd have a base for the English polo playing season between May and July. One day, he surprised Victor by turning up at lowly Brighton races where "he won a lot of money off us. Mickey Fletcher [a bookmaker better known as The Asparagus Kid] tipped him a couple of winners and got a good present out of it."

Packer was often generous to those that helped him. One night, he and his entourage were late leaving the polo at Cowdray Park. On their way back to London, they tried to stop off and have dinner somewhere in the country, but the first three restaurants they called at all said that they were closed. The fourth one was more accommodating, opening up the kitchen and cooking them a hearty meal. At the end of it, Packer left a £10,000 cash tip on the table.

After dark, the Aussie tycoon was more usually to be found in a Mayfair casino in a private room, playing three tables at once. Baccarat, blackjack and roulette. He'd be enjoying himself, shouting and getting excited as the cards came out, and he didn't appreciate being told to quieten down. One night, in Las Vegas, a rich, disgruntled Texan allegedly told him to cut the racket. "How much are you worth?" Packer asked contemptuously. The Texan mentioned a significant sum. "I'll toss you for it," said Packer, at which point the American folded.

Not every big 1980s gambler was as impulsive as Kerry Packer, or as clueless as Alan Bond. Some of the shrewdest punters of that era were followers of Guy Harwood's stable at Pulborough in West Sussex. The trainer enjoyed a golden run with horses of the calibre of Kalaglow, Sandhurst Prince, Lear Fan, Warning and the incomparable Dancing Brave, winner of the 1986 2,000 Guineas, Eclipse Stakes, King George VI and Queen Elizabeth Stakes and Prix de l'Arc de Triomphe. Dancing Brave ran in the colours of Prince Khalid Abdullah, but some of the other horses in the yard were owned by the accountant Tony Ward, who was the chairman of a public company; his brother Brian, who was a professional gambler; and the art dealer Anthony Speelman; and when Harwood gave them the green light, they backed their runners to the hilt.

The commission, which could be anything from £5,000 to £50,000, would be handled by Victor's fellow rails bookmaker Dudley Roberts and the bookie-punter Johnny Lights, who Victor acknowledges was "very clever and terrific with figures." They were the 'enemy' aiming to take as much as £300,000 out of the ring, and their bets landed enough times for VC to feel the pain.

An equally smart set of professionals followed Henry Cecil's yard, though Bill Tye remembers one surreal day at Sandown when "the Harwood people all wanted to back the Cecil runner and the Cecil punters all wanted to back Harwood's." The race was for maiden two-year-old fillies and neither of the big two stables won.

Tony Ward's touches were mainly in top-drawer races with potential stallion and broodmare values on the line as well as betting money. Charles and Edward St George, and the Hong Kong-based Ivan Allan, were other gambling owners who tilted every bit as much at the bloodstock market as they did at the ring. All three of them had horses in training with Henry Cecil in Newmarket at some point and enjoyed regular dealings with his early 1980s stable jockey. The former friend of Victor Chandler senior, the hero of Young Victor's Parisian youth and the greatest flat racing jockey of all time. Lester Keith Piggott.

Chapter Thirteen

Men Behaving
Badly

———

I n the course of his 47 years with a riding licence, comprising 11
jockeys' championships, 30 English classic victories and countless
unforgettable moments, from his first Derby on Never Say Die in
1954 to winning the Breeders Cup Mile on Royal Academy in New
York in 1990, Lester Piggott was the man. There were other outstanding jockeys too, of course – Sir Gordon Richards, Scobie Breasley, Bill
Williamson, Pat Eddery and more – but Lester was the one that every
owner, trainer, punter (and bookmaker) wanted to have on their side
if they could.

The Long Fellow's prodigious skill and ability to deliver when the
money was down has been documented many times over, along with
his indifference to authority and sometimes pathological meanness.
But what the old owners, gamblers and odds-makers also loved about
Lester was that priceless store of peculiarities, prejudices and eccen-
tricities that became, over the years, the stuff of weekly and even daily
comment, from the weighing room to the press room and the paddock
to the rails. One of the earliest Lester anecdotes Victor remembered
hearing was told to him by his father when they had supper together

one night in London. "He said he was standing talking to him in the rain one day at Lingfield Park when they saw Willie Carson come out of the weighing room in an old-fashioned plastic mac. 'I bet that's the first time you've seen a c... in a French letter,' says Lester, gleefully."

The champion's language was equally pungent one afternoon at Kempton where the punter Dougie Goldstein (who later became a bookie) had asked him to ride a horse belonging to him and some friends in the final race on the card. Lester's bets were taken care of by his gofer, a bookmaker from Rottingdean called Robert Callaghan, but there was still the delicate question of his fee, which was well over the nominal retainer and had not been satisfactorily agreed, as he walked into the parade ring. "'If it was just me Lester, I'd pay you,' said Dougie, 'because I think you're the greatest. But the other two, well...' 'What about them?' asked Piggott, scowling. 'Well, they think that £2,000 is an awful lot of money.' 'Well, they're c...s then, aren't they?'" came the reply.

Lester still took the ride. But no doubt entirely coincidentally, it finished second.

Dougie Goldstein's friends weren't the only ones to find Lester frustrating. One of Victor's wealthiest clients in the early 1980s was a Middle Eastern punter called Mr Wakim, who "was overweight and sometimes wore a Fez, like Sydney Greenstreet in Casablanca. One Saturday he invited Alan Kinghorn and me to dinner at this place he'd spent millions on near Newbury. There was a gatehouse with two guards, a huge great fountain outside, like Versailles, and a polo field he'd made for his son at the bottom of the garden. We sat on cushions on the floor to eat. A whole lamb was barbecuing on a spit and I've never seen so much caviar in my life. It really was James Bond, and after dinner he insisted on taking us down into the basement, which he'd turned into a shooting gallery. He had hand-guns, semi-automatic rifles, the lot, and when we looked at the targets, we saw they were all pictures of Lester Piggott. Apparently, Mr Wakim was convinced that Lester cheated him whenever he backed one of his mounts. So, to vent his frustration, he'd go down into the basement afterwards and blaze away at his image. He thought it was hilarious. When I told Lester about it he just shrugged and smiled. 'There have always been people like that,' he said."

Geoff Lewis, who rode Mill Reef to win the Prix de l'Arc de Triomphe at Longchamp in 1971, used to travel over to Paris with Lester for all the big Sunday race meetings between April and October each year. "The same two or three of us – Lester, myself, Jimmy Lindley – would share a taxi ride together from the airport to the course and back. We'd take it in turns to pay the fare but Lester always used to try and get out of it or get away with paying less than he should. One Sunday, the man was late to pick us up after racing. Well, of course, Lester had been in charge of the arrangements on the way in and he hadn't left a tip, and this was the driver's revenge. He drove very slowly all the way back and we very nearly missed our flight. Lester was furious. When he got out, he opened up the boot to get his riding kit and there was the man's supper just sitting there. A nice joint of meat it was, in a shopping bag. So, quick as a flash, Lester picks up the lamb or beef or whatever, unzips his own bag and slips it inside. 'That'll teach him,' he says, grinning, and off he went to check in."

Lester was partial to a free pair of shoes too, as Charles St George discovered when he took him to meet Mr Cleverley one day in the Royal Arcade. Lester was impressed and ordered six pairs, but when he came back to collect them he said that St George was paying and walked out without settling the bill.

Lester was indubitably the best, as well as the most singular, jockey of Victor's lifetime. Geoff Lewis, who hung up his saddle in 1979, was never quite on the same plane but he still won most of the big races, and during his training career, which lasted from 1980 to 1997, he enjoyed a party and a bet with the best of them. "Geoff was in our box one day at Sandown, saying how much he fancied this particular horse of mine. He wanted a monkey on (£500) each way. Then he said, 'Hell, make it a grand.' I said 'Steady on, Geoff. Are you sure about this? It's 40-1.' But he was adamant. So we all backed it. I think I had a couple of grand each way. It was called Night Dance and it was like watching Harpo Marx's ride in *A Day At The Races*. It was plumb last coming into the straight, then it went from last to first, passing the whole field on the wide outside, and it ended up winning by about six lengths. Geoff was all over the place. 'Now you can see what kind of trainer I am,' he kept saying. Much drink was taken and by the end of the afternoon, Geoff was absolutely legless so I tried to take his car keys off him. Big mistake. Geoff threw a punch and knocked me out cold. He may have been drunk, but he was incredibly fit and we all ended up in a heap wrestling Geoff to the ground."

On another occasion, in the box at Ascot, the convivial trainer was "equally plastered and he and his wife Noelene were having an argument. She called him 'short legs,' which really upset him. 'You don't mind them when they're wrapped around you, do you?' he says. 'You've got a fucking long memory,' she replied."

Lewis was always sensitive about his size and never more so than one day when he hosted a racing lunch at his home near Epsom. He was sitting up one end of the table and enjoying plenty of liquid refreshment when he heard an aristocratic trainer, who was sitting further down, making a disparaging comment. "You jockeys," said the trainer. "If it wasn't for horse racing, you'd all be in the circus." The furious Geoff, incensed at what he saw as an insult to his profession, jumped up and ran down the table to aim a punch at the abuser. The two of them both crashed to the floor, pulling the tablecloth, glasses and china down with them. It was the end of lunch.

There was another day, a midweek afternoon, when Geoff had three horses running on the same card. He told Victor he thought that they all should win. The bookmaker was waiting by the phone, expecting Geoff to ring in with his bets, but the call never came. The trainer didn't answer Victor's calls either. "I had that extra bottle at lunchtime," confessed Lewis later, "and I fell asleep and didn't hear the telephone." He was as good as his word, though. All three horses obliged with VC, who'd initially been sceptical, sticking "a few quid on the last one."

By this point, it was somehow typical of Victor that he should be at the centre of such *Carry On* racing escapades. Drunken trainers.

Frustrated wives. Jealous girlfriends. Lustful bookies. Devious jockeys. Incompetent Stewards. Pissed journalists. Misfiring coups. Bacchanalian celebrations and commiserations. These are the stuff of the Turf, or they certainly were 30 years ago as any reader of Jeffrey Bernard's Low Life columns in the Spectator will know, no matter how much they are airbrushed out of the picture by today's more bland and anodyne accounts. Jeff, as his friends called him, detested earnestness and scorned the bland and the unadventurous while chronicling racing with a passion and a savage wit that has never been surpassed.

Victor was an avid Low Life reader, just as he loved stories about the colourful characters in racing's past, like the Edwardian gambler Bob Sievier and the notorious betting syndicate, the Druids Lodge Confederacy. But books of all kind, and not just dry scrutiny of the form book, had been part of Chandler's life since his Millfield days, and he had a similar love of art, nurtured initially by his father's friendship with men like Lucian Freud and developed further during his time in Paris after leaving school. He liked the painters as well as the paintings and was naturally attracted to the whole boozy, scandalous, scabrous world of Soho where Jeffrey Bernard spent almost as much time as he did going racing. "On the Turf, there are men for all occasions," wrote Bernard in his 1987 book Talking Horses. "There are cultured men, kind men, good men, hooligans and absolute bastards." Jeff was never one of the bastards, but he was one of the semi-permanently skint, and his frequent periods of insolvency, accompanied by alcoholic remorse, amused Victor as much as they had his father before him.

One day, shortly after Bernard got to know Victor senior, he was approaching his pitch at Ascot when he heard him saying to his clerk Val Powell, "Good news, boys. Here comes the lunch money." Another day, 10 years later, the journalist owed Young Victor over £2,000 and had been avoiding him for weeks as he couldn't pay. From time to time he'd bump into him at the races and give him £20 as if he was doing him a favour. Then he'd wait for Victor to go away and insist on having a credit bet with Val Powell or Bill Tye. One Saturday in the 1980s, he'd just gone into the old ground floor Members Bar at Newbury, which only had one entrance, when he saw VC walking in with Bill and the team. Jeff promptly pretended he'd dropped something on the floor and hid under the table. After a couple of minutes, a hand appeared, wearing a very nice watch and signet ring and holding a large vodka and tonic. Victor's face appeared a moment later. "Hello, Jeff," he said, grinning. "I should think you're about ready for this now."

Victor's worst experience in Jeff's company was also at Newbury on Hennessy Gold Cup day in 1988. They were on the verge of leaving and the low lifer was in search of a lift back to London. Just as they were coming out of the Members Bar, the Queen Mother was coming down in the lift from the Royal Box. "Jeff chose exactly that moment to throw up in front of her. It was awful, and there was absolutely nothing anyone could say to make it better." It was almost as bad when Victor took Bernard to the Stable Lads Charity Boxing evening in a smart Park Lane hotel. He turned away for a second to call a waiter, and when he turned back, Jeff had just passed out, face first into the melon. It really should have been the soup, as he spent so much of his life in it. But what superlative evocations of jockeys, trainers, punters and horses he left behind. One of the last times he was ill in hospital, Victor went to see him, and Jeff recorded the occasion in print. "Before he left, he said, 'You'll be needing a few quid for things like buying toothpaste and the newspapers in the morning.' He then shoved £100 under the pillow," which, as Jeff conceded, "goes to show there are such things as generous bookmakers."

Generosity or not, VC was there to run a business and to try and show a profit. But he was also determined to enjoy himself and, unlike that other gambling maverick John Aspinall, he was happy to do business with punters from all corners of the social spectrum, including 'gentlemen' who might not be, and assorted racy characters attempting to evade the attentions of the law.

One weekend in the mid-Eighties, Victor and Alan Kinghorn were staying at the Bibury Court Hotel near Cirencester. They were down in the Cotswolds for one of the non-Festival meetings at Cheltenham, and there were a number of big punters staying in the hotel too.

"One evening after dinner, about half a dozen of them were sitting round a table playing cards. It was a big game but they're all being very quiet and well behaved in this smart, country-house setting, and they're tipping the waiters £20 every time they bring another bottle. I was on nodding terms. I'm not playing. I'm sitting nearby reading the paper and I'm the only one who hasn't done time. Well, all of a sudden, this rowdy lot of Hooray Henry types come into the bar. They make a lot of noise and start throwing things around and upsetting the staff and the other guests. One of them, about six-foot six, the hard man from the Rugby Club, doesn't like cigar smoke and starts telling the card players to put their cigars out. One punter, who used to be a bare knuckle boxer, advises him very politely to behave himself, but the rugger bugger gets louder and more obstreperous. 'Do you want to step outside?' he asks, squaring up drunkenly. 'Son,' says the other bloke. 'I ain't been outside since I was 14 years old.' The hooray throws a punch and misses. Then our man throws a right and the rugger player's gone straight up through the air and into the Christmas tree. A few minutes later, three of the Hoorays are laid out on the floor with the card school showing minimal damages.

The police were called, but when they arrived, the rugby players' girl-friends and the hotelier, who was known as Jimmy the Hunchback, all backed up the punters, saying the other lot fully deserved it. The local constabulary were happy to believe them and nobody was charged. The funny thing is that if these local police had realised who it was they were talking to, they could have arrested two or three of the most wanted men in Britain."

Victor enjoyed those Cotswold soirees, sometimes at Bibury Court, sometimes at the Lygon Arms in Broadway (though from 1978 onwards the firm moved to the equally comfortable Dormy House for all Cheltenham meetings), and he named a greyhound he'd bred after one of the hotels. "I had this dog, called The Lygon, and nobody wanted to buy it, so I sent it down to Derek Knight (the Sussex-based greyhound trainer of Victorious Star), as he'd just lost an owner. After a few months, he reported back that it was too clever to run up the straight and he thought it was a hurdler and that nobody had spotted its potential yet." VC grins, that mischievous, conspiratorial look once again. "I remember the first time that it ran over hurdles at Hove. I'd promised Carole I'd be home by eight but instead I was down on the track watching Derek for signs of encouragement as the dogs paraded. Sure enough, he kept turning round and nodding and then turning away again. So, of course, I had to back it." Of course. The grin broadens. "It just got up in a dead heat."

There were to be more memorable nights at the dogs for Bill Chandler's grandson, though his favourite track wasn't the family-owned Walthamstow, where his father had fallen out so badly with his Uncle Charles. The bookmaker-gambler preferred White City, the connoisseur's venue and home of the Greyhound Derby until, sadly, the stadium was closed in 1984 and later demolished. The site had been sold for redevelopment, but with no stadium plan attached, and went on to become part of BBC Television Centre. But in happier times, Victor used to go there a couple of times a week, cheekily making a book at a table in the restaurant (as did John Banks and Michael Tabor), and while there was no formal arrangement with the stadium, nobody tried to stop them. "It was a lovely place back then. A real atmosphere and very social. You'd see all kinds of people there, from Frankie Howerd in his toupee with his boyfriend Dennis, to Charles 'Better Box' Benson working his way from table to table."

In 1965, Victor's father had owned the Greyhound Derby favourite Hi Joe, but he was stolen a week before the final and only found a year later in a garage in Dunstable. The man accused of taking him was subsequently tried and acquitted, but there remained suspicions that Hi Joe had been kidnapped to make things easier for a rival. In 1983, VC had a Derby finalist and was full of hope that it would avenge his father's misfortune. "The dog was called Amazing Man. I bred it myself and we named it after Dougie Goldstein, who had gone into partnership with Carole's father Izzy, who really was a lovely man and had been a rear gunner in a Lancaster in WW2. Izzy was fascinated by Dougie, who always seemed to have lumps of cash in his pockets, and nicknamed him an 'amazing man.' Derek Knight trained it, and the night before the Derby heats began, I had £1,000 on it at 100-1 with Tony Morris. I also had another £27,500 to £1,500 after the first round. Uncle Ronnie came over from Ireland to watch it and thought it was a wonderful dog. We just needed a little bit of luck…but we didn't get it."

The volume of betting on the Dog Derby back then was still massive. One track bookmaker, John Power, took £200,000 running up to the Final in 1983, and a further £100,000 on the night. Long before then, dozens of Victor's friends and colleagues had joined in the punt on Amazing Man. "If that dog had won, I think most of the Chandler firm would have retired on the proceeds," reckoned Bobby Edwards.

Amazing Man stayed on strongly to win his quarter-final despite being slowly away, confirming Ronnie's and Derek Knight's estimates of his potential. "At Wimbledon you were always looking for a sprinter because the track was so sharp, but at White City you'd want a stronger, galloping type. You'd also need a dog that wouldn't go to pieces on the night because the noise when they were loading up there was phenomenal. I thought Amazing Man had everything." Ronnie came over again for the semi-final and saw his nephew's dog put in another powerful finish, getting up to beat the favourite by half a length. "He won so easily that he practically ran another circuit of the track before we could get hold of him," said Knight. "It didn't affect him until afterwards, but when we took him out the following morning his back had stiffened up and his back legs were sore. Ronnie and I tried to treat him, and Victor was very good about it. 'If you feel that the dog shouldn't run…don't run him,' he said."

The 1983 Final took place on June 25th, the same day as cricket's World Cup Final between India and the West Indies at Lord's, and was broadcast live on BBC2 with Harry Carpenter in the commentary box. It was a last-minute decision of Derek Knight's to let Amazing Man take his chance, "but he never really got into the race and finished fifth. The saddest thing was that he had his perfect draw in trap six, and he'd beaten the eventual winner, I'm Slippy, in the semi-final." The

Derby wasn't the end of Amazing Man's track career. The following March he won the Ladbrokes Golden Jacket at Harringay, and afterwards, VC, complete with curly hair and camel-hair velvet-collar coat, was presented with the trophy by the Labour leader of the Opposition, Neil Kinnock and his wife Glenys, who were being entertained by the sponsors. Amazing Man returned to Harringay in 1985 to win the 2,000 Guineas before beginning his new career at stud.

By the mid-Eighties, Victor was also making frequent visits, rarely profitable but always richly entertaining, to the Irish Derby hare coursing meeting at Clonmel in County Tipperary. In Ireland at least, ignorance had not yet relegated the ancient sport of coursing to a status somewhere between crack dealing and child abuse, and VC had been brought up on stories of his father's long days and nights at the Waterloo Cup (including the big poker games in the Prince of Wales Hotel in Southport), which continued to be staged at Altcar near Liverpool until coursing was banned in the UK in 2005.

Especially fond of his Uncle Ronnie, and charmed by all things Irish, he loved the comparable blend of conviviality, gambling and madness that can be found at Powerstown Park in February. A long-standing friend of the Newmarket racehorse trainer and coursing devotee Sir Mark Prescott, Victor had sponsored a special coursing event for track dogs at Swaffham in Suffolk, and Sir Mark and Stephen Little were just some of the many familiar faces he'd see at Clonmel. Not that his visits were ever profitable ones, unless you count the two occasions when he beat Stephen Little at backgammon. "The first time I went there, I think I backed 36 consecutive losers. Then, in 1983, I had the favourite for the Derby and the Oaks, both trained by Ronnie, and they both went out in the first round."

Victor's chauffeur on the way down to Tipperary used to be his father's old friend Gerry Albertini, who had left Ibiza and bought a house in Ireland in County Kildare. It was a converted Piggery in the grounds of Stacumny House, a Georgian mansion which belonged to Count Vincent Poklewski Koziell, an eccentric Polish aristocrat and raconteur who'd escaped from the Nazis in 1939. The locals were somewhat bemused by Gerry, who wore cowboy boots and said he was an American, but looked and sounded like Terry-Thomas. With the Troubles raging in the north, there were mutterings that he might be a British spy, and when he was away at one point, his house was turned over by the IRA. Fortunately, they didn't find anything that displeased them and they didn't bother him again.

Political and religious rivalries were set aside in Clonmel where owners, trainers and punters from Northern Ireland were as prominent as their southern Irish and British counterparts. There were bodies in the lobby of the Cashel Palace Hotel at breakfast time, but they were victims of alcoholic excess rather than gunshot wounds. Priests blessed dogs in barns and the backs of cars before their course. Bishops and the Protestant aristocracy mingled with Catholic publicans and bookmakers, and 10-year-old boys dressed up like Chicago gangsters and ran Find the Lady games on the way in. Victor went back every year.

Joining up with Ronnie Chandler in his adopted homeland meant sharing the company of his many bacchanalian friends. All of them horse and greyhound racing and gambling fanatics. There were natural comedians like the late Dave Cahill, a Kerryman who emigrated to the US as a teenager and made a fortune in the house-building business in Chicago before returning to live in County Limerick and own coursing dogs and horses. One of Cahill's greyhounds was of a nervous disposition so his trainer Ronnie used to give him a nip of brandy to calm him down. "'Did it make him run any faster,' Cahill was asked. 'Not really,' he'd reply. 'But you could say that he was the happiest dog at the meeting.'"

Then there was the Coolmore connection – the John Magnier, Tommy Stack and Billy McDonald syndicate – for whom Ronnie trained Believe Him to win the Irish Derby in 1979. An Ulsterman by birth, McDonald was the bloodstock agent who bought Robert Sangster's dual Prix de l'Arc de Triomphe winner Alleged as an unraced two-year-old for $120,000 in 1976, as well as the filly Fairy Bridge, who went on to become the dam of Sadler's Wells. A long-time resident of Los Angeles, where he doubled as a Rolls Royce salesman, Billy's circle of friends included Sangster, Albert Finney and Frank Sinatra. In full flight, he was like a cross between Richard Harris and Brendan Behan and, as Victor saw for himself, his capacity for excess was phenomenal. "One year at Clonmel, I was in the bar of the Cashel Palace at about two in the morning. It was in that big upstairs room back then. John Magnier was the owner and they had a huge Augustus John painting on the wall and a lot of other pictures too.

The whole place was packed and it was a real rip-roaring party. Billy was standing next to me with a champagne bottle in his hand. Then, all of a sudden, he collapsed, just keeled over on the floor. The staff carried him outside very carefully and laid him down in the back of somebody else's car. But a couple of hours later, the party was still going on when I looked up and there he was, grinning, and ordering another bottle. He'd just woken up and walked back into the hotel and was carrying on again as if nothing had happened."

McDonald was a punter as well as a drinker. A big punter. "One year in the early Eighties, he came over for Royal Ascot and stayed in London with my friend, the racehorse owner Michael Buckley. The first night he went to Aspinall's and won £250,000. But by the end of the following day, he'd lost the lot at the races. He spent the rest of the week in bed in his underpants, seriously depressed and sending out for takeaways."

It was a similar story one Derby Day at Epsom. "We used to go into the underground bar in the old Members Stand. They had a Polish waiter who would always let you book a table in advance and make sure the sandwiches and drinks were ready when you arrived." One year, Billy McDonald, who was "pissed before lunch," cornered Victor in the bar and said that he'd got something for the first. "He wanted £2,000 on this 25-1 chance ridden by someone I'd never heard of. I asked my form man if he knew anything about it and he said the rider was the Canadian champion jockey. So I put on Billy's money and doubled up with another £2,000 for myself. Well, it won easily and it was only afterwards that Billy said that he'd meant to back the favourite but had got the name wrong. By the second race he was flying, and at the end of the afternoon he was still up by about £25,000. I left him still celebrating in the bar, but later that night I found out that he'd finished up in Epsom police station after trying to proposition some woman on his way out."

McDonald was no stranger to police accommodation. "There was another time in Barbados when he got roaring drunk and got into a fight with a large local man. Michael Buckley had to go and bail him out. Billy was in the cells when he arrived. 'I'll fight the lot of them,' he was yelling. 'No you won't,' said Michael. 'Now just shut up and behave yourself.'"

Billy McDonald died in Belfast in 2009, aged 65.

There were so many long nights and so many roaring boys – and girls – in Clonmel and Cashel, and sometimes Victor put his London life with Carole out of his mind for the duration of his stay. One year he met "a very attractive woman who had just come back from working in the States. I took her to supper at Chez Hans, the smart restaurant at the foot of the Rock of Cashel. My Uncle Ronnie was there too, along with Gerry and Tommy Stack and one of Vincent O'Brien's daughters. The conversation got on to politics and we discovered my new girlfriend had radical views. She ended up standing on a chair and singing Irish Republican songs. We were nearly thrown out by the owner Hans, who's German, but Ronnie managed to smooth things over."

Ronnie and Gerry Albertini's good offices also assisted in the case of the Irish politician, a Fianna Fail cabinet minister, who, a bit like Jeffrey Bernard, collapsed face first into the soup one night at dinner in the Cashel Palace. "'Ah, Raymond,' said the head waiter, as he and Gerry escorted the minister from the scene. 'He's a martyr to the drink.'"

Most of those Clonmel and Cashel Palace revellers were martyrs to a bet too, and they started seeking out Victor when they came over for the Festival at Cheltenham in March. Irrepressible characters like the cattlemen John and Jim Horgan, Mick and Danno Heaslip from Galway, who pulled off a famous touch when their horse For Auction won the 1982 Champion Hurdle, and the trainer Mick O'Toole who would ring up to place bets every year even though he still hadn't settled the previous year's account. "Couldn't you just give me something, even if only for appearances sake?" Victor used to ask him. Micko and the Heaslips were wild men but the young bookmaker was convinced by now that, if he kept his nerve in that adrenalin-charged rodeo, he could successfully take on the Irish favourites. One or two bankers might go in but, provided he ducked the other bullets, as Butch put it, he was sure to come out ahead over the three days.

It was a bold strategy but, in March 1986, it encouraged him to seriously overreach himself and take on "what felt like an entire country" who all wanted to back one horse.

Dawn Run.

Chapter Fourteen

The Roaring Eighties

I t would be difficult to exaggerate the spine-tingling sense of drama and emotion that surrounded the 1986 Cheltenham Gold Cup. If you were there that day you will never forget it. If not, you should forever be respectfully in awe of what was a truly epic occasion.

The Blue Riband of steeplechasing had attracted most of the top staying chasers in England, including the 1985 winner Forgive 'N' Forget, whose Irish trainer Jimmy FitzGerald was without equal when it came to bringing a horse to its peak in the third week of March. Then there was the magnificent Wayward Lad, trained in Yorkshire by Monica Dickinson and a three-time winner of the King George VI Chase at Kempton, but thought to be vulnerable over the Gold Cup's extra distance. Combs Ditch, representing Desert Orchid's trainer David Elsworth, had only been beaten a neck by Wayward Lad in the King George, and also in the mix was Run And Skip, the tough as teak winner of the Welsh Grand National. Any one of those four would have been a worthy victor, but lining up against them was Dawn Run – 'the mare beyond compare,' as the *Sporting Life* called her.

Triumphant in the 1984 Champion Hurdle, she was bidding to be the first horse ever to complete the Champion Hurdle/Gold Cup double. She had won three races over fences impressively, but her jumping was still novicey, and in a trial race at Cheltenham in January she had unseated her jockey Tony Mullins, brother of Willie and son of the mare's trainer Paddy Mullins of Goresbridge in County Kilkenny. At the insistence of her owner, Charmian Hill, Mullins was replaced at Cheltenham by Jonjo O'Neill, who had been aboard when she won the Champion Hurdle in 1984, but he too was unseated during a schooling session at Gowran Park 10 days before the race.

Undeterred, ante-post, and especially Irish punters, conscious of the five-pound weight allowance the mare would be getting from the others, continued to back her, whetting the appetite of Victor Chandler, who was convinced she was the biggest false priced favourite of his bookmaking career to date. "I couldn't see her winning. I just couldn't believe that she would get round. I thought she was too inexperienced, so I took on the ring, trying to be clever. I kept laying her all through the season. I had plenty of chances to back her back, but I didn't take them."

Victor's confidence in his own judgement had been boosted by his record in the big races, which was an impressive one. On Derby Day at Epsom in 1984, he had taken on the brilliant 2000 Guineas winner El Gran Senor, who was meant to be the best horse Vincent O'Brien had ever trained. Victor doubted his stamina and saw similarities between the Senor and Nonoalco, the Guineas winner beaten in Snow Knight's Derby 10 years before. Laying a string of £10,000 to £11,000 bets on the odds-on favourite, he put his money on the more stoutly bred Secreto, trained by O'Brien's son David, and tipped by Lester Piggott. By the off, he'd taken £16,000 to £1,000, £14,000 to £1,000 and £10,000 to £700 each way with rival bookies. When El Gran Senor coasted into the lead with a furlong to run, it looked as if VC had made a costly blunder, but Secreto was running on strongly and, in a sensational finish, he got up to win the Derby in the final stride.

At Aintree the following March, Victor had opposed the Grand National joint-favourites, Greasepaint and West Tip and, on the advice of his form man, had backed a 50-1 outsider called Last Suspect. The outsider won by one and a half lengths.

Now it was time to be similarly bold at Cheltenham. "When you go there, you've got to play the game," he said 33 years later. "You don't go to the Festival thinking of the negatives." There was nothing negative about the outcome of the first race of the week, the Supreme Novices' Hurdle, in which Knockelly Castle, trained by Paddy Prendergast junior and owned by a syndicate led by Sue Magnier, was meant to be an Irish banker. "Is he ready, Paddy?" Peter O'Sullevan asked on the gallops on the morning of the race. "Peter," replied the trainer, "he's as cocked and ready as a cowboy's gun. If I don't win with this one, I never will. All we need is the rub of the green." But unfortunately for 'Long Paddy,' the necessary luck was with the bookmakers instead, including Victor who laid the favourite heavily. Knockelly Castle was well behind early on and ran on late, but too late to catch the winner, River Ceiriog, a 40-1 outsider whose trainer Nicky Henderson professed himself "absolutely staggered" by the result.

Victor got it right again in the Champion Chase on the Wednesday when the Irish favourite Bobsline, brilliant winner of the Arkle Trophy in 1984, was outgunned by his fellow countryman Buck House, trained by the canny Mouse Morris, who had a second winner of the meeting on the Thursday afternoon when Attitude Adjuster won the Foxhunters' Chase half an hour before the Gold Cup.

As the runners in the big race paraded in front of the stands, the tension rising to levels not seen since Arkle and Mill House clashed at Cheltenham in 1964, the trading in the ring and along the rails was frenzied. Again and again Victor laid the mare from 2-1 to 9-4 to 85-40, and then back into 15-8. £20,000 to £10,000, £21,250 to £10,000, £10,000 to £5,000 twice, £5,000 to £2,000, £4,000 to £2,000 three times, £7,650 to £3,400, and scores of smaller cash bets up to a monkey and a thousand a time.

As Maureen Mullins, the trainer's wife, said later, her husband had "worked tirelessly and worried endlessly" to ensure Dawn Run went to post in the best possible condition, and it was clear from her appearance in the paddock that she could not be an ounce fitter. When the starter sent them on their way, it was Run And Skip who made the early running, but with Dawn Run right there at his side, travelling at a searching pace on the fast ground and jumping fluently. Jonjo was banking correctly that her stamina, as well as her guts, would prove the decisive factor, and as they raced down the hill for the last time, she was in the lead. But then, as they swung into the home straight, both Wayward Lad and Forgive 'N' Forget were closing and, as Run And Skip began to falter, it looked as if the mare was beaten too. But as Maureen Mullins also said afterwards, "Dawn Run was never beaten," and after they'd jumped the last fence – Wayward Lad seemingly finally destined to win the Gold Cup at the fourth attempt – Jonjo angled her across to the stands-side rail and she started to run on and, within 20 yards of the line, raw courage carried her past Wayward Lad to claim the prize by a length.

Pandemonium overcame Cheltenham racecourse as Jonjo and the mare returned to the unsaddling enclosure amid unprecedented scenes of jubilation. But down at the Victor Chandler pitch on the rails, there was stunned silence as punters began queuing up to be paid out and, not for the first or the last time in his life, the bookmaker reached for another pack of Winston or Marlborough Red and told his clerk to 'just turn over the page' in the big field ledger. When Wayward Lad took up the running, Victor had put down his binoculars and started counting his winnings. Moments later, he was consumed by a feeling of "utter stupidity. You just want to kick your ego in the bollocks." Dawn Run's victory cost Victor in excess of £250,000 in 1986 money, which would be more like £6.5million today, and "in terms of percentages of losses to assets, it was my worst ever result." He subsequently paid £1,500 at an Injured Jockeys Fund auction to buy the boots that Jonjo had worn on the mare – who was tragically killed in a fall in France that summer – along with O'Neill's whip and a signed photo of Jonjo saluting the crowd as he came in. The photograph had been signed by Paddy Mullins too. "I hung the boots on a pedestal in the office so that I could see them all the time. They taught me a lesson never to be too opinionated."

So did the chastened gambler decide to change tack? Back down? Adopt a more conservative strategy in future? Not a bit of it. Not VC. Not the fourth generation Chandler to lay the odds. 'Keep 'em coming and keep your nerve.' That was his approach. And as the 1980s wore on, the Conservative Chancellor of the Exchequer Nigel Lawson continuing to cut taxes, privatise state monopolies and deregulate the City, the economy continued to boom, racecourses were awash with easy money and it was a great time to be a bookie.

In the summer of 1986, Victor and Carole bought a semi-detached late Georgian house in tree-lined Hamilton Terrace in St John's Wood. Carole's children had grown up and left school by now and Victor had grown tired of commuting between London and Sussex. Living together seven days a week was a new experience for the couple, but one that Victor professed to embrace. The now 35-year-old bookie admitted to having had affairs at times when Carole was down in Hove and he was in London and Ireland, but assured her that sort of thing was behind him now.

The Chandler firm had a new home too, moving to Linhope Street near Marylebone Station. Victor bought a pair of Georgian terraced cottages and had them converted into an office. It was run jointly by Roger Jenkins and Mick Saunders, another old friend and family retainer who had previously worked under Joe Dunbar and, before that, for Victor's father in his Great Portland Street office. Victor senior would surely have been impressed by his son's new set-up. Linhope Street had thickly carpeted stairs, and walls lined with equine prints and sporting cartoons. Victor's office on the second floor was furnished with dark wooden bookshelves, leather-lined chairs, an antique desk and more elegant prints, etchings and drawings. Visitors were struck by the personal intimacy of the set-up, in sharp contrast to the corporate HQs of the big high street betting shop chains, and the feeling that VC was "one of us and not one of them," as Ian Carnaby put it in an article in the London Evening News in March 1987. "His clients may include a high proportion of racing's inner circle, including professional faces and media types, but the human factor is still very much a part of the Chandler business."

Victor's desk-top was invariably strewn with calendars, diaries, old newspaper and magazine articles, form guides yellowing at the edges, and empty coffee cups. "Indeed, Chandler inhabits the sort of lived-in office his famous namesake envisaged for Philip Marlowe," observed Carnaby before adding that it didn't take long to realise that the occupant was every bit as shrewd as the legendary private eye.

Victor's turnover soared with new clients every week, though his biggest problem continued to be getting paid. But in the era of Dallas and Dynasty, rising property prices and conspicuous consumption, there were days and nights when it seemed as if everyone had cash to spare, or were pretending they did. "I'll never forget one Monday evening at Windsor in June 1986. We took a million on the card. It was the Monday before Royal Ascot and it seemed as if all my big customers went into premature big punting mode. We lost £150,000 on the first two races, but there was so much money around we still finished the night over £100,000 ahead."

The atmosphere on those warm summer evenings beside the Thames was hard to beat. London punters leaving their offices in the afternoon, taking the train from Waterloo down to Windsor and Eton Riverside, and then the river taxi up to the course. City boys packed into the tented champagne bar around the paddock. Bottles of Krug and Veuve Clicquot, and plates of Barrie Cope's cold poached salmon and crab claws, and Cuban cigar smoke drifting up between the trees. Sharp men, hard men, faces, touts. Money to bet with, money to play with, money to burn. The favourite always mysteriously winning the last race, and then the Rollers, Bentleys and Mercs speeding back up west at the night's end.

It was intoxicating and irresistible but, alas, it proved all too addictive for some. The decade's most notorious plunger, and one of the biggest gamblers in the history of British racing was the mullet-haired commodities trader Terry Ramsden. The Enfield boy made good, started out in the City as an office boy in the late 1960s and went on to make a killing in the Big Bang heyday in the complex world of Japanese warranty markets. For a few years, his personal investment vehicle, Glen International, seemed to be accruing spectacular wealth, which he spent largely on racehorses, football clubs and gambling, allegedly working his way through £58 million worth of wagers by 1990. "Terry used to bet with me, but then at one point or another he was betting with just about everyone, including Ladbrokes. He had this character called The Butcher who used to put his money on. His real name was Bobby Cox and he really was a butcher, supplying the meat to the restaurant at Walthamstow Stadium. But Terry's bets were insane. He'd want £5,000 Yankees that were beyond everyone's limits."

The big companies like Ladbrokes and Coral all had a daily limit or maximum payout that could not be exceeded, but Terry Ramsden behaved as if they didn't exist. "One day, he had three parts of a Yankee up, which had already taken him over the limit, but he kept putting bets on the last leg even though there was no way they'd have paid him, even if he'd won."

The stock market crash of 1987 hit Ramsden hard and, in 1988, he was warned off for non-payment of debts by the Jockey Club. In 1990, he spent a traumatic six months in prison in Los Angeles awaiting extradition back to the UK following the collapse of Glen International, and he served a further 10 months in Britain seven years later for breaching the insolvency act. 'Bish, Bash, Bosh,' as Victor used to call him, reappeared briefly at the races in 2003, having relaunched himself thanks to a loan of several million pounds from Michael Tabor. The gambler moved to Spain where he was supposed to be presiding over a new trading system to simplify equities transactions, but Victor remembers him spending "most of the day gambling on horses and dogs. The bets were mad. Super Yankees when the racing was on and in the end, we just looked at him and thought 'you're potty.' He'd come from nothing, and he was clever enough to speak fluent Japanese, but his gambling really was a disease."

'Tel-Boy' was the biggest but by no means the only high-stakes punter of that era to choke on the bone. There was a London property developer who was forever wanting to back short-priced favourites and, at Cheltenham in 1989, he thought he'd found one that couldn't lose. The meeting had started in great style for VC thanks to that tip from Martin Pipe's owner Jim Ryan to back Sondrio, the stable's runner in the opening race. The novice hurdler, deserted by Pipe's stable jockey Peter Scudamore but well clear on Terry Kirk's speed ratings, went off at 25-1, and Victor backed him with £2,000 of his own money. But after the Gold Cup on the Thursday afternoon, the firm was in trouble once again.

The famous victory of Desert Orchid, who had failed to win at Cheltenham in five attempts, sparked scenes of wild celebration similar to the ones that had greeted Dawn Run two years before. But for Victor the result was another disaster. It had been raining and snowing all afternoon and the ground was soft and, as a three-mile Kempton specialist, Victor didn't think Desert Orchid had any chance, laying the grey from 7-2 down to 5-2 favourite. The losses weren't as heavy as 1986, but painful all the same. But consolation was at hand. Rusch De Farges, running in the Cathcart Chase, the penultimate race of the day, was supposed to be a Festival banker. The five-year-old French-bred gelding, trained by Martin Pipe and ridden by Peter Scudamore, had a huge reputation, and opened up in the ring at 4-9, but then drifted on the rails to 4-5. The property tycoon was determined to recoup losses from earlier in the week and wanted up to half a million pounds on Rusch De Farges, beginning with £40,000 to £90,000, and Victor laid him. "It had never done a time, and our form man, who'd been studying it in the paddock, kept coming up to me and saying, 'this isn't going to act on the going.'"

The form man was a good judge. Rusch De Farges hated the ground and finished a well-beaten fourth. The punter was cleaned out, though Victor later had to settle "for about two-thirds of what he owed. He was so far behind by then that I suppose it didn't make any difference to him." Terry Ramsden, the property mogul, and the Northern Ireland poultry dealer Brendon Kearney, "who smoked even more than me," were all what were known as 'top of the book punters,' which meant that the bookies were happy to play them for even a portion of their theoretical profit and losses, knowing that accepting 50 per cent of £200,000 is still better than turning the punter away. But the mid to late-Eighties were also the period when Victor had to be on the lookout for the ambushes and cunning moves of two or three exceptionally shrewd characters. Professional gunslingers who rarely missed. Men in black.

Victor first met Michael Tabor in April 1978. "I had to go up to Wembley dogs one evening and we started chatting. Everyone had heard of him. He was well known at the time for the bets he was putting on greyhounds, fourfolds and trebles, and he already had quite a reputation. I was still in my twenties. He was in his thirties and he asked me if I could give him a lift home afterwards. He lived in a flat in the same block as his mother by Baker Street station. The interesting thing about him was that if he'd got a plan before he went to the races, he didn't know it, but when you went through a card with him, you realised how good he was at separating the relevant stuff from the dross."

Tabor hadn't always intended to be a punter. He grew up in Forest Gate in East London and his father was a glassmaker. Leaving school at the age of 15, Michael was at one point a trainee at the Morris School of Hairdressing in Piccadilly. Founded by 'Professor' Alf Morris, the school was one of London's most respected private hairdressing academies in the 1950s and 60s, and many of the graduates went on to start their own salon. But Michael Tabor also developed a precocious interest in, and understanding of, odds and betting, and he had the nerve and wits to make it pay. There was a setback in 1970, when he was warned off by the Jockey Club for allegedly paying two jockeys for information, but three years later the ban was overturned.

Not long before he met Victor, Tabor became the owner of a small off-course bookmaking firm called Arthur Prince. "Henry Cohen helped him to expand the business. 'You don't look at the deal,' Michael used to say. 'You look at the man.' By the Eighties, he was having bets with us at the racecourse, and one evening, Carole and I bumped into him and his wife Doreen in the Villa Bianca, the old-fashioned Italian restaurant in Hampstead. She was a former model who was brought up in Peckham in South London. When they moved to Monte Carlo years later, she learned to speak French, and she also played the piano. That night, she'd managed to drag Michael out to an art house film at the Hampstead Everyman, which was the sort of thing she loved but he hated. I remember another time I went up to see him in their house there, and Michael was in his office and practically had to have his supper passed into him on a tray. He didn't want to come out, and he only drank in moderation when I first met him."

In his 2015 biography of John Le Carré, Adam Sisman described a dinner in the upstairs room at Villa Bianca to mark the novelist's 60th birthday in 1994. Guest of honour was Strobe Talbot, the Deputy Secretary of State in Bill Clinton's administration and the man responsible for America's policy towards the Soviet Union. Talbot brought a friend with him, his Russian opposite number Georgiy Mamedov, a big Le Carré fan who was rumoured to be a KGB agent. Apparently, it was a very convivial evening, and it seems rather appropriate that, 12 years earlier, the same Villa Bianca, with its timeless black and white frontage and bread sticks on the tables, should have been the setting for an encounter between Victor Chandler and Michael Tabor, men who – at the time – were also immersed in a world of intelligence-gathering and information.

1994 was when Michael Tabor sold his Arthur Prince betting shop chain to Coral for £27.4million and began his spectacular ascent of thoroughbred flat racing's rock face. In 1995, he won the Kentucky Derby with his American-bred horse Thunder Gulch and he went on to become John Magnier's partner in Coolmore Stud and a leading shareholder in the countless blue-blooded stallions and mares the syndicate has raced and bred from since then. Tabor was never afraid to wager £100,000 on a horse as long as the conditions were right, and providing he could get on without a bookmaker trying to halve his stake or reduce the odds, and Victor unhesitatingly rates the Russian immigrant's grandson and his Irish confrere JP McManus as different class to the generation of mainly internet high rollers that followed them. "They'd give any of them a 10-break start and still beat them with one hand tied behind their backs. JP's got the most incredible brain, and Michael's the same. He's tough and he could kid the kidders. They used to employ the best form men and pay the best money. To beat them you had to be as armed as they were, which is partly why I was the first independent bookie on the rails to have a guy doing computer ratings."

In the late 1980s, Tabor invested in his first deal with Victor. "I was approached by Yannis Andreou, a Greek Cypriot who was known as 'Fat John.' He wanted me to open some betting offices with him in Cyprus. There was a lot of interest there then in betting on football, but I could only have 10 shops. So I enlisted Alan Kinghorn, and he opened some too, and to begin with, things were going very well, but then three or four weeks in, we got hit badly. Every old First Division favourite won and I had to cobble together the money to pay the bill. About six months later, I bumped into Michael Tabor at the July meeting at Newmarket. I told him we were lacking structure and management with these Cypriot shops but that there was the chance to expand. Not long afterwards, I flew out there with Michael's associate Frank Irish, and as a result of his recommendation, Michael bought into it with a £200,000 stake. There were times then too when he asked me to put a few bets on horses for him, though sometimes we were closing accounts that we'd realised were really proxy punters betting on Michael's behalf."

There were other dangerous professional bettors in that era as well as Tabor and JP. Jack Ramsden, for example, the Yorkshireman and ex-stockbroker whose son James is the landlord of the popular racing pub, the Sydney Arms in Chelsea. Jack Ramsden was "a hard man," according to VC, and fellow rails bookmaker Colin Webster was his punter. "He came to me first and asked me to put six £50 doubles on for him one day and a £50 treble. But there was a non-runner and we couldn't get the bet on as requested. He didn't accept that and he went with Colin instead. Jack would do the card for him and they backed a lot of winning horses together, and Jack was another one who was very big on speed figures."

One Friday evening in the 1990s, Victor went to the July course at Newmarket having been alerted to a Jack Ramsden-owned runner that Terry Kirk reckoned was "an absolute stand-out" on his computer ratings. As Victor got out of the Mercedes in the car park, Colin Webster's son David was just getting out of the car next to him. "'I know what you're here for,' I said. 'I know what you're here for,' he replied." The big two made their way to the rails and duly got the prices they wanted to good money. The horse won easily and "we all had a drink together afterwards."

The enigmatic Stephen Little, who stood only a few feet away from Victor on the rails at Ascot and Cheltenham, took similarly big risks, laying Jack Ramsden's accumulators and £100,000 bets to Michael Tabor. But as individuals, he and Victor could hardly have been more different. A skilled mathematician like the Frenchman Patrice des Moutis, Little never enjoyed a misspent youth and wasn't asked to leave his public school, Uppingham, under a cloud. He would rarely ever take a view or offer an opinion about a race or a horse, preferring to rely on his assessment of the market as to what he would lay, and the instantly recognisable fur coat he wore in winter was to keep the cold out rather than foster any notions of glamour or style. "He's the coldest fish I've ever come across," said Victor. "But he was a bloody good bookmaker. He played…and he paid, and racing's the poorer without him."

Little's determination not to pay more than was strictly necessary was sometimes the cause of much amusement to the clerks and workmen, the Sergeants and NCO's of the racecourse bookmaking trade. Alan Mills remembered a day at Chepstow when the 'Little Man,' who cycled everywhere to the races in the early days, "got on his bike straight after the last and pedalled down to the station to try and intercept two Cardiff-bound punters who'd left early. There'd been a mistake settling up and they'd been paid something like £70 instead of £7. Stephen couldn't see them at first, but the train had just pulled into the platform so he got on and walked up the corridor until he found them. He got his money back too."

Then there was the day when the bookmaker and his wife and children were moving into a splendid Grade One Listed property in Bath's Georgian Royal Crescent. The removal men discovered that Stephen's effects included numerous tea chests packed with old copies of the Sporting Life, and each weighing about half a racehorse. They intimated that an additional cash payment might be in order to compensate them for carrying them upstairs. Little felt he'd already paid them enough and told them to load the tea chests into the lift despite their warnings that the antique elevator would struggle to take the weight. The lift duly broke down, leaving the tea chests stranded between floors, and the eventual bill was some way in excess of what it would have cost him to pay the removal men to carry the chests upstairs in the first place.

Money owed, money paid, debts, bets, readies and the lack of them, were a constant theme for Victor and his bookmaking colleagues. Jackie Cohen, the old stager whose Rolls Royce VC had rescued at Hove dogs in 1973 and who had taken a liking to the young hustler, would look on with a kind of mordant satisfaction when punters walked past his pitch to bet with another bookie further down. "And what's wrong with Jackie Cohen?" he'd call out to them indignantly. "What's wrong with me? I don't know. It's no good. No good for a Jewish boy."

If the results contrived to go against him, Cohen would turn his mis-anthropic Walter Matthau-style wit against his fellow layers as well as the general public. Victor escaped, but others weren't so lucky. "Fuck me," Jackie began one afternoon at Sandown. "Is there a fog over Esher today?" "It's me Jackie," a neighbouring bookmaker replied. "I'm smoking Three Nuns." "Three Nuns?" says Jackie, fixing him with a disgusted look. "What did they do…shit in it?" The red-faced bookie immediately stubbed out his pipe.

The inimitable Lewis 'Lulu' Mendoza, who was Carole's uncle, was another eccentric who provided the betting ring with plenty of entertainment down the years. With his distinctive shock of curly grey hair and his diminutive stature, he bore a striking resemblance to the comedian Charlie Drake, who was a household name in the 1960s, appearing regularly at the London Palladium, and seemed to wear a similar expression of permanent bafflement and alarm.

Lulu, who claimed to be a direct descendant of El Cid, had pitches in the south of England, and for a while he even popped up on the rails next to Victor at Cheltenham, though Fontwell and Plumpton were more his level. Even there he tended to regard punters with the same kind of nervous agitation a wagon train boss might display at the first sign of smoke signals on the horizon. As long as he wasn't personally under fire, he enjoyed playing the role of the grand seigneur, sporting correspondent shoes and a Panama hat at Brighton and Goodwood, but somehow where Lulu was concerned, embarrassment was never far away. "There was one Monday at Plumpton where he's somehow laid a much bigger bet than he wanted to," remembers Victor. "When he realised how much he stood to lose, he panicked and started tearing round the ring, trying to get on at the same price that he'd laid. He ended up, badly out of breath, standing in front of this board and asking for a bet of £520 to £80 (odds of 13-2). 'Dad,' said a voice…it was his son Paul, 'this is your own pitch.'"

On a bigger day at Ascot, Lulu felt sufficiently prosperous to light up a Corona, every inch the bookmaking big shot, between races. Victor was standing nearby. "After a while, Alan Kinghorn and I noticed he'd thrown the cigar away. Then all of a sudden there's smoke and flames behind his back, and Lulu realises he's thrown it, still alight, into his money bag. So he and his workman have to turn the bag upside down, tip everything out and stamp on the readies, like a pair of tap dancers, in an attempt to put the fire out." The sight of the two of them jumping up and down and desperately trying to salvage their charred bank notes will live forever in the memory of their old betting ring colleagues.

Mendoza's misadventures were not confined to Kent and Sussex either. He sometimes crossed the channel. "One August in the late 1980s, Carole and I took my sister Liz and her kids over to Deauville for two weeks," explained Victor. "The losers and credit account punters hadn't paid after York because it was August, and now they'd all gone away, so the bank was on the phone to me all the time, but you could say Lulu brightened up our holiday. We were staying in the Normandy Hotel and Lulu was there too with his wife Judy, and Lulu's son Paul and his girlfriend were staying too. Lulu was in his linen suit and his Panama with the two-tone shoes, calling himself the Count of this and the Count of that, but he wasn't getting on well with the hotel manager. He'd accidentally walked backwards into the big china vase they've got there in the foyer and, in his efforts to save it from breaking, he'd fallen into a palm tree. Then he came back early from the races the following afternoon, having eaten something that disagreed with him at lunch, and found somebody else in his room. The manager assured him it was all a mistake and that they'd just mixed up the bookings, but Lulu was convinced it was intentional.

A few nights later, Carole and I had been out to dinner with Paul and his girlfriend, and we were all sitting downstairs in the bar having a drink after midnight when Paul gets this idea. He slips into the manager's office, which wasn't locked, finds a sheet of headed Normandy Hotel notepaper and types out this letter to his father. 'Dear Monsieur Mendoza,' it begins. 'In order to compensate you for the inconvenience you have suffered in the last couple of days, we would like to offer you your entire stay at the Normandy free of charge.' Paul signs it with the manager's name at the bottom, then takes it upstairs…it's about 2am by now…slips it under his father's door, knocks loudly and hides in the corridor with me hiding behind him. Sure enough, after a few minutes we hear shuffling sounds inside the room and then the door opens and Lulu comes out in his dressing gown and pyjamas holding the letter. He can't see us, but we can hear him talking to his wife. 'Here, Jude,' he says. 'You won't believe this. They're giving us the whole week free.' 'Who are?' she says. 'The hotel,' he says. 'As compensation. Don't tell the others though, or Paul will want his bill paid too.'

Of course, Paul's loving that, and when it was time for his dad to check out on the Saturday morning, he made sure he was well placed to watch the fun. A porter comes down first, carrying Lulu's luggage and takes it out to the Bentley. Then Lulu comes down with Judy,

ACCOUNTANT

LICENSED
TING
FICE

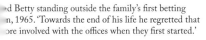

...d Betty standing outside the family's first betting
...n, 1965. 'Towards the end of his life he regretted that
...ore involved with the offices when they first started.'

Victor's father, Victor Chandler
senior, 1960s. 'He had such a
huge love of racing and being
there at the racecourse but
commerce, in the narrowly
acquisitive sense, was not his
strong suit.'

Young Victor's tearaway friend
Fernando Ponce-Torré, right with
moustache. 'A midget Mexican
and possibly the most sexually
athletic man I've ever met.'

Young Victor, the sulky teenager, with his friend Nick Cook at Millfield School, 1968.

Young Victor and fellow students at the Glion Catering College, Switzerland, 1971. Another day of double pheasant, hotel staff plans and a patisserie practical.

Young Victor living it up at a party in Switzerland

A nervous VC on the rails at Newmarket, 1976. 'It was scary to start with. I hadn't the slightest idea what was going on. I felt like a real fish out of water.'

Curly-haired VC in tails at Epsom, 1977. 'As a young man he was possibly a little naive but he was never a fool.'

VC, Amazing Man and trainer Derek Knight (far right) at the presentation after the William Hill 2,000 Guineas at Harringay, 1985. A moment to savour but 'if Amazing Man had won the 1983 Greyhound Derby Final most of the Chandler firm would have retired on the proceeds.'

Left, fellow bookmaker Alan Kinghorn with Benno Miller and Victor at VC's 50th birthday party 2001. Kinghorn was a bright, droll man with a mischievous sense of humour. Above, Victor and Carole Masters at the same party. 'I thought it might last six weeks if we were lucky. Instead it lasted 30 years.'

VC at work on the rails. 'There were
days and nights when it seemed as if everyone
had cash or was pretending they did.'

Coursing dogs at Clonmel.
Rarely profitable but
always entertaining.

VC, the Gentleman Bookie, sponsoring a
coursing meeting for track dogs at Swaffham
in the late 1980s. Victor's friend and clerk
Bill Tye is on the left in a flat cap.

The Chandler party leaving Aintree racecourse after the bomb scare on Grand National day, 1997. (From left to right) Benno Miller, Alan Kinghorn, VC, Gerry Albertini in sheepskin collar coat, Bill Tye and Alan Mills. Aside from Cheltenham and Royal Ascot, Aintree was Victor's favourite meeting.

VC and Carole at Ascot on Victor Chandler Chase day, early 1990s. A hundred and fifty or so big hitters mixed with old friends and members of the Chandler family.

Carole's uncle, the bookmaker Louis 'Lulu' Mendoza, far right, at Victor's 50th birthday party. Lulu enjoyed playing the role of the Grand Seigneur but invariably came unstuck.

Before the good times. The pokey top-floor room of Victor senior's betting office at 151 Great Portland Street.

'REVOLUTION.' Victor shaking hands with the Gibraltar first minister Peter Carauna at the official opening of the VCI offices on the Rock, May 1999.

VC and Carole with George Best and his wife Alex (on Best's right) at the Victor Chandler Hong Kong launch party in April 1998. Mike Carlton is on Alex's right. Best's visit turned in to a marathon of man-management.

VC at Royal Ascot in the 21st century. 'Business and bloody hard work with all the entertaining.'

The invite to a gala evening at Walthamstow Stadium in 2006 celebrating the 60th anniversary of the Victor Chandler firm

The Valiant Cowboy. VC and his favourite horse Fabuloso not quite ready to ride off into the sunset. Spain 200[ ]

both of them looking very grand, and they walk right out through the foyer and down the steps. They're just about to get in the car and drive away when the concierge and several receptionists come charging after them and one of them flings herself on the bonnet of the car to block their escape. 'Monsieur, Monsieur,' they're crying. 'L'Addition.' Everyone goes back inside and the manager's there angrily demanding payment. Lulu tells him the bill has been waived and shows him the letter. Of course, the manager's outraged and accuses Lulu of writing the letter himself. Meanwhile, Paul's there in the background trying to keep a straight face. Lulu had to pay in the end, but it wasn't until they were all back in England a few weeks later that Paul confessed."

Victor and Carole's trips to Deauville were really less about racing and all about the continuing good life of the 'Gentleman Bookie,' as Victor had now been dubbed. A few lunches and dinners at Chez Miocque or Le Drakkar or Ciros on Les Planches. Evenings at the casino. Shopping in town. They might even take a dip in the sea, though the Caribbean was more Victor's temperature. But, back in London, he was now just as likely to be found in the company of the raffish, often impecunious but never boring old Soho bohemians who had found their way into his father's circle in the 1950s. Artists, authors, journalists, drunks, and many of them habitual gamblers. Victor's old clerk Val Powell was friendly with the painter Francis Bacon and "sometimes the three of us would have supper together in Wheelers in Old Compton Street. I remember one night, when for some reason, the actress Thora Hird was there too. She and Francis both got very drunk together and they were both very funny. He was really a casino punter though. He only ever had one proper bet with me on racing." Unlike his friend and contemporary, Lucian Freud.

The greatest figurative painter of his generation, grandson of Sigmund and estranged brother of Clement, was a man who, in Victor's words, "only really cared about three things. Art, racing and women, and not necessarily in that order." Gambling on horse racing cost Freud millions in the 1960s, '70s and '80s, and one ungrateful firm, Ladbrokes, even went so far as to have him warned off. Not so VC, who, like his father, laid many of the artist's biggest bets.

In 1987, Freud said to Victor that he owed him so much money that he'd paint him, to make good the loss, and the bookmaker could have first option on the picture. "It was meant to be just a head and shoulders. It ended up being five-foot by four, but he let me have it for the same price. I sat for him for over 18 months, three nights a week."

It was to be one of the most fascinating experiences of Victor Chandler's life.

Chapter Fifteen

Dinner With Lucian

The photographer and picture editor Bruce Bernard – who was the *Low Life* scribe Jeffrey's older brother – knew Lucian Freud well and sat for him several times. They first met during the war and Bernard was immediately struck by the artist's "exotic and somewhat demonic aura." That element of danger was still there when Victor first encountered him on "another night at Wheelers with Jeffrey Bernard and Guy Packer, the bookmaker's son and former jockey who later changed his name to Guy Hart. He introduced us. Lucian used to have an account with my father, and Benno Miller put his bets on for him. Once, when he owed Benno some money, he gave him a painting, but Benno didn't like it and sold it for around £2,500. Today, it would be worth three or four million. Lucian stopped betting for a while after Dad died. But then he started up again with me in the 1980s. He wasn't what you'd call 'nice' by any definition of the word, and he fell out with most people. But I just seemed to be able to talk to him and we became really good friends."

Despite his natural shyness, Victor was never intimidated by Freud, or overwhelmed by his personality, and that was one of the things the artist liked about him. They also had plenty of interests in common... notably art, racing and women. "He was still punting right up until the day he died (in 2011). I don't think he could live without it. I always felt he had a passion to lose because it put pressure on him to work in some way. The money didn't mean anything to him really. It was all about the thrill." The only time the artist and sitter ever went racing together was one evening at Sandown in 1990, after the picture had been completed. "He'd been warned off by Ladbrokes by then for owing them £20,000 ,so he says to me, 'I suppose I'll have to wear a fucking ginger wig and a beret.' He was as good as his word and turned up with a false moustache and a beanie on his head. He was terribly frightened of being caught, but he relaxed after he backed several winners. The favourites all won and the firm lost heavily on the night, and so did most of the other bookies."

Freud and Chandler spent hours talking together, both during the sittings and afterwards. "He lived on the top floor of a big house in Holland Park at the time. He had a four-foot high Rodin bronze of Balzac, and a Michael Andrews painting, and beautiful furniture. But it wasn't homely. He always had the whippet, Pluto, with him. There was rarely anyone else there other than the sitter, though afterwards one of his daughters might turn up or a young female muse hanging around cooking grouse or partridge. He loved game. One night he rang me up around three o'clock in the morning and said he needed a cleaner. So I sent him round a nice Portuguese woman. She came running back a few days later saying, 'Oh, Mr Chandler. I can't go back there.' She said the sheets were filthy and there were no cleaning materials. I remember once I was going to cook for him myself, and when I opened the oven door, there were a couple of half-eaten pheasants inside with worms in them."

Freud's studio was Spartan with old rags and naked light bulbs, and very bright halogen and tungsten lighting. "The whole studio wall was covered in paint and there were brushes everywhere, and all the other canvases he was working on were standing around covered in dust sheets. I used to try and take a peek at them when he was on the phone. He used to wear unlaced walking boots, chef's trousers and an old denim shirt to paint in. If he made a mistake, he'd jump back suddenly. 'Oh, fuck,' he'd say. You were working for him when you sat for him, but he liked a conversation while he was painting."

The artist, who still had a faint German accent, recounted the story of his father, Ernest, who had been an architect in Berlin in the 1920s. The Jewish family had got away to England when Lucian was 12 years old, living in St John's Wood, not far from Victor and Carole's house in Hamilton Terrace.

The teenage Freud was expelled from several schools, accused of being a disruptive influence, just like Victor at Highgate, but in WW2 he served in the Merchant Navy. "He'd been called up by the army first and he went to the interview wearing pink boots. He said he never realised that the Merchant Navy would be far more dangerous. He was on Atlantic Convoys to Canada and the States, and one year he and the rest of the crew were snowed in for several months. On New Year's Eve, they went to a very rough bar in a black neighbour-hood in some port on the east coast. Everyone had to do a turn, so he got up on a table and sang a song he'd heard a couple of sailors singing in the mess the day before. By any standard the lyrics were highly offensive and racially charged but he said it was the only song he could remember at the time. Unsurprisingly about 30 locals jumped on him and smashed him to pieces.

He could recite things like Stanley Holloway's monologue *The Lion And Albert* and his 'stick with the horse's head handle.' And he made up these little rhymes about himself and Bacon. 'The Russians were visibly shaken/by the paintings of Francis Bacon/Perhaps they'd be less visibly annoyed/ by the paintings of Lucian Freud.' Then, the next minute, he'd be telling you about portraits by the likes of Orpen or John Singer Sargent, or why he preferred Matisse to Picasso."

The sittings were a major undertaking and sometimes they would go on until one or two in the morning but, on other nights, Freud would finish a little earlier and then they'd go out to dinner. There was a strict protocol. Freud paid one night, Victor the next, and "sometimes we were going out three times a week." The artist liked places like Bibendum and Annabel's because they stayed open late. "The only problem was that after he'd been painting for two or three hours, he was often very hyper. One night, we were in the River Café. Lucian was wearing a dirty old coat and a scarf covered in paint. Two nice North London couples came in and were shown to the table next to us. I think they were celebrating somebody's birthday. As they walked past, Lucian suddenly starts saying, 'I can't stand fucking perfume. I always say women should smell of one thing and one thing only, and that's c....' You should see the looks we're getting from the boyfriends. 'For Pete's sake, Lucian,' I said. 'Steady on. They're big fellas. They're not small. You'll get us both punched on the nose.' One of the men got up and was coming over, so I got up too and tried to calm things down. 'My friend's had a terrible breakdown,' I said. 'They've only just let him out.' In the background, I could hear Lucian laughing and saying 'I haven't had a fucking breakdown.'"

Another night, the pair were in Bibendum late, and a waiter was just pouring them some special champagne. "'Been to the theatre boys?' he asks nicely. 'Why don't you just go home and fuck yourself?' says Lucian. Of course, the waiter's practically in tears and runs off back to the kitchen and, as usual, I have to try and calm things down. There were a whole crowd of Americans in there too, and you should have seen their faces. It didn't help that he often looked like a tramp. He'd always wear a shirt, sometimes with a scarf tucked in, but he only liked suits when they'd got a hole in the elbow. But he did love evening scarves. I went to Charvet in Paris one year when I was over for the Arc and bought him three new ones. I went up to his studio with them when I got back, and he came to the door with a black eye. 'I can't paint you tonight,' he said. 'What happened?' I asked. 'I called a taxi driver a c...,' he said. 'But I'm going to get a great self-portrait out of it.'"

Freud's absolute dedication to his work, and equally fierce protection of his privacy, meant that he rarely socialised with sitters in their own homes, but he made an exception with Victor. "One day he just called me up at midday and asked if he could come for dinner at our house in St John's Wood. It was the time when he was painting his mother when she was dead. She was up in the morgue in the Royal Free Hospital in Hampstead and he wanted to come down to us afterwards."

Carole got what she describes as "the usual five-minute warning," from Victor that a guest was coming. "'What does he eat?'" I remember asking nervously. "Victor suggested oysters and a lobster afterwards, adding that he also liked fruit tarts."

VC got home from his Linhope Street office around 6pm to find several dozen oysters, packed in ice, waiting for him, as requested, in the kitchen. But while Victor liked eating oysters, he had minimal experience or skill when it came to opening them. "I've got the knife out and started to try and open one, but nothing's happening. 'How do you do this?' I'm saying to Carole. In the end I got out a hammer and the kitchen floor starts looking like Brighton Beach. Of course, when Lucian walked in he just picked up the knife and opened all the oysters, no problem. He's got incredibly strong wrists from holding the brushes and from when he was a sculptor. And he was talking nineteen to the dozen all the time. You couldn't keep up with him."

Carole served everything as requested, culminating in a raspberry flan from the patisserie counter at Selfridge's food hall: "As I was bringing it in from the kitchen, I tripped and bumped into the door frame, and the whole lot fell onto the floor, face down. Without stopping talking for a moment, Lucian just leaned down, scooped it up with his hand and ate it off his fingers."

"He was the same scooping out the green bits of the lobster," remembers Victor. "It was like watching him with paint. He was very sensual."

One night, after another daytime sitting followed by a West End dinner, Freud took his sitter to the National Gallery for the ultimate private view. He was one of a handful of artists who were invited to make a personal choice of work from the permanent collection that would then be exhibited in one of the rooms. As a result, he was entitled to visit the Gallery outside normal hours. "It was about eleven o'clock in the evening and he got the place opened up just for him. He had a special pass and all he had to do was phone up and say how many we were going to be, then the night porter let us in. Other than the security men, we had the whole place to ourselves for about three hours. It really echoes when you're there on your own. To walk around from room to room and have him talk about each picture was unforgettable. He loved Sargent (John Singer Sargent, the Edwardian-era expatriate American), "especially his painting of Lord Ribblesdale, who was Master of the Buckhounds and a Trustee of the National Gallery. He was happy to stand in front of his picture for ages. 'Just look at those riding boots,' he'd say. 'Those are the best pair of boots ever painted.' We went there three times in all. I remember one night we were both a bit drunk and in fits of hysterical laughter trying to correctly pronounce the surname of the French artist Jean Ingres."

Freud's portrait of Victor – '*Man in a String Chair*' – was finished in 1990. It shows him sitting on a chair, legs crossed relaxedly, wearing a cardigan, an open-neck shirt, white trousers and deck shoes with no socks. It's not an illustration. It's physical, sensual and evocative of something open and vulnerable yet devil-may-care. It has never been displayed in public or hung at any retrospective shows. Victor has a copy at his house in Spain. "I do still have a couple of his other paintings, though they're kept in the bank rather than on the walls." At one point, Victor owned seven Freud paintings in total and he and Carole hid about 30 more "under the beds and in the cupboards at Hamilton Place when Lucian was being pursued by the Inland Revenue." (Not that VC was the biggest collector of Freud's work. That distinction belonged to the Northern Irish bookmaker Alfie MacLean, who sat for Freud in the 1970s and reportedly amassed nearly £100 million of canvases in lieu of debts).

Their artist and sitter relationship may have ended, but Victor remained a friend and confidante for years after. "He would sometimes ring me up and say, 'shall we go out for a dish?' meaning supper. You'd arrange a time and a place and then he'd say, 'see you then.' It was his catchphrase, and the triple Champion Hurdler See You Then was named after it." As well as dining companion, Victor's roles continued to range from bookmaker and tipster to occasional chauffeur. "I had a Bentley at the time and he liked riding around in it. There was one day, in 1990, when he'd just made some etchings and he wanted me to drive him up to the printmakers' studio in Camden. It was wonderful turning the handle on the press and watching as they came out, but I could tell immediately by the expression on his face that he wasn't sure about them. We left there and drove round to his friend the artist Frank Auerbach's house in Camden Town. 'I want to see what Frank thinks,' he said. He took two inside, but then when he came back out later he just tore them up. 'Frank didn't really like them either,' he said. He'd left a few in a bag on the back seat of the car and I was thinking of keeping two or three for posterity, but he wasn't having it. 'Have you got those other prints?' he said a couple of nights later. 'I'll look in the back of the car,' I said. 'I know you've got them,' he said, and I had to give them back."

A few days later, Freud phoned Victor at the Linhope Street office but, for once, he didn't want to talk about betting or racing. "'That Bentley,' he said. 'Can you get me one?' Well, Victor Barclay, the old luxury car dealer in Berkeley Square, was still alive at the time, so I went to see him. He used to bet with me and he found another Bentley that was quite similar to mine and had done about the same mileage. The only difference was that this one was new and had a rather garish interior. I drove it round to Lucian's so that he could take a look at it. 'Yeah,' he says. 'It's alright…but I prefer yours.' So, of course, we ended up doing a swap. He got my nice old one and I got the other one with the red leather upholstery…and it was from the day I sold that car that everything seemed to go wrong."

Chapter Sixteen

Close To The Edge

A t first, it looked as if the new decade would be every bit as enjoyable and rewarding as the Roaring Eighties had been. Aside from Cheltenham and Royal Ascot, one of Victor's favourite race meetings was the Grand National Festival at Aintree, and he went up to bet there every year. The whole racing circus was staying away from home for three nights and there were so many characters to see, like the Graham Brothers from Belfast, and Sandy 'Pickles' Rice, who'd once looked after Uncle Ronnie in Ireland. The Chandler family's involvement with the big race went back to Victor's grandfather's day, while the quality of the supporting cards was getting better each year and all the big gamblers came out to play. In 1998, the firm would lay JP McManus a £130,000 bet on Istabraq at 8-13 in the Martell Hurdle, only for the champion to be beaten a head by Tony McCoy on Pridwell.

The atmosphere at Aintree was less intense than Cheltenham, and there was partying every night. Bill Tye fondly remembers the bomb scare in 1997, when the course had to be evacuated on the Saturday afternoon and a Blitz spirit ensued. The firm's chauffeur at the time was an ex-policeman called John, but nobody was allowed back into the car park from the grandstand, so they all had to start walking. After a mile or two, "Victor found a bloke in a pub and gave him £200 to drive us to a station," but Bill ended up staying over in Liverpool until the rescheduled race on the Monday, catching a game at Anfield along the way. On the Saturday night, all the jockeys, still in their riding silks, were in the Adelphi Hotel dancing until the early hours with a couple of girls on each arm.

Not that every big bookmaker and punter was fond of Merseyside. In the 1980s and '90s, memories of the Toxteth riots yet to fade, some of the Londoners referred to Liverpool disparagingly as Beirut, and the local Scallies became adept at casing out the hotels where the smart money boys were staying and targeting their valuables. There were several instances of bookies coming downstairs in the morning to discover that their Mercs and Jaguars had disappeared, or that the hubcaps had been stolen, necessitating negotiation with the representatives of the light-fingered thieves and the paying of reward money in exchange for the return of their wheels.

Victor liked staying at the Prince of Wales Hotel in Southport, an easier drive to Aintree than from the city centre and long a favourite of the racing and coursing crowd. He always remembered his father's friend Charlie Maskey – son of Charlie The Hammer – telling him of the time Victor senior lost his shirt at Altcar but managed to persuade a wealthy bookmaker called George Dexter to play poker with him – with Charlie looking on – in the bar of the Prince of Wales until the early hours. At which point, Dexter finally got up and said, "Have you got enough of my money now? And can I go to bed?"

One year, Victor, Bill Tye and Alan Kinghorn arrived in Southport together on the eve of the National meeting to find police cars everywhere. "There had been a fight outside a coffee bar and the whole place felt like Dodge City on a Friday night. We went out to dinner, and when we were walking back from the restaurant, kids were running past throwing stones through windows." It wasn't until the following day that Victor realised he'd been robbed. "I'd put my float in the safe downstairs, but my briefcase in the room had been broken into and some money had been taken along with a banker's draft from JP McManus. That same night, Stephen Little had thousands of pounds worth of cash stolen and Alan Kinghorn had been robbed as well." A police constable came round to the hotel the next morning, just as the bookmakers were having coffee. "He looked about 12 years old. 'Haven't you got anyone more senior?' I asked him. 'No, sir,' he replied. "All the senior policemen are on the beach. We've just found a dead body there."

It could be Bandit Country at the racecourse too, which didn't faze Victor, despite having his raincoat and binoculars stolen at least twice. The year after the bomb scare, there was a big security check as he and the boys were coming out of the car park, and there were extra-long queues on the way in. It looked as if they were going to miss the first race, so Victor "tapped a bloke in a high visibility jacket on the shoulder and offered him £50 to let us in a side entrance. He turned around very slowly and I saw his jacket had the word 'Police' on the back. He thought it was very funny." That ploy may have failed, but a further 50 yards along the perimeter, an enterprising Scouse chef had cut a hole in the back of a tent and, for a price, was permitting certain racegoers to pass through. Cockney and Jewish bookmaking voices handing over their readies, nicknamed the chef 'Schindler's List.'

As well as Last Suspect in 1985, Victor backed the 1987 Grand National winner Maori Venture at 28-1, and at Aintree in April 1990, he landed a spectacular 100-1 touch on the first day of the meeting. The Sandeman Chase over two and a half miles was the sixth race on the card and there were 11 runners, including Multum In Parvo, who had finished second in the Cathcart Chase at Cheltenham, and Martin Pipe's Rusch De Farges, who had cost the property developer so much money in the Cathcart the year before. Victor's form man advised him to back a 100-1 outsider called Sure Metal, who was trained by Red Rum's handler, the legendary Ginger McCain, and had been pulled up last time out. The seven-year-old, who was getting weight from all the other runners, was said to need time "to properly warm up," but if he got an undisputed lead, he was hard to catch. Victor had £50,000 to £500 each way three times, the bets placed by the ever-dependable

Bobby Edwards, and Sure Metal made all the running and won by six lengths.

But other results at that time were more worrying. The Chandler firm sponsored numerous horse races and other sporting contests during Victor's career. The flagship event was the Victor Chandler Chase, run over two miles at Ascot in January. It was meant to begin in 1987, but the first two runnings were both lost to bad weather. It's belated debut in 1989 saw a thrilling race in which the indefatigable Desert Orchid, conceding weight all round, got up in the last strides to beat the game and genuine Panto Prince by a head, and subsequent renewals were won by champion two-miler chasers like Viking Flagship, Martha's Son and Master Minded. The occasion was extremely popular with the 150 or so big hitters Victor invited to lunch in the biggest hospitality suite at Ascot, where they mixed with old friends and members of the Chandler family, VC passing among them, once the big race presentation was over, a bit like Tony Soprano blessing the faithful.

The 1990 Victor Chandler Chase was won by Jimmy FitzGerald's Meikleour, a 10-1 chance who held off the well-backed Irish challenger Feroda, with Panto Prince back in third. It was a day when the sponsor lost heavily, but not directly because of any losers he'd backed or winning favourites he'd laid, but because a fellow bookmaker defaulted on his liabilities to the ring. "When Carole's father Izzy Mendoza died, his friend Dougie Goldstein took over his pitches. Dougie was in the aircraft maintenance business. He'd been a punter with me and now he said, 'I want to be a bookmaker.' On the face of it, he was playing big at all the main meetings. He had a Bentley too, and a Merc. He even turned up at Windsor one evening in a stretch limo. He had a house in Camberley worth millions. He had staff. Everyone thought he was like the Bank of England."

Goldstein was a storyteller, and one of his most frequently told anecdotes concerned the misfortunes of his 17-year-old nephew the year he got a Christmas holiday job with a firm of accountants in Jermyn Street. The teenager went to the office party and got extremely drunk. The following day at work he was still feeling under the weather and had an unfortunate accident in his trousers. He tried to clean himself up but, too embarrassed to remain at the office, hurried round the corner to Simpsons of Piccadilly, which was still a department store back then and had not yet become a bookshop. It was only a few days before Christmas Eve and the shop was packed. The distressed nephew made his way to the menswear department and asked for a pair of trousers, declining to be measured. 'Yes, sir,' said the salesman. 'Would you like to try them on?' 'Definitely not,' said the boy. Thrusting some money into the salesman's hands, he grabbed the Simpsons carrier bag and carried on to Victoria Station where he boarded a train to Haywards Heath, which was where his parents lived. Once the train was under way, he shut himself in the lavatory at the end of the corridor and began to change his clothes. Diesel trains in the 1970s had windows that opened even in the loo, so the nephew decided to throw his soiled trousers and underpants out onto the track. He then opened up his Simpson's bag, only to discover that it contained not a clean pair of trousers, but a V-necked pullover. Horrified, he realised that in his haste to get out of the shop, he'd picked up the wrong bag. There was nothing for it other than to remain in hiding until the train arrived at Haywards Heath, where he had to make his way along the platform and out of the station naked from the waist down other than for the V-necked pullover which he'd tied around his middle.

At Ascot 13 years later, it was Uncle Dougie who was, at least metaphorically, in the shit. "It was Victor Chandler Chase day," remembers Victor, "and we were all there. I'd looked at the card in the morning with the team and I thought it was one of the most dangerous I'd ever seen. I decided I was going to have all sorts of insurance, including a couple of big doubles and trebles. I was walking down to Ladbrokes on the rails, but Dougie saw me first and said, 'I'll lay it to you.' Well my selections in the first, second and third races all won, and then the fourth and fifth won too. I'm scrambling around in the box trying to work out how much I'm going to win. I was on a 5-2 favourite in the last, and if that had gone in too, the total would have come to over £300,000. It got beat, so the accumulators went down, but I still finished £56,000 ahead. But Dougie 'knocked.' He gave me a cheque for the winnings and I paid it into the bank a week later, but it bounced. He did phone up and apologise, but I suppose I should have seen it coming. I wasn't the only bookie or punter who got hit either. It was the beginning of bad times for the ring."

It seemed Dougie Goldstein had ended up owing everyone on the rails and on the boards, and he couldn't see a way out of it. He left Ascot that day and never set foot on a racecourse again. His transformation didn't end there. The following year, his wife died, and he responded by becoming more reclusive than ever. But then, one day the next summer, Victor and Carole were walking back from lunch at a friend's house in St John's Wood when they saw Dougie's Mercedes Sports go by with a blonde woman at the wheel. "'Oh, Dougie's got a new girlfriend,' said Carole. Well this figure got out, tall, in a skirt with high heels, and walked up to the entrance to Dougie's flat, and I said 'Hang on a minute. It's Dougie.' 'I don't believe you,' says Carole, trying to get a closer look. 'It's either Dougie or Dick Emery,' I said. 'You're right,' she said. 'It is Dougie.' It seems he'd decided to start wearing his late wife's clothes." Perhaps he just couldn't afford any of his own anymore, his fortunes having plummeted still further at the onset of the recession. He wasn't the only one.

Already, steepling debts built up in the good times became towering massifs of ruin as the new 1990s interest rates climbed horribly to a high of 15 per cent on the morning of Black Wednesday, September 16th, 1992. Householders, shareholders, entrepreneurs and punters were hit equally by the fall-out, and the racehorse owner and Chandler family friend Charles St George was one of the casualties. He had to sell his London house near Brook Street and move into Claridges, which may not have been too much of a hardship. But the diminishing funds impacted on his horses too. In the summer of 1990, he sold his good three-year-old Saumarez to Wayne Gretzky and Bruce McNall, who moved the colt from Henry Cecil to Nicolas Clement's yard in France. That October, Saumarez won the Prix de l'Arc de Triomphe, the race that St George had longed to win above all others. Victor felt that "Saumarez broke Charles's heart.Mind you, he used to say that 'I don't suppose Henry would have run it in the Arc anyway.'"

The horses St George had in training with Cecil in Newmarket were housed in the historic Sefton Lodge stables on the Bury Road, and St George told Victor that he'd recuperated the entire purchase price by selling the Chippendale cabinet that had belonged to the former owner Jim Joel. The Sefton Lodge stable lads were paid directly by St George and, when the money ran out, it was his bookmaker, Victor Chandler, who ended up "giving him lumps of cash" to make sure the wage bill was met. "He used to call into the office on Friday nights."

When Charles St George died in 1992, his brother Edward took over the horses, saying to Victor, "tell me the worst. How much do I owe you?" Victor had been supporting the stable for about a year, and the total had mounted up, but "to me, Edward was always absolutely straight and he paid the full figure." He retained Sefton Lodge, running it under the banner of Lucayan Stud and installing David Loder as trainer, and Victor had "a terrific relationship with him when he was backing the Loder horses. They had terrible arguments, but they always made up the next day, and they won money every season, bar one, from selling their two-year-olds." When Victor was beginning his research into offshore gambling jurisdictions in 1995, Edward invited him out to Grand Bahama in his private plane. Carole had stayed behind in London and VC ended up there on his own on New Year's Eve. He was sitting at a table in his hotel, shades of Don Draper in Mad Men, and at the table next to him were four very attractive women, all wearing identical watches. Edward's nephew, James, tactfully explained to him that they were all his uncle's mistresses.

Edward St George died in 2004 and Victor went to his funeral in London, walking out afterwards in the company of Lester Piggott and the trainers David Elsworth and Richard Hannon. "How many people do you think were there?" Piggott asked. "About 500?" guessed Hannon. "Yes," said the jockey, "and 499 of them hated him." "A bit unfair," said Victor. "He and his brother always looked after you, and he supported a lot of people down the years." Lester didn't reply.

Not every gambling owner was as fortunate or well-connected as the St Georges. "Another of our biggest clients went under. 'It's all over,' he said to me. 'I'm finished. I'm going mini-cabbing.' He actually came back a year or two later and sent me a cheque for the lot. But a lot of people didn't survive and I saw loads come and go. Our worst ever loss was in 1979. A punter called George Greene who designed and built oil rigs. He was the first person I ever met who had a private plane. He was an absolute lunatic gambler. A binge gambler. He used to pay half-yearly and he always brought the cash with him in a carrier bag to the Stafford Hotel behind the Ritz. We'd arranged to meet there one day, as usual, but there was no sign of him. I waited in the bar and then telephoned his secretary, but she didn't know what had happened. Eventually, I went back to the office. Well, it turned out that he was being chauffeur-driven up to London in his Rolls Royce when he had a heart attack on the way and died right there. I tried to enquire, very delicately, whether he'd been carrying anything at the time, but nobody seemed to know. His wife didn't know he gambled and I never did get paid. We always suspected that the chauffeur made off with the money."

Some of Victor's customers, when unavoidably strapped for cash, also paid in kind, and a top-floor cupboard at Linhope Street became a sort of depository for boxes of cigars, cases of wine and even the odd antique. One punter up in Lancashire owned a factory that made Christmas crackers – very good ones, with swanky novelties and presents inside – and, whether it was December or June, he used to pay Victor with boxes of crackers when he lost. Other struggling clients unloaded their assets onto their bookie, which is how he temporarily became the proprietor of "all kinds of funny businesses," including a stonemason's firm that had a royal warrant and specialised in carving and restoring gargoyles on the stonework of Oxford colleges. One of the firm's other clients was Woburn Abbey, home of the racing-loving Henrietta, Marchioness of Tavistock, and her husband. A few years later, Victor stayed there during the British Masters golf tournament, which he sponsored. When he walked into the house, he "looked down at the floor and realised that we had put all the new stones in. When I told Henrietta, she didn't believe me." For a time, Victor and a double-dealing partner also owned a range of vintage cars – Ferraris and Aston Martins – that they bought off the banks who, in turn, had acquired them from customers decimated by the slump. But the bookmaker's biggest headache continued to be individuals who could afford to pay, but didn't, month after month, while still flaunting cash and plastic all around the West End. "One man kept telling me to fuck off over the phone and boasted that he'd never pay me." In the end, the exasperated odds-maker, unable then to go to law to reclaim the debt, resorted to 'specialised assistance' in an effort to collect.

One of Victor's oldest clients was a North Londoner, with underworld connections, who had gone into the property business. But he remained in touch with people who, for a fee, could arrange the demise of unpopular characters. One day he told VC about the time a man came to see him and started to talk about how difficult his marriage was, how impossible his wife had become and how, to put it frankly, he wished she would just disappear. When Victor's friend looked under the table, he saw a hold-all full of cash that the man was nudging in his direction. The hint was loud and clear, but Victor's friend was horrified. "I told him," he said, "I don't do women and children."

When Victor explained his problems with the non-paying customer, his friend put him in touch with a couple of debt collectors, ex-soldiers, who would get the job done. "They had both been in the army in Northern Ireland and they were both over six-feet tall. One of them, a guy called Prince, had been shot in the leg, and he walked with a limp. They arranged to meet this client at the Carlton Towers. 'Where's Mr Chandler,' he asked, when they got there. They pointed to a large blacked-out Mercedes that was parked outside the hotel. 'He's in there, waiting for us to come out,' they said, which was nonsense. Half an hour later, they returned to the office. The man had given them his car keys and his Cartier watch. 'No, no, no,' I said, with my hands over my eyes. 'It wasn't meant to be like this.' The account was settled, but we never used them again."

There turned out to be a less threatening but very effective way of persuading Jimmy Chung, a Chinese restaurant owner in Chelsea, to settle his long overdue account. Victor decided that he and the firm would eat their way through Chung's arrears and "I kept having parties there, including one New Year's Eve dinner for 20 people." There would be a fat cash tip for the waiters but, when the bill came, it was simply deducted from Chung's account, a bit like Boss Meyer's school fees at Millfield. Casinos were Jimmy Chung's downfall and, overwhelmed by debt, he finished up selling Victor a flat he owned in Spain. But at one point, he had three or four restaurants, including one in Majorca. "I used to take Lucian Freud to dinner at the one on the river near Lots Road. He loved it, eating the lobster with his fingers, and Jimmy often came over to our table with a bottle of wine."

Jimmy Chung wasn't the only restaurateur whose gambling got him into difficulties. Mr Ferrari, the owner of the Villa Bianca in Hampstead, was also a hopeless punter, and whenever Victor tried to reach him on the telephone to discuss settlement, his secretary would report that he was "down the William," meaning the William Hill betting shop on South End Road. The long hours spent in the Bill, along with the big card games with other Italian restaurant owners, only added to, rather than diminished, Mr Ferrari's losses, while Victor's account remained unpaid.

By the end of 1992, Victor was in grave danger of a visit from the debt collectors himself. What was pushing him towards the edge was not just the problem of non-paying clients, but a series of ruinous demands from the Lloyds Insurance market. The 1988 Piper Alpha oil rig disaster, which killed 167 people, had resulted in a £1.7billion loss, the largest insured man-made catastrophe in history. A series of big asbestos and pollution claims in the US added to the damage. The syndicates run by Charles St George's Oakley Vaughan agency were dangerously exposed and many names were hit hard. Carole had become a Lloyds name in the 1980s, encouraged by Victor's old punting and dog-racing friend Roger Barby. Fatefully, he introduced her to the underwriters Anthony Gooda, who was a racehorse owner with a house in West Sussex, and his partner Derek Walker, whose syndicates were now facing a £1 billion loss amid allegations of negligence and grossly incompetent underwriting. Their names were expected to pay up well in excess of a million pounds each. "I'd underwritten her position personally, guaranteeing it with the house and several of my paintings, and it couldn't have happened at a worse time. The day I finally realised how serious the situation had become was the day I got the letter from the bailiffs saying they were about to come round and take everything away." Somehow Victor staved them off, drawing once again on that reservoir of luck and good friends, and stiffening the mix with something of his grandfather's nerve. Victor had borrowed money to buy the betting shops in Cyprus with Alan Kinghorn. The shops had to go. Michael Tabor bought them for £200,000, and lent Victor a further £100,000 on top. Victor owned a building, a long-term property speculation, on the south side of the Thames. The building had to go too. The total Lloyds bill was in excess of £20 million but, in the end, "they settled for an awful lot less," thanks to the negotiating skills of Gerald Hyam, an ex-accountant and private investor "who saved a lot of names."

Victor being Victor, he continued to play for high stakes on the racecourse. In May 1995, he fancied Peter Savill's colt Celtic Swing to win the 2000 Guineas at Newmarket, but Barney Curley advised him to think again. "Peter was a personal friend and I always got on very well with him, including when he became Chairman of the British Horseracing Board a few years later. He'd backed Celtic Swing with me to do the Guineas/Derby double over the winter, and there were cartoons in the racing press suggesting I was getting worried. But Barney said that the horse would make the running in the Guineas until there was about half a furlong to run and then something would catch him. He really liked the French colt Pennekamp, and Peter O'Sullevan backed it with us too. He [O'Sullevan] was formidable when he wanted to get a bet on, and in those days before mobile phones, he'd always track me down at sparrow fart, no matter where I was, and insist on getting his preferred price. I backed Pennekamp myself at 9-2 on the day, and

I tipped it beforehand to John McCririck on Channel 4. The race panned out exactly as Barney had said it would, but I was sweating for the first seven furlongs."

Six weeks later, Victor landed another coup, scooping over £250,000 from backing Mick Channon's colt Piccolo at 25-1 in the King's Stand Stakes at Royal Ascot. The mount of Richard Hughes had finished a creditable third on unsuitably soft going in Germany last time out and was expected to be much happier on the faster ground at Ascot. In August 1994, Piccolo had won the Nunthorpe Stakes at York, albeit after a Stewards Enquiry, and according to Victor's speed figures, the Ascot odds wildly underestimated his chance. It was another double-whammy for Chandler, who also stood Jack Berry's horse, the 8-11 favourite, Mind Games "for bundles," and saw it finish third.

The occasional big winners, along with the Bentley and the evocative Linhope Street office with the phones purring from early morning onwards, continued to give the impression of wealth and style, and of trading just within the rules. It was an image that Victor was happy to play up to, telling a journalist from the *Racing Post* that his ideal companion on a desert island would be Naomi Campbell, and that if he could have one wish, he'd "like to be Michael Tabor for a day… just to see how he does it." Not all the coverage was so favourable. In 1994, an article in the Times by Julian Muscat, which could have been written by the Highgate housemaster Norris Butcher, described Victor as having "something of the scoundrel about him." But Jockey Club members, choking over their breakfast toast and marmalade, were reassured that "he speaks well enough to be comfortable in the company of Lords." Phew!

But as the 1990s economies continued to bite, gambling Lords and Ladies were becoming a rarity and Victor Chandler was one of the only big punters still active on the domestic stage. A long line of wealthy individuals, who had patronised British racing and bookmak-ing stretching back to before WW2, had been all but wiped out, ravaged by Eighties overspending and the Nineties backlash, and recoiling from the 9 per cent rate of off-course betting tax, with the result that illegal tax-free bookmaking was the only side of gambling that was thriving. Victor had to keep going to the races and betting there with his fellow layers because no thinking or numerate punter was still prepared to bet heavily on racing in Britain off-course or by phone. But where were his future customers going to come from? And what would they bet on?

The answers came to him during the 1994 FIFA Football World Cup, and they didn't involve horse racing at all. 'Go East, young man,' they said. 'Go to the Far East…go to where the big boys play.'

Chapter Seventeen

Follow The Money

The car journey took them north from Singapore City, past the war memorial and the site of the new racecourse at Kranji, across the thousand-metre causeway where the Japanese invaded in 1942, and on up the Malaysian peninsula. They sped past the smog-clouded tower blocks of Johor Bahru and carried on up the west coast highway towards Kuala Lumpur.

About an hour south of the old colonial city of Malacca, they turned off down a side road lined with palm oil trees, leading to a modern one story building with cheap tables and chairs outside. It could have been just a forgettable roadside restaurant, except that there were dozens of luxury cars – Mercs, Jags, a few Rollers – parked outside too, their drivers hanging around smoking and chatting and all kitted out smartly in suits and dark glasses. Victor's ageing chaperone 'Kai Ming'(not his real name) who "had very little hair and bad skin, yet was one of the most genuine people I've ever come across," led his guest up the steps and into what turned out to be two private air-conditioned rooms. One of them was filled with women and children, but VC, presumably whistling the theme tune to *You Only Live Twice*, was conducted into the farther room where he was confronted by about 20 smartly dressed men all sitting at a round table, smoking furiously and arguing in loud voices.

The assembled company were some of the biggest illegal bookmakers in South East Asia (thanks to Apps and the internet, one Taiwanese operator now has an annual turnover in excess of US$13 billion) and they were there for one of their weekly settlements when they reckoned up who owed what to who.

Not long after Victor arrived, the arguments suddenly ended and the men shook hands, their cigarettes replaced by the finest Havana cigars as bottles of ice-cold Chablis appeared, followed by a lavish buffet supper, served on a Lazy Susan by uniformed waiters. The English visitor, who was "just along for the ride," was introduced to everyone and took a seat at the table, nodding and smiling politely. The food was mostly delicious, except for one mysterious-looking fish dish, an agglomeration of scales and fins that was unlike anything Victor had ever seen at Wheeler's and which aroused Kai Ming's suspicions. "He leans over the plate, sniffs and then looks at me and shakes his head. 'Long time no swim,' he says."

As the meal drew to a close, the diners lit more cigars and then their drivers-cum-bodyguards started walking in and out of the room carrying Marlboro duty-free boxes stuffed with cash. The money was packed into suitcases and loaded into the boots of the various luxury motors. Then everybody shook hands once again and the convoy of high rollers, VC and Kai Ming among them, pulled back out into the heat and humidity of the Malaysian night.

Victor Chandler would probably never have been at that power brokers dinner had he not become the favoured bookmaker to an Asian billionaire, who was also one of the biggest casino gamblers in the world. And he might never have tried his luck in the Far East at all had it not been for the surging popularity of football in the late 20th century and the gambling boom that accompanied it, especially east of Suez.

When the BBC chose Luciano Pavarotti singing *Nessun Dorma* as the theme song for their coverage of the 1990 World Cup in Italy, it seemed to mark the beginning of the detoxification of football in middle-class eyes. The soaring passion of Puccini's aria won over not just a British, but a global audience, banishing bleak 1980s images of hooliganism, the Heysel Stadium riot and the Hillsborough tragedy. The wall between high and low culture had been breached, and just as the five-year ban on English clubs competing in Europe was coming to an end. Advertisers sensed the commercial potential with the advent of Sky Sports in 1991 and the formation of the Premier League a year later. Television revenues, eventually adding up to billions in domestic and international rights, would henceforth enable clubs like Manchester United, Arsenal and Chelsea to attract players from all around the world. The biggest teams were followed with fanatical enthusiasm in the Far East, where all the games were watched on satellite TV, and among those Asian supporters were seemingly limitless numbers of high-stakes punters.

The government-backed monopoly run by the Hong Kong Jockey Club was the region's biggest legitimate bookmaking system, but in the background was a vast illegal industry with varying degrees of honesty, reliability and customer service. Many South East Asian sports betting fans had spent time in Britain at work or at university. They had read the sports pages and gone into betting shops and watched football live as well as on pub TV, and they had heard about Victor Chandler and his reputation for laying a proper bet. If the name behind the brand could safely establish a presence on the ground, in places like Hong Kong, Macau and Singapore, an enormous opening beckoned. As Victor himself puts it, "successful people are generally the ones that take advantage of the opportunities that present themselves. We had to follow the money. By that point, we had no choice. We had to go where the punters were."

During the 1990 World Cup, VC and Michael Tabor had "done a bit of football business together," and it had gone well. But it was four years later when the tournament was held in the US that "the fireworks started." It began with a Hong Kong lawyer named Tommy Chiu (not his real name) who sent Victor a £1 million deposit on behalf of an anonymous Chinese punter who wanted to bet on the first round of games. Then an existing client, a Londoner called Barry who was in financial services, arrived at the Linhope Street office with a briefcase containing a million in cash. The money had been wired to his account by another Hong Kong gambler who had deputed Barry to bet on his behalf. Victor wasn't there at the time. It was a Saturday and he was about to set off to Newbury races. Barry, who like all the other big hitters was going to place his actual bets at the racetrack to avoid paying betting tax, set off for Newbury too, only for his car to be stopped by a road-block on the M4. It transpired that Barry's bank had been suspicious of the £1 million deposit and had relayed their concerns to the police.

Victor, whose car was some way behind, belatedly discovered that armed officers had turned up at Linhope Street and taken away the million pounds. "They had been watching the office and seen our female telephonists coming in and out for a cigarette. They thought the whole place was a brothel." The police raided Barry's house too, and found another £200,000 in cash under the mattress of his baby's cot. They suspected Barry of being a gangster, money laundering drug deals, but letters were duly faxed from Hong Kong confirming the existence of the football-loving Chinese businessman and eventually the £1,200,000 was returned.

Victor was under no illusion and realised that he was dealing with "a punter on the fringes, but there were loads of them around at that time and loads of illegal bookmakers too." Barry wanted £200,000 bets, which was too big for Victor, as he had no football odds specialist to advise him, so he shared the business again with a few colleagues and they ended up enjoying an extremely successful extremely successful World Cup.

Victor had rarely seen betting on this scale outside of the Cheltenham Festival, and it made him realise what a huge market in football there was in the Far East. If he was prepared to take it on, it would make his financial problems at home seem like a mere hiccup. Like his grandfather, he understood that a business had to keep growing and that a bookmaking and gambling enterprise couldn't maintain itself just by repeating today what it had done yesterday. He was up for the challenge, the scout on the Oregon Trail, and his first trip to try and recruit new customers was to Hong Kong after the 1994 World Cup. It was his first ever visit to South East Asia, and to begin with, it was quite a shock to the system. "It was early autumn and there were these wonderful smells of street food in the air. There was this feeling of industriousness and purpose, and everyone looked as if they'd got somewhere to go and something to do. It was all very exciting, but I soon realised that it was every man for himself in Asia and that there was no social net if you fell."

The Englishman "knocked on as many doors" as he possibly could, using contacts among the firm's existing clients to try and find out who was betting. He met the lawyer Tommy Chiu, who introduced him to a big property developer whose headquarters were in a backstreet building behind the Mandarin Hotel. "His office looked dilapidated from the outside, but the inside was huge and luxurious with lots of photos of him in the winners' enclosure at Sha Tin. He introduced us to a few more people, who we followed up on." Victor was invited to the races too, mindful of the fact that within an hour of his arrival in the former crown colony, a letter from the security department of the Hong Kong Jockey Club had been slipped under the door of his room at the Grand Hyatt Hotel. The HKJC knew all about Victor Chandler and wanted to enquire, politely but firmly, what was the purpose of his visit?

The honest answer to that was that he wanted to see if he might be able to open an office there with sales staff, and recruit customers without being accused of breaking the law regarding illegal bookmaking. The key to it all was to find an offshore jurisdiction through which he could legally channel the bets, simultaneously ensuring his Asian punters didn't have to pay UK betting tax, and in the course of the next 12 months, he scouted dozens of possible locations. Antigua, Costa Rica, Guernsey, Jersey and the Isle of Man were all considered, but then in May 1995, Cyril Stein phoned up and arranged to meet him for a drink at the St James's Club in London. "Cyril had always helped me with advice before. His wife Betty was a very nice woman and the families had known each other for three generations. Carole's father had worked for him, and Cyril – who was a big punter when he was in the mood – used to bet with us. We'd see his money coming down to the racecourse masquerading as Ladbrokes. He used the firm as his own vehicle, and when he won, some of his on-course men would return his bets at, say, evens, when the official price was 11-10. They were skimming off the top, and that's how they ended up retiring with a house in the south of France."

Cyril Stein knew what Victor was looking to do. Ladbrokes had a license in Gibraltar which they took out in the early 1990s so that they could use it to trade with one big international client not resident in the UK. "He told me that I should talk to a man called Alex Dembeniotis, who had moved to Gibraltar and successfully applied for a casino license. Apparently that also gave him the right to a bookmaking license, which he didn't want. So, I flew out there to see Alex, who'd been a big punter with Alan Kinghorn and used to have a club in London but lost it during the Ladbrokes-Playboy licensing battle. He was quite a character, and he used to chew, rather than smoke, long thin Monte Cristo cigars. He agreed to sell me the license for £100,000, and then I talked to Michael Tabor, who was in Monte Carlo, and he said he'd put in a few million in time for Euro '96, which was going to be the next big football tournament. So, we set up the office there at Leanse Place with about 16 people, and Michael and I going 50/50 each. Michael provided the finance and I did the work."

Michael Tabor had just won the Kentucky Derby with Thunder Gulch and was about to join the all-conquering Coolmore Stud syndicate in Ireland. Victor felt it made sense to talk to him rather than a recognised lender "because he was someone who would take a decision very quickly, and we needed that. If we'd gone to Deutsche Bank or Barclays or HSBC, it could all have taken months and we'd have missed the moment."

Initially, the Chandler Gibraltar office seemed rather drab and uninspiring, like the rest of the colonial outpost hanging on to the Rock at the southern edges of Europe. The internet was still in its infancy in

1996 and the skeleton staff were dependent on Teletext, 10 landlines and a lot of mobile phones. But, once again, the level of Asian business on Euro '96 was staggering, far exceeding turnover on the tournament in Britain.

Mike Saunders, who had been running Linhope Street with Roger Jenkins, was involved in the early stages of the Gibraltar move. But the sums of money at stake and the legal challenges were suddenly way beyond what they had been used to as a rails bookmaking firm with an office in Marylebone. At the time, Victor had about 5,000 credit clients in Britain and an annual turnover of around £40 million. Now he was considering tilting at business worth many hundreds of millions, and it was plain he needed a full-time Chief Executive to assist him. Bookmaking, he always believed, was "a lot to do with finding the right people and having them around you." Victor's business, like his father's and grandfather's before him, had originally been built around a small network of close-knit personal and professional relationships, from Joe Dunbar and Val Powell, to Bobby Edwards and Bill Tye. These were men who worked together every day, knew each other well and were also deeply and passionately knowledgeable about racing and book-making. The challenge if he was going to move offshore would be to try and replicate that structure as far as possible in the far-flung world of global gambling.

Fortunately, there was a candidate for the job of CEO who had known Victor since he was an eight-year-old boy. Michael Carlton had grown up in Brighton and Hove where he was a good friend of Carole's son, Danny. Now, having completed 13 years with Ernst and Young, he was about to make the move from chartered accountancy to Turf accountancy. He flew out to Gibraltar on his first day on the job in 1998. There was a judicial review of offshore gambling going on at the time and it was by no means certain that the firm would be able to continue operating an office there, though Victor and Mike received a sympathetic hearing from the Chief Minister Peter Caruana when they met him. "I've got nine lives," he said, "and so far I think I've only used up two of them." By now, Victor must have been on to at least his third or fourth life, the indebtedness of the early '90s slump forgotten and deal-making in the air. "A bookmaker must be an optimist," he told another interviewer. "I don't think you can afford not to gamble." In 1995, the Beijing Jockey Club came to a similar conclusion.

News of Victor's initial Asian foray had rippled around the Far East and reached China where the Communist authorities were looking to build a racetrack in the capital city and set up the gambling infrastructure to go with it. Out of the blue one day in 1995, Victor received an invitation from the Beijing Jockey Club to fly out to China, first-class, as their guests for exploratory discussions, all expenses paid. It turned into one of the strangest overseas trips of Victor's career, beginning with a request by the chairman of the BJC to bring him a set of bagpipes as a present. It seemed he was a big fan of Gaelic music and wanted to learn to play the pipes himself.

China in the 1990s had not yet embarked on anything like the full tilt modernisation that would follow in the next decade, and Chandler found himself in a hotel in Beijing with a splendid exterior but a bizarre and sparsely furnished interior. The sitting room in Victor's suite had just two objects. "A TV set and an armchair. No one spoke English. It was the same when I walked out into Tiananmen Square. I couldn't see another European anywhere. I was there for a number of days and went out to see the site of the proposed racecourse, where they had a huge model of what they wanted to build, complete with a dressage and showjumping arena. There were more talks in their offices, where they wanted to know all about odds and gambling."

At the weekend, the chairman, who was Northern Chinese and very tall, asked Victor to join him at his compound in the country. "It was about two hours out of the city and in the middle of nowhere. His wife and children were there, but the facilities were what you might politely call limited." On the Saturday morning, the chairman got a call ordering him to return to the city, but he told Victor to stay on, saying that he'd rejoin him as soon as he could. But he didn't come back that night and he didn't return on Sunday either. "There were no mobile phone networks where I was and no one spoke English there either. I was starting to feel as if I was wandering around in a maze. It wasn't until Monday morning that he finally returned, and I've rarely been so relieved to see a car."

Back in the capital, they worked all day on a business plan, and then on the Monday evening, the guest was treated to what was described as an honorary English dinner at the Snooker Club. "We had steak and chips, warm glasses of Asti Spumante and the most terrible corked red wine. I was trying to pour it into the plant pots. Everyone had to stand up and make a speech and say how they thought the week had gone, and the longer it went on, the more drunk and incoherent the speeches became. When I got home to Britain, we submitted our proposals, as requested, but then about a week later we were informed that the chairman had been moved to another government department and that was that. He asked us to send him a book on how to play the bagpipes and some tapes, but we never saw him or any of the others again."

China may have proved unrewarding territory for VC, but back in London he was thinking it would be a good time to merge the company with a spread betting business and take advantage of the upsurge in global wagering on financial markets. He'd been in talks with Stuart Wheeler, the financier and founder of IG Index and a major donor to the Conservative Party. The 60-year-old Wheeler was an astute and respected gambler, his specialities card games and bridge, and the pair saw potential for both sides from a blending of their upmarket clientele. In the event, the merger never happened, Wheeler deciding to float his company in 2000 (at a valuation of £125 million), and a few years later Victor was in discussion with Compton Hellyer and Lindsay McNeile, founders of Sporting Index, instead. But, by then, considerations of merely British-based trading had been pushed off VC's agenda again as he began an extraordinary two-year embrace of an Asian 'whale' whose gambling was off the scale.

It all began with the Yorkshireman Keith Stone, who 20 years before had been the head lad at Peter Easterby's stable at Habton Grange near Malton. It was the fabled era of the Cheltenham Gold Cup winners

Alverton and Little Owl and the dual Champion Hurdlers Sea Pigeon and Night Nurse, who Stone used to ride regularly on the gallops. Stone left Britain to try his luck at training in Malaysia and Singapore, and he saddled a few winners out there for VC. In December 1996, he was back in England for one of his periodic visits when he phoned Victor to say that he knew a punter – a very big punter – he was happy to introduce him to, providing the bookmaker would pay for his stay down in London. The meeting took place in Les Ambassadeurs, the luxurious casino and club in Hamilton Place where the manager, the Greek businessman Sotirios Hassiakos, was a fanatical punter and racing lover and one of Victor's best friends. From time to time, international high rollers like Alan Bond would come for an evening at the casino and express an interest in going racing. Sotirios would pass them on to Victor and sometimes it would work the other way.

That first evening at Les A, Keith Stone's contact – "a personable looking man and very intelligent" – was "laid back, but very well dressed too, with a look of power about him, and he was drinking large brandies before dinner." Kai Ming, who was "a player" as well as the tycoon's right-hand man, was there as well.

The meeting was considered a success, and the gambler – codename 'Swordfish' – asked Victor to have lunch with him in his London apartment the following day. There were staff, and the meal was to be served in the dining room, but Swordfish kept telling the waiters "we'll be another hour," because he wanted to watch a football match on television first. It was a game in the Scottish Premiership, about which Victor knew next to nothing, but "he had a £20,000 bet with me on the correct score. I think he was just testing me out. He lost, but that was only the beginning."

The billionaire invited Victor and Carole to stay in Las Vegas with him over Christmas, offering to fly them over there in his private jet. Carole, who loathed Vegas, was horrified by the idea and refused to go point-blank, but in late 1996, VC made his first trip to Singapore at his new client's behest, and that was it. The start of two years of living dangerously, which lasted until the Pacific Rim stock market crash in

April 1999. There was no easing in gently. The second big test came on a hot, wet, humid afternoon at Bukit Timah racecourse where Victor and his assistant Richard Thomas, who had formerly worked for Coral and Sporting Index, were the gambler's guests in his private box. The brightly lit stands were packed with high rollers, all of them wining, dining, smoking, and betting on their mobile phones. Bookmaking was officially illegal in Singapore, just as in Hong Kong, and all citizens and visiting racegoers were meant to bet solely at the Tote windows of the Malayan racing association. Yet at Bukit Timah, the gambling-mad populace seemed to ignore the restrictions at will, and for every dollar traded with the legitimate operators, they were wagering up to three times as much with the illegals.

Victor's host didn't need the black market. He had Victor Chandler, the renowned gentleman bookmaker from Britain and Gibraltar to play with, and play him he did. "He wanted £20,000 on a 66-1 shot in a mile and a quarter handicap, so I laid it to him. It had been raining heavily by the time the race got underway, but it was still very hot. Well, this horse, which was supposed to be a total outsider, led all the way into the straight and was still four lengths in front with two furlongs to go. I nearly fainted. We were looking at a payout of over £1.3million if it won, and for a moment I thought we'd been set up."

Richard Thomas couldn't bear to watch. "He was practically lying on the floor with his eyes closed. I was sweating heavily, but then in the final furlong it tired and dropped back to finish third. Fortunately, he (Swordfish) wasn't on each way. Richard and I were like gentleman about it and smiled graciously, but the important thing was we hadn't backed down, and that's what he'd been looking for. So, from then on, he went absolutely potty. There were so many bets. I couldn't lay it off."

Asian punters pay less regard to the form book than their European and American counterparts. They believe in the power of luck and cosmic forces, and that, with the aid of omens and lucky charms, they can channel it in their direction. Richard Thomas was deputed to be personally on hand whenever Swordfish was feeling lucky and wanted some action. There could be no slacking either. Richard was expected to keep his phone on night and day, and had to be provided with two assistants to enable him to get some sleep. The gambler played golf, and on Sunday July 20th, 1997, he summoned both Victor and Richard to attend him at his favourite karaoke club in Singapore where he was watching the final round of the Open Championship at Troon on satellite television. Over the course of the next three hours, he proceeded to wager £1.6million in bets, which Richard had to write down on a series of napkins. "Ten grand to hit the fairway. Ten grand to miss the hole. They just kept coming. By the end, he'd lost £75,000."

Football was his favourite. The karaoke clubs featured live satellite coverage of Premiership games at the weekends and on Monday nights, and Swordfish started having £50,000 and £100,000 bets every Saturday, the wagers channelled through the Leanse Place office in Gibraltar. He had a million at even money on Brazil in the 1998 World Cup Final against France. The holders lost 3-0, but the punter kept playing, sometimes commanding Victor's presence at short notice, be it in London or the Far East. And from his handling of staff to his views on politics, finance and business, he continued to comport himself like a James Bond villain. On one occasion, Victor was in Singapore and ended up accompanying Swordfish on a trip to Vanuatu (formerly the New Hebrides), the island archipelago in the South Pacific. They travelled in the tycoon's private plane, stopping to refuel at Cairns in Northern Queensland. The flight time was 13 hours. As well as the pilots and stewardesses, the party included the gambler's mistress and his inscrutable male secretary, which added to the 007 atmosphere. There was a casino in Vanuatu, so Swordfish set up a competition, giving everyone US$5,000 each to see which of them would fare best. But when their patron had had enough, they were ordered to be "on parade" and ready to depart at 7am in the hotel lobby. Except that 7am, 8am, 9am, 10am and 11am would come and go with no sign of the severely hungover billionaire.

Eventually, they flew on to the Gold Coast, where Swordfish decamped to a private room in a casino and played baccarat with a credit line of AUS\$ 20 million. But when "a particularly obnoxious casino manager," refused to allow Victor to play with the same discounted chips, the gambler exploded. "I was starving and we were about to have a steak sandwich and a very good bottle of wine. But he was so angry with the croupier that he tipped the table over and the food and drink all went flying through the air. It was 3am and the women had all gone to bed, but they were told to get up at once and get dressed as we were leaving. But then the pilot called and said that we couldn't take off from the airport until nine o'clock in the morning, so they went back to bed. Of course, when 9am came we were all up and ready, and he was still asleep. When we did finally take off, the pilot was told to fly to Sydney, but then, when we were in mid-air, he was ordered to change course and return to Singapore instead."

Kai Ming was the tycoon's essential accomplice, even on the most confidential trips. But when he went away on more formal journeys, all the staff went with him. "They had to wear black uniforms with stars on their shoulders denoting their rank. He was very fond of books like Machiavelli's The Prince and Clausewitz's (the 1914-18 Prussian Military strategist) On War. 'Business is like running an army,' he'd say to me, 'and I am the five-star general. You've got cadres in your business who are not loyal. You have to have spies at every level.' I think he wanted me to shoot someone to encourage the others.

One day, at Bukit Timah in Singapore, he was wearing jeans and a safari jacket when he was denied entry to the racecourse stables for being improperly dressed. 'You know who I am?' he says to this official. 'I've got 20 horses in training here. If you don't let me in inside five minutes, I'll line them all up on the track and shoot them, one by one, in full view of the public. And I think they'll find it a lot more interesting than your racing.'" The official, who wasn't at all sure that the tycoon was bluffing, let him in at once.

As Victor was discovering, "money is king in Asia, and everything goes on there," and the billionaire's wealth and power could open doors and protect his confidantes and friends, whether from criminals or the law. When Richard Thomas was fielding their client's bets in

Singapore, he "had to leave the country every few weeks to keep the police happy." But there was never any problem coming back in again because Swordfish had squared it with the people who mattered.

When the working day was over, the tycoon's largesse continued in the nightclubs and karaoke bars of Jakarta, Bangkok and Singapore. "He'd be saying to us, 'how many girls do you want tonight?' remembers Victor. "You could do pretty much whatever you liked out there. There were casualties, but they also had this saying everywhere we went: what happens in the east, stays in the east.'" One night, they were in a gigantic sports bar with karaoke going on up at one end and a Manchester United game live on the big screen. "Everyone was smoking and betting like mad, and they all wanted prices in running. Richard and I could hardly keep up with them and we resorted to writing the bets down on more napkins and the back of fag packets. '£50,000 to £20,000 Roy Keane to get a red card. Down to the fat bloke with the mole. £40,000 to £10,000 Beckham to score from a free-kick. Down to the little one with the beard.' The atmosphere was incredible."

VC's new customers were determined that he should be fully inducted into their rituals and wouldn't let him leave the bar until he'd taken a turn on the karaoke stage. And the Westerner's choice of music? Bobby Darin singing *Mack The Knife*.

Part of the initial excitement of those nights was the realisation on both sides that, due to the restrictive nature of legal gambling in the Far East, there was a vast, pent up demand for the services of a legitimate offshore bookie with a famous name and reputation. Victor was the pioneer, and thanks to its new Gibraltar office and call centre, Victor Chandler International was ideally placed to meet that demand, especially with the sudden rapid development of online trading in the run-up to the Millennium.

Before then, though, Swordfish's one-man spree came to a halt, at the punter's own choice, when the East Asia slump shaved more than £250 million off his assets in April 1999. Over the course of the previous two Russian Roulette years, he'd worked his way through millions trying to beat his bespoke English bookie. "He'd already paid £10 million, and we eventually settled on another £15 million when I met Kai Ming at the Shangri-La Hotel in Singapore. We agreed that he'd pay us off monthly. He bounced right back a few years later and had a million pound bet with us – another losing one – on Portugal in the final of Euro 2004."

The billionaire may have been the biggest single punter in Chandler family history, but he was by no means the only big hitter in the Far East and, travelling repeatedly throughout the region from 1997 onwards, VC met plenty of others, including just as many sharks, snakes and hustlers as he'd encountered in Britain when he'd first started out on the bookmaking trail more than 20 years before.

Chapter Eighteen

Heads Or Tails

Wherever Victor and Mike Carlton went on their Asian journeys, they followed the same pattern. Meetings with lawyers to see if they might be able to operate legally in their jurisdiction, followed by more meetings with middlemen, brokers and bankers, and entertaining in hotels and restaurants to get introductions and make contacts.

In 1998, Victor flew out to Kuala Lumpur especially to meet some of the new customers he'd been introduced to by Kai Ming. The first night, his chaperone took him out to dinner in a thousand-seater restaurant serving Chinese, Japanese and European food. Some of the punters there were convinced that Victor was Tom Jones and insisted on him signing autographs accordingly. The next night, VC was entertaining clients in another KL restaurant and, this time, one of the other guests knew exactly who he was. "There was this Chinese guy who came over and introduced himself. 'Hello,' he said. 'I'm Paul.' 'Alright,' I said. He claimed that he was developing an off-track betting business in Malaysia. 'Do you remember me?' he says. 'I'm afraid not,' I said. 'You know who I am?' he says, grinning. 'I'm the man who turned the lights out.'"

What 'Paul' meant was that he was the underworld fixer who arranged for the floodlights to fail just after the scores had been levelled in a match between West Ham and Crystal Palace at Upton Park in November 1997. Asian bookmakers, unlike their British counterparts, pay out on the result as it stands if a game has to be abandoned in the second half, and Paul's syndicate were believed to have won an eight-figure sum from their East London coup. They pulled it off again during a Wimbledon-Arsenal match a month later, but a third attempt, when Charlton hosted Liverpool in the new year, was foiled, and four men – two Malaysians, a Chinese man and a Charlton security supervisor – were jailed for between 18 months and four years. Paul, though, was clearly proud of his achievements. "'I'm planning something else, you know,' he said, laughing. 'Oh yes?' I said. But he never did tell me what it was. 'What did you do with the money you won last time?' I asked. 'I went up to the Gold Coast in Australia,' he said 'and lost it all in the casinos.'"

Flagrant con men like Paul were operating openly outside the law. Others were partners in criminal enterprises with the full knowledge of the authorities while purporting to be friends and helpers of the English visitors. The first office the firm opened in Asia was in Bangkok in 1997, and it was set up by Harry Kwo (not his real name), a smooth talking Chinese man who had been recommended to them as a go-between who could bring in customers and get things done. The office, conveniently close to the airport for quick getaways, was to be the base of what might be described as a deep-cover operation designed to facilitate turnover from Asian punters on the 1998 World Cup in France. A small select team was sent out from England, four young men, all of them football fanatics and good at numbers and, as Victor put it, "all nice boys who hadn't been away from home that often and were all good to their mothers."

The key member of the team was the now internationally renowned poker player, sports betting analyst, investor and Chairman of Brighton and Hove Football Club, Tony Bloom. The 27-year-old Bloom had only been working for the firm "for about three or four weeks," but Mike Carlton was friendly with his racing loving father Ronnie and had known the Bloom family for years. Tony's grandfather, Harry

Bloom, who moved to Brighton from the East End in 1947, was a greyhound racing enthusiast and served as Brighton FC's Vice-Chairman in the 1970s, when Victor and Carole were living in Hove. Tony went to school at Lancing College and took a degree in mathematics at Manchester University. But when he was growing up, he often played the slot machines in Brighton's West Street arcade, and that kindled his interest in gambling. His older brother Darren used to make regular and successful visits to Hove dogs. One night Tony found where he had been hiding his cash and took £2,000 and went greyhound racing himself. When his brother got home, Tony was waiting for him. "I've borrowed two grand," he said, beaming. "But don't worry…I've turned it into three."

Bloom's punting skills were destined to yield spectacular returns for Victor's business, but that first posting, the boys ensconced in a couple of apartments near the Bangkok airport runway, was to prove dangerous as well as profitable. Their brief, sleeping by day and working by night due to the time difference in Europe, was not just to man the computers and cell phones, but to help set the markets and odds that the Gibraltar office would offer on the World Cup games, especially to their new high-rolling Asian punters.

There were a lot of grey areas and the set-up wasn't strictly illegal at the time, or at least not according to Harry Kwo, though many South East Asian governments would later try and forbid their citizens from trading with what they called "offshore robbers." But Victor was under no illusions about the possible obstructions he might encounter from the local illegals and their friends in law enforcement, many of whom were paid off regularly, just as British police forces had been looked after by Bill Chandler, William Hill, Joe Coral and their like in the old days of street bookmaking, before the legalisation of off-course betting shops. And so it was that officers in the Bangkok police were cut in directly for a stake in the Chandler enterprise. Their interests were watched over by an alarming character called Colonel Bob, who sported a moustache and military fatigues, and an entirely bogus air of jovial camaraderie.

HEADS OR TAILS

Harry Kwo was in charge of the arrangements and making sure everything functioned smoothly, out of sight and out of sound. To begin with, it all went very well. Tony Bloom had been quick to spot the potential of the so-called Asian Handicap (not yet available with bookmakers in the UK), which sought to create a level playing field in a football match and eliminate the draw as a possible outcome. The odds were expressed in decimals rather than fractions, and for betting purposes, one team would be given a virtual start of, say, half a goal (0.5) which would mean that if the game ended 1-1, that team would be deemed the winner. Approaching it like a modern day Stephen Little, and deploying his knowledge of statistics and probability, Tony Bloom consistently found the Asian handicap's weak points. His familiarity with English football and the depth and intensity of his statistical analysis of a team's form, fitness and record was simply greater than anything the Asian bookies could muster, and the information he provided enabled Victor to lay bigger prices than his rivals. Come the World Cup final, his bold calls on behalf of the firm had racked up gains totalling over £10 million. High stakes held no fear for him. When Victor asked him what position he should take on the decider between the holders and hot favourites Brazil and the hosts France, Bloom's response was unequivocal. "Stick everything we've got on the French," he said. "Everything?" queried Victor, mildly shocked even by his buccaneering standards. "Everything," said Bloom. He believed that France, with home advantage and Zinedine Zidane, had been grossly underestimated by the market, while the Brazilians were overhyped. VC decided to back the man, as Michael Tabor used to say, and placed £3 million on France to win with the bookmakers in the Far East, and laid bets on Brazil, including one of £1 million at even money, out of the Gibraltar office. By the time the game was over, the French having triumphed 3-0 with Zidane scoring twice, the firm were nearly another £10 million pounds better off.

Tony Bloom had left Thailand about a month before the World Cup began, difficulties having surfaced in the firm's relationship with the Thai policeman Colonel Bob and his friends. Not satisfied with their remuneration, they'd started demanding winning football tips every week. They were very bad losers, as Victor saw for himself when he stopped off for dinner in Bangkok with Tony Bloom and the others on the way to one of his rendezvous with Swordfish. "Colonel Bob had been drinking heavily all through the meal and popping pills as well. We were in a club near the end of the evening when all of a sudden he takes out his gun, grabs Tony by the hair, pulls his head down and sticks the pistol in his mouth. 'You'd better stop tipping me losers,' he says. 'Or else.' He's miming pulling the trigger and going 'bang, bang' like it's all a big joke. But I decided there and then to close the Bangkok operation down and pull the boys out. I was trying to imagine what I'd say to their families if anything happened to them."

Tony Bloom and his colleagues were on their way home within 48 hours, relocating to the office in Leanse Place, Gibraltar where, thanks to Michael Tabor's investment, there were soon to be millions of pounds worth of new software and hi-tech phone links in preparation for the big move. Bloom continued working there for Victor for another two years, his footballing and Asian Handicap knowledge right on the money, though by the time he left to start his own business in 2000, he was betting as much for himself as for the firm.

By that point, he'd also began his transformation into one of the biggest and most successful tournament poker players in the world. His nickname, 'The Lizard', a reference to his cool and unemotional demeanour at the table, also harked back to his enthusiasm for American sports like baseball and the NFL, and his preference for spending part of the winter studying the form in warm weather training camps in places like Florida and Arizona. His old Jewish bookmaking friends, who enjoyed a joke against themselves, had another name for his poker-playing alter ego. They called him 'The Cincinnati Yid'.

Victor may have ducked the threat represented by Colonel Bob, but business transactions in the Far East were never less than eventful, and the next problem was the middleman. Harry Kwo continued to be a nuisance, demanding further payments and percentages for him and his right-hand man, who was an agent for the MGM Casino in Macau, and submitting expenses claims to Mike Carlton "as long as our arms. He did introduce us to all the established credit bookmakers in the Far East, but it went to his head. He loved to impress and always met us with motorcycle outriders and police cars and bikes which just clogged up the roads. When I went through the accounts, I couldn't believe all the things he was charging for. I told him I wasn't going to pay them, and he just tried to ignore us."

Victor told Kwo that he no longer needed his services and was going to end his association with the firm. Kwo responded by claiming that he was owed US$4 million worth of commission on bets struck. Victor dismissed the figure as preposterous and offered him US$110,000 (around £81,000) to go away. The dispute dragged on until in the end, Victor, Kwo and Mike Carlton met to discuss the situation in a private room in the Grand Hyatt in Hong Kong in November 2000. "After a lot of wrangling, he reluctantly came down to £500,000. So in the end, I said we'd toss him for it, and he agreed. Mike had a coin in his pocket. Harry Kwo called heads. The coin came up tails. It was only after Kwo had gone that Mike took another look at the coin and we noticed that it had tails on both sides."

Mike Carlton kept the lucky coin and had it set in two silver magnifying glasses and presented to Victor as a souvenir. He had it framed and placed on his office wall, along with a photo of a five-franc casino chip from Évian-les-Bains, evoking memories of Fernando Ponce-Torré, and "a florin that was found in Grandpa's pocket when he died."

The year 1998 had been a very good one for the House of Chandler, thanks largely to that fabulously successful World Cup and, for a while, the company was doing as much business with punters in the US as it was with the Asian market. "We set up an American trading office in mid-'98 and recruited three Americans – Rich, Al and Marty – to run it. We had a special staff of about 40 people taking calls, plus a lot of internet business, and we were just about to launch an enormous marketing campaign too. It revolved around a documentary we'd had made for the major US TV networks. It was all about bookmaking in the UK, and there were interviews with us and film of our offices in Gibraltar and Hong Kong, and also interviews with our competitors and the Gibraltar Chief Minister, Peter Caruana. The idea was to show the general public in the US that regulated and taxed betting was perfectly legal and that legitimate businessmen were involved in it." Unfortunately, the American Department of Justice took a less enlightened view and, in late 1999, they started a crackdown on what they considered to be illegal bookmaking, culminating in legislation prohibiting US financial institutions from transferring money to online betting sites. Michael Tabor, who had been following what was happening, had property, bloodstock and other investments in the States and was worried they could be jeopardised if the company continued to accept American bets. He asked Victor to pull out of the US trade and, in due course, the 40-strong staff were paid off and the custom diverted elsewhere, Antigua temporarily becoming a new offshore location. There were problems there too, until Victor managed to sell the office to his fellow Englishman Mark Blandford, founder of Sportingbet, for $7million.

The wisdom of Michael Tabor's action was underlined eight years later when David Carruthers, a former Ladbrokes middle manager, became entangled in the US legal system. Edinburgh-born Carruthers had taken a managerial job with a US online firm called BetonSports, which was trading out of Costa Rica. Travelling back there from Britain in 2006, Carruthers was arrested while in transit at Dallas-Fort Worth Airport and found himself in court the next day, wearing an orange jumpsuit and facing Federal charges relating to illegally taking wagers over the phone and online from US citizens. Transported to the investigation's headquarters in Missouri, he had to post a $1 million bail bond in order to be released from custody, and spent three years there under house arrest while the case proceeded. He eventually pleaded guilty to racketeering and was sentenced to 33 months in prison, serving 14 of them in a US jail before being transferred back to the UK.

It was widely accepted that Carruthers, who had openly made the case for online gambling in the US media, had been used as a pawn by the Department of Justice to try and catch his boss Gary Kaplan, who was alleged to have links with organised crime. But the story reminded Victor of one of his father's experiences when he and Betty had passed through Miami on their way to the Bahamas on one of their holidays with Lester Piggott in the 1960s. "When the American immigration official found out that Dad was a bookmaker, he looked at him and said 'And are you carrying a gun?' Dad was horrified."

Trading safely with sports bettors inside the US may have been off the agenda, but with the scent of the new money getting stronger by the week, the search for a secure offshore location from which to handle the booming Asian and European business intensified. In January 1999, Victor had flown over to Dublin for a meeting with the bookmaker and racehorse owner Joe Donnelly (who would go on to enjoy back-to-back Cheltenham Gold Cup victories with Al Boum Photo). That evening, Donnelly, an old friend of the trainer Mick O'Toole, a long-time Chandler customer, organised a dinner with Ireland's racing-mad Finance Minister, Charlie McCreevy. An ardent punter who never missed Cheltenham or Galway if he could possibly avoid it, McCreevy had presided over a significant cut in Irish betting tax, while allowing bookmakers based there to bet into the British market at the lower rates. McCreevy would have welcomed Victor's presence in the Republic, and VC was seriously considering opening up there. But then came what he described as his 'Eureka' moment, and the inspiration was all thanks to Carole. "She was reading the newspaper in the bath one day and she came upon the story about Irish bookmaking, and she said to me, 'why is it that Irish bookmakers can advertise their prices in the UK, but you can't from Gibraltar?' and a lightbulb went on in my head." Why not be bold and move the entire telephone betting operation offshore and give British punters the same service as clients in Asia and elsewhere.

A much expanded set-up at Leanse Place looked the best option, despite some concerns about bandwidth and telephone reliability, and within a week, Victor and Mike Carlton had their first meeting with the lawyers David Oliver and David Lord at Lincoln's Inn and were assured by them that there was no legal objection that could prevent them from moving the business en bloc to Gibraltar. They, nonetheless, counselled absolute secrecy until all the preparations were complete.

By now, Victor had amassed about "ten to fifteen million pounds to invest in the move. I'd won a lot of money off Swordfish, and so I said to Michael Tabor, 'now I suggest that you take half of the old business, the debtors as well as the creditors,' and he agreed and bought 45 per cent. I had 45 per cent and Mike had the other 10 per cent, and it was on that basis that we went ahead."

There was a comical moment when the Gibraltar minister newly responsible for gaming had to go home and use his child's computer to print off the licence, numbered 001. Then, on Friday May 14th, 1999, there was a dramatic front-page headline in the *Racing Post*. 'REVOLUTION,' it proclaimed in capital letters. "Victor Chandler stuns the betting industry with dramatic move that could change the face of gambling in Britain." Describing Victor as "an institution of the Turf" and "the dominant figure on the rails," the reports mixed genuine excitement at the implications for British punters with disbelief that a man whose "year culminates with the high-rolling battles of the Cheltenham Festival," could feasibly be turning his back on the old world of the racecourse and everything that went with it.

The move was the lead story in many of the broadsheets too, including the *Telegraph*, which ran the story on the front page, including Mike Carlton's comment that going offshore was "the only sensible commercial move we can make," and predictions that Britain's "outdated gambling taxes" would be routed. From now on, Chandler punters – both UK callers and overseas clients – would be subject to just a 3 per cent service charge (with a proportion going to British racing) rather than the existing 9 per cent rate, which would continue to apply to bets placed with other bookmakers without an offshore presence.

It was the kind of bold, winner-takes-all play that Bill Chandler would have approved of, and his grandson had seen it through without blinking. Overnight, Victor Chandler International became the largest private employer on the Rock, the Leanse Place HQ now occupying three floors staffed by 140 people tasked with operating the multi-million pound investment in new software. It was a bit different to the cheerful muddle that had characterised the Linhope Street office back in London. The trading room desks were lined with Dell computers. Banks of television screens around the walls relaying sporting events from four continents, and the miles of blue and red cable beneath the carpets humming with electronic tic-tac messages from around the globe. The uninterrupted flow of news and information like a digital version of The Blower in Victor's grandfather's office in Wardour Street before the war.

Most of the staff were English, but many of their clients were not. From day one, the firm was taking calls from Britain and Ireland, and there was also a Greek-speaking desk, a Russian desk and a special hotline to the Middle East. But the greatest volume of business was coming from Asia, and a team of specially-trained Cantonese and Mandarin speakers had been recruited to field their bets. Victor's and Mike Carlton's offices were one floor above, next to the conference room. Open plan and stylish, with dark blinds, soft black leather chairs and sofas. From VC's office window, there was a panoramic view of the Gibraltar harbour and waterfront. A British warship lying at anchor in the naval dockyard. Ferries and freighters heading out to sea. The mountains of Spain rising up in the background and the Moroccan coastline hidden by a heat haze across the Straits.

It was difficult to adjust for the first couple of years. Victor had an apartment in Gibraltar, but he and Carole spent most weekends at a house they bought in Spain, half an hour up the coast near Soto-grande, while also keeping their London home in Hamilton Terrace. On Monday mornings, a taxi collected him around 9am and drove him back down to the frontier, where he walked through the barrier to avoid the traffic queues, and then another taxi met him and drove him up to Leanse Place.

In October 1999, Ladbrokes followed suit, hiring 250 people to staff a new Gibraltar call centre; within a year they had been joined on the Rock by a spate of other bookmaking firms, including Stan James, William Hill and Coral. Gambling suddenly supplanted cigarette smuggling as the principal economic activity of the unlovely garrison town, with its swarthy looking policemen in British bobbies' uniforms, its Angry Friar pub, and red double-decker buses rumbling incongruously through the narrow streets. The 1970s ambience (which has changed enormously in recent years), complete with fry-ups and cheap cigarette smoke, feeling as if one of the Channel Islands had been transplanted to the Mediterranean, and Jersey Jim Bergerac was about to come striding round the corner in his Burtons leisurewear.

The exodus of British business and loss of a much-valued sin tax made a deep impression on the Treasury, and in his March 2001 budget, the Chancellor, Gordon Brown, scrapped the official 6.75 per cent betting duty, rounded up to a 9 per cent tax to cover the bookies' payments to the Betting Levy which helps to finance British racing, and replaced it with a 15 per cent gross profits tax. Punters thanked Victor, not Gordon Brown, for their good fortune, and celebrated being able to bet tax-free in shops and off-course without having to go racing or offshore anymore to take advantage. Not long afterwards, Victor was invited to an official reception at the Governor's mansion in Gibraltar where the guest of honour was the Princess Royal. "Oh," she said, as she shook hands with the bookmaker. "You're the man who upset our Chancellor, Mr Brown." Victor smiled politely. There were honeyed words from government sources, saying they hoped that the bookmakers who had moved away would come home now that the duty had been abolished. For some of the big high street betting shop chains, going back seemed a sensible move in the short term, but VC wasn't interested. The company put out a statement describing the new 15 per cent charge as "another stealth tax," and affirmed they had no plan to close its offshore operation. Within a year, they had cut their 3 per cent handling charge to zero, and increased their marketing spend. Victor was keen to make further inroads into that potentially vast Asian market, and this time he was taking aim at the biggest prize of all. Hong Kong.

Chapter Nineteen

The Wild, Wild East

With a combined population of over seven million people living within 427 square miles, Hong Kong was the premier financial centre in the Asia-Pacific region. The city state pulsed to the tune of risk and speculation, and never more so than at its two racecourses. Sha Tin in the New Territories opened in 1978 and races every Sunday during the season between September and April. With a crowd capacity of nearly 80,000 people, it stages the biggest races of the year, including the Hong Kong Derby and the prestigious Longines International meeting before Christmas. The smaller but more atmospheric Happy Valley, right in the centre of the island, races mainly on Wednesday evenings under floodlights and opened in the age of empire in 1845.

Since the handover at midnight on June 30th, 1997, the People's Republic of China has been happy to keep the decadent racecourses open as long as the betting revenues continue to flow and as long as the former Royal Hong Kong Jockey Club continues to act as monopoly gambling provider.

The HKJC, as it became, has enjoyed almost unprecedented power in the colony, both socially and financially, ever since its incorporation in 1884. By the end of the 20th century, the Club was presiding over annual revenues from the eight-month racing season in excess of HK$10 billion, and contributing the equivalent of £405 million a year to public and charitable projects. Yet, running alongside that legal Hong Kong gaming industry, there was a parallel black market worth up to HK$30 billion or HK$40 billion per annum.

Victor Chandler reckoned it was high time that both the HKJC and the illegals faced a bit of legitimate competition. Why shouldn't their captive punters enjoy the option of trading with a recognised offshore bookmaking firm? One with a long history and reputation able to offer a wider range of markets than the HKJC, and one that would free them from the necessity of taking their custom underground? He sought the opinion of Jason Webber at the multinational law firm Slaughter and May, who'd had an office in Hong Kong since 1974. Webber, who "was about five-foot two-inches tall and a London cabbie's son, took notes at the meeting in Greek because he said it wasn't testing enough for him otherwise." His advice was that it would not be breaking the law were Victor Chandler International to open an office in Hong Kong as long as no bets were taken there on site and locals were merely advised of the Gibraltar phone numbers and online service.

A VC office was duly set up in Causeway Bay, and in April 1998, there was a launch party attended by George Best, supposedly on the wagon at the time and still as much of a footballing legend in Hong Kong as he was in Britain. Unfortunately, rumours of his newfound sobriety turned out to be misplaced, and the 48 hours Victor spent in his company turned into a marathon of man management. "Mike was only about six weeks into the job and Harry Kwo was in charge of customer recruitment. He organised the party at the Shangri-La Hotel and I thought George would be a good guest of honour. I first met him in the Dover Castle, back in the Marylebone era, and I liked him.

The party was costing us a lot of money. There were 150 people invited and Mike and I were in a suite at the Peninsula having dinner with customers for a week leading up to it. Tickets were changing hands on the black market, especially when it got out that George was attending personally. Mike went out to the airport to meet him and his wife, and when all the other passengers had disembarked and there was no sign of them, he assumed they must have missed the plane. Then, finally, he came out with a luggage trolley. Mike went to take it from him only for George to say that he needed it to lean on, otherwise he'd fall over. His wife, Alex, said that he hadn't slept at all on the plane and that he'd drunk five bottles of Chablis on the way over. We were meant to be having dinner with him that evening in the Chinese restaurant in the Peninsula, and all the food had been ordered beforehand. But halfway through, George did a Jeffrey Bernard and fell face first into his plate." At that point, Victor feared the worst, but the next day, Best was on top form, doing TV interviews, signing dozens of autographs and generally charming everyone. But the following day – the day of the big party – he was down again, and demanding more money. "We were paying him £20,000 in cash. He'd had half upfront – and first-class plane tickets – and he was going to get the rest when it was over. He said 'I want the other half now.' So Mike got up and got a pair of scissors and cut the other £10,000 in half. 'You can have the rest when you leave,' he said. 'But you'll have to stick the notes back together.' Best reluctantly accepted it, but I could see the warning signs. 'Tonight you must not leave his side,' I told Mike, 'and you must keep him away from the bar, at all costs.'"

The party began with Victor making a speech, something he never enjoyed, and then he had to tour every table chatting to the high rollers and performing a traditional 'Yam Seng,' or Chinese toast. Best, meanwhile, was meant to sign 100 footballs and kick them into the audience but, when Victor looked up, he saw the footballer heading to the bar before dinner had even begun and Mike Carlton running after him. "What shall I do?" he asked Victor, desperately. "He's signed four or five and then he fell asleep during your speech, and now he wants a drink." "Go back in there and sign them yourself," came the reply.

After the film show, it was Best's turn to go up on stage. Despite his already considerable inebriation, "he made a fantastic speech and charmed everyone again, posing for photos with all the kids." He then proceeded to kick the balls into the crowd with all his old flair, ecstatic guests catching them, and Victor realised he was "sweating with relief."

But it wasn't over yet. Harry Kwo had organised a block booking at a nightclub, and when they all got there, the Kung Fu star Jackie Chan was sitting with his entourage at the next table, and they all wanted their pictures taken with George Best too.

For the final day of the visit, Barclays Bank had organised a junket for Best in Stanley Harbour and laid on the best food and drink. They'd even provided a ski boat for Alex. "You've got to be down here at 11.30am," we told him before we all went to bed. But, of course, when midday came and went, there was no sign of George, and when Mike Carlton went up to his room to investigate, he discovered he'd ordered more bottles of Chablis on room service and was lying insensible on the bed. Mike had to ring the expectant bankers and tell them that, unfortunately, "George has eaten something that disagreed with him and won't be able to make it."

The next day, they all saw Best and his wife onto a plane back to London, relief that the trip was over soured by the £40,000 bill that the middleman Harry Kwo presented Victor with for the nightclub. It seemed that Jackie Chan's party had put their tab on the Chandler account.

It was around the time of the Hong Kong party that Victor's new aide-de-camp and Far Eastern emissary Peter Beaton-Brown joined the firm. The 32-year-old was Victor's second cousin and, in his own words, had spent "several years always nagging Victor for a job." His nickname, 'Butch,', had been bestowed by "Old Man Chandler, Victor's Uncle Charlie, after he put his hand on my mum's tummy when she was pregnant and felt me kick him hard."

By the late 1990s, Victor had decided he needed a polished and presentable number two with Far Eastern experience, much as Jean Bouquin had been looking for somebody "charming, sensible and bi-lingual" to work in his Boulevard Saint-Germain menswear shop in Paris in 1970. Butch, like Victor in his Parisian phase, was charming and sensible – sort of – and if not exactly proficient in Cantonese, he did have a good working knowledge of Hong Kong from the three years he'd spent there in the employ of a boutique finance house. "All ex-pats drinking pink gin and reading the *Racing Post* with the *Evening Mail* in the Captain's Bar of the Mandarin Hotel."

Butch used to get teased remorselessly and called 'Filth' (Failed in London, tried Hong Kong). He admitted he had a lot to learn about bookmaking and racing when he began, and he was the butt of many a good-natured joke by the racecourse team in the UK. One day, they were in the car on their way to the races when Butch looked up and asked Steve Wilson if the firm had any representation at Steeple Downs? Steve looked across at Bill Tye and smiled. Bill smiled back. "No, Butch," said Steve. "I don't believe we do. But maybe we should. They could be your pitches and you could go there whenever the racing's on." As the grins broadened, Butch realised they were winding him up, and they duly explained that Steeple Downs was not a real racecourse but only a virtual racecourse used for a betting shop computer game. He took it well. Butch's new VCI role was primarily as a greeter, deputed, in Victor's absence, to look after the high-rolling clients in London and Asia, and to try and recruit new customers for the firm. In Hong Kong, it kicked off with a particularly delicate task. He had to meet and entertain another launch party guest. A retired sportsman every bit as famous as George Best and a man who had been known to reduce owners, trainers and Stewards of the Jockey Club to gibbering wrecks. Lester Piggott.

To meet Lester, who was 62 in 1998, is to encounter immense charisma. A lifelong friend of several generations of the Chandler family, he smiles and nods and shakes hands politely. But the great jockey – still trim, still sharp, still deaf – doesn't bother with superficial chit chat. You talk, he listens, and you suspect he's thinking what an idiot you are.

The trainer Captain Ryan Price was once so infuriated by Lester's general foxiness that he tried to shunt him off the road at a roundabout near Findon in Sussex. He didn't succeed. Lester Piggott has encountered every imaginable kind of pressure in his personal and professional life, from irate trainers and punters, to death threats and a term of imprisonment, and none of it has broken him.

The Long Fellow has been a regular visitor to the racecourses of the Far East, where he enjoys God-like status. Yet what was perhaps Lester's finest hour as a jockey in Hong Kong came not in some celebrated classic race, but in a run-of-the-mill contest at Happy Valley that would have meant little to the average punter. But to the owner, trainer and gambler Ivan Allan, whose horses Lester used to ride at Henry Cecil's stable in Newmarket in the 1980s, it was a million-dollar affair.

Allan, who was born in Malaysia in 1941, was a very wealthy man with interests in property as well as the Hong Kong form book which he owned. He was betting heavily with the illegal bookmakers, and was going for a touch on a moderate 10-furlong handicapper at odds of 10-1 or better. It was the early 1990s and Lester, still a few years shy of final retirement, took the reins. Allan had assured him that as his horse was guaranteed to stay every yard of the trip, he should jump out of the stalls, kick on early and try to make it a proper test of stamina. Imagine Allan's horror then when the rider completely ignored his instructions, taking a pull when the stalls opened and virtually anchoring his mount in last place for the first half of the race.

Lester still had only two or three behind him as they made the turn out of the back straight, by which point the infuriated Allan had kissed his investment goodbye. But 20 seconds later, despair had given way to elation as he saw Lester, all guns blazing, come with a brilliantly timed run on the outside that, like Geoff Lewis's gamble that summer day at Sandown, carried him from last to first place inside the final two furlongs.

There was a photo-finish, but the verdict went Lester's and Ivan Allan's way, and that night there was a big celebratory dinner. At the climax of the evening, Allan was presented with a brown paper parcel. Inside it was a blown-up version of the photo showing Allan's horse just shading it on the line. Underneath, Lester had written 'Did you ever doubt me?' Allan flashed him a look that said 'yes…but no.' Piggott just smiled.

Allan lived dangerously, and one day he was shot at his home in Singapore when he opened the front door and was confronted by an irate gambler who believed the owner-trainer had double-crossed him. As he lay on the ground, blood running from the wound in his chest, his devout Catholic mother dropped to her knees, clutching her crucifix and exhorted him to pray for deliverance. "Mum," gasped Allan, who was terrified of his mother. "I don't need deliverance. I need an ambulance." Fortunately, he made a full recovery, and the following year, Lester accompanied him on a trip to Malaysia, and this time it was Piggott's turn to have a brush with mortality. As he sat in the weighing room at Penang racecourse, getting changed for the next race, a gunman walked in and shot dead the Malaysian champion jockey who was changing right next to him. Presumably one photo-finish that went the wrong way, but not exactly an everyday occurrence at Kempton or Sandown Park, even in Darby Sabini's day.

Getting to know this tough, canny and complex genius had never been easy, not even for men who were officially close to him, like Ivan Allan, Charles St George, Sir Peter O'Sullevan and Victor Chandler. Now it was to be a learning experience for Butch too. Things didn't get off to a propitious start. "So, Lester?" Butch enquired politely in the bar of the Mandarin Hotel. "Did you know Charles St George well?" "Who is this c…?" Lester is meant to have responded, addressing Victor over Butch's shoulder.

Things didn't improve when Butch called on Lester one day at his house in Newmarket. A friendly and evidently very capable woman served them coffee and biscuits, with Lester stamping his feet on the floor each time he wanted a refill. "She seems very nice, Lester," said Butch. "Does she come in every day?" "That's Susan, you idiot," replied the jockey. Poor Butch. How was he to know that, in spite of leading long and independent lives, the first Mrs Piggott still sometimes shared Lester's modest bungalow abode.

Victor assured Butch that Lester could be tricky with everyone, himself included. Like the time when VC was in Hong Kong and took Piggott and Ivan Allan out to dinner one night at the Mandarin Hotel. "I met Lester beforehand in the bar. I'd brought a box of cigars over with me from England as a special present for Ivan. While we were chatting, I left them on the bar stool. But when Ivan opened the box at the end of the meal we saw that several of them were missing. We both knew at once who had to have them. 'Have a cigar, Lester,' I said, simultaneously reaching across and pulling back his jacket to reveal the missing Cohibas sitting snugly in his inside pocket. 'Oh, look,' I said. 'You've got some already.' Lester just ginned. Ivan shook his head, and we all laughed."

Learning how to handle Lester Piggott was one thing. Dealing with the uninvited guests who turned up at the Victor Chandler office in Causeway Bay one day in 2001 was quite another matter. "It was mid-August, about 10pm local time," remembers Butch. "I was staying in the Mandarin Hotel, but that evening I was working late in our office, which was on the 13th floor of a shiny new building overlooking the yacht club. All of a sudden, half a dozen Chinese men walked in as if from nowhere. They all had long hair, T-shirts and tattoos on their arms." The office manager, an expatriate Englishman called Murray Burton, guessed at once who the intruders were. They were members of triad gang 14K (the number referring to the 14 members of a Kuomintang anti-communist 'action group' formed in 1945 or, if you prefer, to their old Hong Kong headquarters on 14 Kowloon Road), one of the biggest and most dangerous criminal organisations in the world. The triads "kicked all of the other people out of the office," recalls Butch, "and just left me in there with Murray and the Chinese secretary. She's busy talking to them for several minutes, so I asked her what she was saying. 'I was asking whether they'd like tea or coffee,' she replies. 'I'm not sure that's important, just now,' I said." What they were really there for was to deliver a message. 'Tell Victor Chandler to stay out of Hong Kong...or else.' The terrified Englishman, trying to play for time, rang Victor in London. "It was about half past two back home. He just listens to what I'm telling him and then says, 'Welcome to the family business.' Can you believe it? 'Just tell them I'll be in touch later,' he said. He seemed pretty nonchalant about it to me."

In reality, Victor was feeling anything but nonchalant. He had been advised that the triads were more than likely to kidnap Butch and take him up to the New Territories. Their specialty was chopping bits off their hostages with a meat cleaver, thumbs one day, fingers the next, toes the day after that, and then they'd post them back to Victor in London or Gibraltar and keep up the deliveries until they got paid. He'd made arrangements for eventualities like this, but he wasn't about to reveal his next move over the phone. But while Butch and Murray Burton continued to do their best to fend off the visitors, who "were shouting in my face one minute and sprawling around on our office furniture, flicking the TV on and off the next," he made a call. To a private security firm called Penumbra, whose services he'd been appraised of by "a very impressive ex-secret serviceman called Charles Webb, who was the senior partner." Within 40 minutes, a people-carrier arrived at the Causeway Bay office block and out jumped "half a dozen men. Some Chinese police, some private security, and all very tough," who ran into the building and took the lift up to the 13th floor, where they managed to 'persuade' the triads to leave and no guns or knives were drawn.

The immediate drama had been contained, but Victor understood that it was still an extremely volatile situation: at that moment it was no bigger than even money that Butch wouldn't be roughed up again or kidnapped within days. Some big punters may have welcomed Victor as an exciting addition to the Far Eastern gambling party, and assorted lesser contacts may have been friendly on the surface. But the reality was that, as far as the triads and their overlords in Macau were concerned, the English gentleman bookie was an interloper whose attempts to recruit high-rolling customers were depriving them of the commission they enjoyed from the region's illegal trade. They weren't about to tolerate his presence unless a tribute was paid, and their collection methods were straight out of the Dutch Schultz and 'Legs' Diamond playbook from Prohibition-era New York.

In the run-up to the Chinese takeover in 1997, Macau had been racked by the so-called Casino Wars, as different triad gangs – whose activities also included prostitution, drugs, illegal bookmaking and loan sharking – battled for supremacy. A police chief's car was blown up and 42 gang members murdered in broad daylight. Many of them on the orders of the triad 14K boss Wan Kuok-Koi, commonly known as Broken Tooth, a flashy dresser who loved long, late nights and casino gambling. In 1999, Broken Tooth had been jailed for 10 years, though he was said to still direct triad affairs from his prison cell on Coloane Island.

The Chinese had attempted to clean up the former Portuguese colony and crack down on the most blatant criminality while also liberalising the ageing casino industry, which resulted in a massive influx of foreign capital. Whereas Macau received three million visitors in 2001, by 2011 it would be welcoming more like 25 million, many of them drawn to the massive new casino resorts like the 550,000 square foot Venetian Macau, built by Sheldon Adelson's Sands Corporation of Las Vegas. The old backstreet atmosphere, along with many of the pink and yellow colonial-era houses, was set to become a thing of the past. But at the time of Butch's encounter with triad 14K, American Disneyfication had yet to fully take effect. The rackets continued to thrive, less visibly than in the past maybe, but not gone, and local shareholders continued to jealously guard their interests.

Victor's first priority was to get Butch out as fast as possible. Penumbra handled the exfiltration in classic MI6 manner. To confuse the enemy, Butch was booked on four different planes out of Hong Kong and into four different hotels, before being smuggled out to the airport on the train service from Central and on to a London flight. Then a few weeks later, Victor flew out to Hong Kong and went to the Peninsula Hotel, where he was told to wait for a call to be summoned.

The most powerful businessman in Hong Kong and Macau was the property and infrastructure magnate Li Ka-Shing, but for decades the official gambling Mr Big had been Dr Stanley Ho, the billionaire founder of SJM Holdings and, prior to the Chinese takeover, controller of 70 per cent of Macau's gambling business. Ho, who died in May 2020, aged 98, fathered 16 children, and "his son Robert and daughter Pansy were pupils at Millfield back in 1969," Victor recalled. "He was a most extraordinary man. Eighty-six years old when I first met him, and totally deaf, yet on to his fourth wife. The thing he really loved was ballroom dancing, especially the tango."

For a rampant capitalist, Stanley Ho was on remarkably good terms with the Communist authorities, the two sides having pragmatically worked out what they could offer each other. Even in 2001, Ho's Lisboa Casino was looking tired and old hat, a bit like a 1950s Blackpool nightclub complete with spongy carpets and stale cigarette smoke. In 2007, Dr Ho and his new US and Chinese partners would unveil the Gran Lisboa, the tallest building in Macau and the most outrageously kitsch and over the top casino-hotel in the world, with over 800 gaming tables and 1,000 slot machines.

But long before the Gran Lisboa opened its doors, the real behind-the-scenes power in the Macau gambling fraternity had passed to a junket operator called Martin Chang (not his real name), who organised trips for big hitters, just like the jaunts fronted by George Raft when the American Mafia bought the Colony Club in London in 1965. Victor had been briefed that Chang was not only a casino big shot, but a leading triad with a controlling influence among the illegal bookmakers, and that he was most likely to have been the man who sent the deputation to the VCI office on Causeway Bay. If Victor wanted to remain safely open for business in Hong Kong, Mr Chang would have to be appeased, and so Penumbra "talked to people on the street" to let them know that the Englishman would like to meet. When the call came, Victor was told to take a helicopter. He was met at the heliport in Macau by a Mercedes. "Is the car bulletproof?" he asked the driver. 'No, sir,' he said. 'It's bombproof.' The doors were so heavy that I couldn't open them."

Martin Chang and his people put Victor up in the Presidential Suite in the Landmark Hotel, which had been used by the Portuguese for the formal handover to China. "No one had ever actually stayed in it before," recalls Victor. "It had all been done up in the most fantastically bad taste, with more gold leaf than you've ever seen in your life."

The big meeting was scheduled to take place the following morning in a private casino and high-rise apartment block catering exclusively to gambling high rollers. Stanley Ho had retained a share, but he'd been obliged by the Chinese to divest himself of some of his casino holdings and the club had since been acquired by Martin Chang, who had big plans for it.

Throwaway as ever, Victor may have seemed on the outside, but he was taking no chances and had hired a personal bodyguard called 'Goose,' an ex-British paratrooper and SAS member who had fought at the Battle of Goose Green in the Falklands War. Goose, who was recommended by Charles St George's son David, who had a security business in Dubai, was about five-foot eight but "as strong as they come," and he arrived with a small rucksack on his back. As two of Martin Chang's men ushered the visitors into the lift, they opened their jackets to offer a glimpse of the guns they were carrying in their shoulder holsters. One of them cockily asked Goose what his favourite weapon was. "Grenades," said Goose, fingering his rucksack. After that, the two triads remained silent.

When they got up to Chang's office, Victor found himself greeted warmly by a man who "was very thin, about five-foot tall, pockmarked and with very bad dress sense." Despite his loud check suits and Dr Fu Manchu moustache, Martin Chang was not just some pantomime villain. As well as owning all the slot machines in Macau, he also owned most of the pawn shops – said to be the most profitable in the world – and explained to Victor that his minder 'Paul' (another one), who bizarrely had a daughter at Roedean, could arrange anything. A hint perhaps that among his other talents, Paul could arrange an unfortunate accident or disappearance.

Chang told Victor all about his ideas for the club and how he was preparing for the laws to change so that he could make it the biggest and smartest casino address in Macau. The conversations carried on over dinner that evening where Victor was "the only one at the table without a gun." The wine was exceptional and from Chang's cellar in the building. They were served priceless bottles of Chateau Petrus 1947 and a magnum of Petrus 1961 but, to Victor's horror, some of the other diners then proceeded to water them down with Sweetex and Coca-Cola. "It was funny," he says. "It was life. China's not the Salvation Army. Unless you've seen it, you can hardly believe it."

Chang and his wife "were charming, and we got on well," and by the end of the night, Victor had heard all about their vision for their high-rollers club. (On a subsequent visit, he agreed to make an 'investment' of HK\$750 000, which was considered sufficient to allow his Causeway Bay office to continue trading free of harassment, at least in the short term).

Chang understood that a lot of the existing Macau casinos were outdated and that times were changing. He believed that Chinese gamblers would be interested in the more sophisticated slot machines available in the West and wondered if Victor could help him. Sensing the possibility of a really big deal, Victor went back to Gibraltar and he and Mike Carlton did a lot of research. "About three months later, we found out that the Sun International gaming group in South Africa had the best technology at the time. So we brought Peter Bacon (then one of Sun's executive directors, now the CEO) over to London and, after we'd built up a relationship, Mike negotiated a 10-year deal with him where, in return for the Martin Chang connection, we'd take 5 per cent of his profits. Peter sent a team of 25 people out to Macau to do a survey. Martin did his research and we were in line to get 5 per cent of his profits too."

Martin Chang wanted the new casino to be shamelessly Las Vegas, with Egyptian décor complete with sphinxes, pyramids and pharaohs. All the work was done, and Sun International was going to get 25 per cent of the profits for running the slots. The parties then progressed to negotiating an exclusive arrangement for Sun to run all the slot machines in Macau, with VCI on 5 per cent of that transaction too. Things were going swimmingly, with Martin Chang in benign form and even laying on a special floor show for his new partners. As well as the private rooms, where rich and powerful men came to play baccarat, the club had a theatre and sometimes Chang would keep the band on after their act had finished and then get up on stage in his check jackets and do a whole Frank Sinatra or Dean Martin set. "He had a wonderful voice, and all the Sun International people came to be entertained there."

The big signing was meant to take place in Macau in early 2002, and "Sun organised a private plane from London to go over for it. It was as big a deal as ever could be imagined. We'd have had the Gran Lisboa as soon as it opened. We'd have had the lot, and Stanley Ho had personally approved it. But then we got a phone call in Gibraltar from Peter Bacon saying we must meet urgently. We went to see him in London and he said that Sun couldn't go ahead with the deal. 'Why on earth not?' I asked. 'You will make hundreds of millions.' 'We've had Kroll (the corporate investigation firm) look into Chang,' he said, 'and they've told us he's a leading member of a triad gang.' 'So?' I said. 'They pay their dues.' But there was no moving him. Mike and I looked at each other and I almost burst into tears. 'You're mad,' I said to Peter. 'You will not be able to do business in the Far East with that criteria,' but he wouldn't budge."

Victor then had the unenviable task of going back to Macau and telling Martin Chang face-to-face that they couldn't go through with it and the reason why. There were no choruses of Volare or New York, New York this time, and the brutal truth was that Victor's Hong Kong and Macau luck was running out.

In April 2002, VC was summoned to breakfast at the Regency Hotel with the head of security for the Hong Kong Jockey Club and told that the Chinese-backed government were about to pass a law making it illegal for any of its citizens to place a bet on racing, football, golf or whatever with anyone other than the officially sanctioned HKJC. At the time, the Club's gambling revenues accounted for approximately 11 per cent of the government's annual tax take, and henceforth "offshore robbers" could expect to be harshly treated. But what the HKJC man really wanted to say was that it wouldn't be him who would be coming after them. It would be the triads. It was meant to be "an absolutely private meeting with no pictures," but the next morning, Victor's photograph was on the front-page of the *South China Morning Post* along with a description of his 'illegal' activities. 'Victor Chandler gets warning from Jockey Club,' began the story. VC realised he'd been set up and was the victim of a not-so-subtle hint by the HKJC and tip-off to any triad bookie who didn't already know his name or the hotel he was staying in.

Accepting the inevitable, the company had to shut down the Causeway Bay office within weeks of the beginning of the 2002 World Cup in Japan and South Korea, making their staff redundant. They relocated their Far Eastern headquarters to Singapore where, according to Mike Carlton, "everything goes on under the surface," only to be forced to shut that down too when the Singapore authorities followed Hong Kong's lead, eventually ending up in Kuala Lumpur "with about 60 people doing customer service. The KL office is still there to this day, though a lot of the staff have moved to other locations." To an extent, though, the offices were already becoming superfluous as, once they'd got the gambling contacts and directed them to their offshore Gibraltar site, they no longer needed an actual presence in the various Asian locations. As the internet powered up, the new century was going to be all about online gambling rather than telephone betting, and whereas it might once have taken several hours for news of a market change to reach Hong Kong or Singapore, it would soon take no more than a few seconds.

The end of the Hong Kong office didn't mean the end of all Far Eastern reconnaissance. "Frank Irish, who was managing director of Michael Tabor's betting shops, wanted to explore a possible joint-venture in Vietnam. So Frank, Butch and I flew out to Singapore and then on to Ho Chi Minh City. Our contact was a local entrepreneur who owned the greyhound stadium in Cholon and also ran the Tote betting concession, the country's only legitimate way to gamble. He wanted to film the dog races and then stream them over the internet and sell the pictures to the major Asian bookies."

The track was about an hour's drive out of the city, going west towards the Cambodian border. It wasn't much to look at. "A concrete bunker with stone benches, newly built to prison standards," but, as Victor discovered, it was packed with punters. "It's Vietnam's one and only greyhound stadium and the whole place is run by an expatriate Aussie called Jimmy, who's got a moustache and a pair of what must be 20-year-old Dunlop trainers. He used to race greyhounds in Australia, and he trained the fastest dog ever to run there. He does everything in Vietnam, including the commentaries, and he wanted our advice on upgrading the racing and the betting. 'You'd love it over here, boys,' he kept saying. 'The local girls are very nice.'"

Victor said that what he'd really like to do would be to see the kennels, so Jimmy arranged a hotel stay for them overnight and then, the following day, he drove them up into the jungle. "The kennels were all very clean and comfy looking, with about 150 greyhounds, but the heat and humidity was stifling, and not surprisingly most of the dogs were lying on their backs with their paws in the air." The travellers also learned that all the dogs had two names, running under one name the one week, and another the next, encouraging the gullible punters to believe there was a greater pool of talent and form to pore over than was really the case.

They made the return journey to Ho Chi Minh City by hydrofoil from the nearest town, passing beaches on one side and offshore oil rigs on the other. "The people were all unbelievably friendly," said Victor, but first-hand research convinced him that conditions in Vietnam were hardly conducive to sustaining competitive dog racing. Even with the sweetener of government legislation to assist the betting side, it wasn't an enterprise he wanted to get involved in, especially as all transactions seemed to take place in cash, with no facility to transfer money offshore. But what all those eventful Far Eastern journeys – to Singapore, Thailand, Hong Kong, Macau, Malaysia and elsewhere – did convince him, was that the gambling-mad populations of south-east Asia would become *the* core business for any wised-up 21st century bookmaking firm with more than bread and butter ambitions. Especially with millions more yearning to join them in mainland China as the technology improved and restrictions on transferring money were lifted.

Those big hitters didn't only bet in the Far East either. Sometimes they came to London. One summer night, not long after the Vietnam adventure, Victor got a call from Sotirios at Les Ambassadeurs. A high-rolling Chinese gambler had taken a private room at the club and was playing punto banco, the American variation of baccarat, for £100,000 a shoe. Jimmy Wu (not his real name), who owned a moped factory in China, was a former Kung Fu movie star who had since gone into the illegal bookmaking business and was a regular punter with VC on football. Wu had a lot of cash on him, but no credit line at Les A. He had assured Sotirios that Victor would vouch for him, so "I signed a guarantee for £200,000. We went to see him there at lunchtime and he ordered a peppered steak and a Dover Sole and proceeded to eat the steak with the sole on top. He played on his own throughout the afternoon, and then in the evening I got another call from him asking me to come down and have dinner with him." Wu wanted, nay, insisted that Victor play alongside him to "change his luck." VC, who was at home in Hamilton Terrace and had been about to go out to dinner with Carole, Butch and Butch's wife Caroline, agreed, and all four of them set off for the West End. The superstitious Jimmy Wu was totally confident that the bookmaker's presence would change his fortunes… and it did.

Within seven or eight hands, which only lasted a few hours, Wu – who was sporting a Versace shirt, a £150,000 watch, a gold toothpick and a triad lucky necklace with 14 miniature Buddhas on it – was £100,000 in front, with Victor, starting from scratch, already up £75,000. "The casino had given us everything complimentary, delicious food, wine, champagne, the lot, thinking he (Jimmy Wu) could never get up," said Butch. "But he and Victor kept winning. Every time a card was turned over, he (Wu) would be busy fingering his necklace and shouting at the table. Victor kept giving me chips to put in Carole's and Caroline's handbags. By the time we left, they were full of them."

All in all, it was quite a night, and one confirming again Charlie Maskey's description of Victor as "a late-night clubs and gambling man," like his grandfather before him. Jimmy Wu took his winnings, and his bad teeth and lucky charm, and went back to Hong Kong, a celebrity hardly known outside the Far East. But, at the same time, another notorious gambler in Victor's orbit was making waves much closer to home.

Chapter Twenty

Sheriff Buffham

O n August 17th, 2001, the Jockey Club confirmed in somewhat elliptical terms that their controversial head of security Roger Buffham had been sacked. Allegations of serious misconduct, including sexual harassment, had been made by members of his staff, who were themselves under strict instructions from their employers not to discuss the matter with the press.

At the time of his dismissal, the 53-year-old Buffham – a short, rather portly man with a self-important, self-satisfied air – had few friends left at the Jockey Club's Portman Square offices. "If anyone had suggested throwing him a leaving party, it could comfortably have been held in a telephone box," according to one jaundiced ex-colleague.

It had all been very different when Buffham was first recruited by the Club in 1992. He was a former bomb disposal expert who had been awarded an MBE for his work in Northern Ireland, where he had also served as an undercover operative in the shadowy world of military intelligence ('a contradiction in terms' in the view of the comedian and satirist Peter Cook).

After leaving the army, Buffham ran his own private security business, becoming weirdly entangled with Dr Wouter Basson, the South African cardiologist and apartheid regime's so-called Dr Death. In the 1980s, Basson had been recruited by the South African Premier PW Botha to head the country's chemical and biological warfare programme, and at his trial in Pretoria 20 years later, he was accused of being behind scores of attacks and assassinations of anti-apartheid figures. Roger Buffham, described in court as "a British secret agent," was said to have supplied Basson with a robot used to disarm bombs, and protective clothing including bombproof suits. The prosecution wanted to call him as a witness, but he declined to travel to the Republic fearing for his safety.

The most popular Jockey Club security chief had been Brigadier Henry Green, who set up Racecourse Security Services in 1962 and brought in the ex-Scotland Yard Detective Inspector Bob Anderson who, along with the Irishman Detective Superintendent Terence O'Connell, had taken down the Bill Roper doping gang. A former Guards officer and MI5 man, the Brigadier got on well with the bookmakers, including Victor's father, and boasted that he could "spot a scallywag at a hundred yards."

As a more austere ex-military type, who had also been a spook, Buffham was meant to dispense with Green's clubbable approach and bring an outsider's sternly dispassionate eye to bear on Turf misdeeds. Yet, in the end, it was precisely his ignorance of racing and its age-old ways that brought about his downfall. He displayed little love of the sport nor interest in its history and characters, and negligible understanding of gambling. Instead of the eagle-eyed Sheriff picking off the bad apples one by one, he came across as a sort of Witchfinder General determined to train a howitzer on an entire industry. In the process, all manner of individuals, some of them innocent, others neither wholly good nor wholly bad, became temporarily caught up in his web. Victor Chandler being one of them.

Buffham spent his first few years at Portman Square re-organising his department. The Jockey Club had been embarrassed by their failure to nail anyone after two proven and high-profile dopings at Doncaster in September 1990. A subsequent TV documentary claimed to have tracked down the doper, nicknamed 'The Needleman,' who had gained access with impunity to racecourse stables. Buffham introduced

CCTV cameras into all racecourse stabling areas. He also set up a special security hot-line, similar to the anonymous phone link for informants in Northern Ireland, and issued a new headmasterly protocol warning all jockeys and trainers about the possible consequences of associating with "undesirables." By late 1996, the security department, Buffham's hand firmly on the tiller, were in the early stages of what was to become a labyrinthine investigation into possible race fixing. Events the following year gave a powerful impetus to their inquiries.

On March 7th, 1997, a horse called Avanti Express, who was trained by Charlie Egerton and ridden by Jamie Osborne (nicknamed the 'Corduroy Cavalier'), drifted from 4-5 to 5-4 before being pulled up in a novice hurdle at Exeter. Three weeks later, a Josh Gifford-trained runner called Lively Knight was sent off the 1-7 favourite for a Plumpton novice chase, but finished a well-beaten second. The duo were both routinely dope tested and, six months later, the Jockey Club revealed that they had tested positive to the fast-acting tranquilliser drug ACP. It was time for the police to be called in, but if anyone had expected that some sage Inspector Morse or Jane Tennison would be in charge of the inquiry, they were disappointed. Unlike Bob Anderson and Terry O'Connell in 1962, the London-based detectives turned out to be even more ignorant of racing and ham-fisted in their methods than the man who was supplying them with their list of suspects.

On January 27th, 1998, Jamie Osborne and his fellow jockeys Leighton Aspell, who had ridden Lively Knight, and Dean Gallagher, who hadn't ridden in either the Exeter or Plumpton races, were arrested and then bailed after melodramatic dawn raids. The following day, the Jockey Club suspended their licences, effectively making it impossible for them to earn a living, though, after a barrage of criticism, the licences were returned on February 4th.

Ray Butler, an unemployed Irish builder living in Cricklewood in North London, was also arrested, and between January 30th and February 13th, three punters – Jason Moore, John Matthews and Glen Gill, all the subject of Buffham's suspicions – were added to the charge sheet.

On April 23rd, the distraught Aspell, who knew nothing of what went on at Plumpton and should never have been arrested in the first place, was told that he was to be discharged without further questioning. But there was no such luck for Osborne and Gallagher, who were first kept waiting until June and then told their bail was to be extended again until October. Osborne feared that his career was being slowly but systematically destroyed by ill-informed insinuations. He had tried to convince his inquisitors that he would have had to be insane to take the mount on Avanti Express if he had known it was doped. In a jump race, run at speed, it would be tantamount to committing suicide. But Buffham and the police weren't just looking into Osborne's or Gallagher's behaviour in the saddle. They wanted to know about their social lives too, including their and other jockeys' involvement with Mr Brian Wright. A man with one of the fattest address books in racing containing the names and telephone numbers of numerous top owners, trainers, riders and bookmakers. One of whom was about to become the object of Roger Buffham's special attention.

"It was early June 1998," remembers Victor. "The World Cup in France was about to happen. The firm had yet to make the full move to Gibraltar, but we were already looking into expanding the offshore office. Carole, Mike Carlton and I had been down there in southern Spain for about two or three weeks. We weren't residents then. We were staying in a hotel at San Roque. Obviously, I'd read all about who'd been arrested, the dawn raids and the rest of it. Well, one morning we were having breakfast on our balcony and Mike was there too, when suddenly my brother-in-law Steven, my younger sister Debbie's husband, rings me up from London. He said the police were at his door because he was a keyholder of our house in St John's Wood and they wanted to search it. It was actually very brave of him to ring me because the police had told him not to. I tried to phone my lawyer, but he wasn't in, and to begin with we couldn't find him.

A few hours later, I got a call from this detective who sounded as if he was auditioning for a part in The Sweeney. "'You know what this is all about, don't you?' he says. 'No,' I said. 'I've no idea. But I presume it's something to do with the racing scandal.' 'We found a large quantity of money in your wife's wardrobe,' he says to me. 'Can you explain where it came from?' 'I've no idea,' I said. It seems it was in Carole's underwear drawer. She was sitting next to me on the balcony. 'Have you been keeping cash in your knicker drawer?' I asked her. She nodded. 'How much?' 'About £40,000,' she said. '£40,000?' I said. It was the first I'd heard of it. 'Where did you get £40,000 from?' 'That's my running away money,' she said. 'I keep it there for a rainy day.' Then she reminded me of the time Barney Curley told me to back a horse for him, and Carole organised a team of her friends to go round all the betting shops in Hampstead and St John's Wood. She got maps out and they planned it like a bank robbery. The horse won and she always said it was one of the most enjoyable things she'd ever done. 'I just put my share away for safekeeping,' she said. 'Everyone has expenses.' Of course, that didn't satisfy the detective, but we did cry with laughter about it afterwards. By then we'd found my lawyer, and then he phoned another top lawyer called Henry Milner and explained the situation. We left it for a day, and then I flew back to London, half expecting to be arrested at the airport, and went through everything with my solicitor Lee Goldsmith."

It was clear to Victor's legal advisors that the Met, egged on by Roger Buffham, were going to infer that there had been a conspiracy to fix the outcome of the Exeter and Plumpton races, with the arrested jockeys and punters in league with the gambling Mr Big – Brian Wright – and his bookmaker, Victor Chandler. But other than one £600 hedging bet on Stormhill Pilgrim, phoned through to the course by Linhope Street, there was no evidence of any financial profit for the firm from the two races, and "after about four hours of conversations, Lee was adamant that there was absolutely nothing for the police to make an issue of."

The conference took place in Lee Goldsmith's office in Jermyn Street, with Henry Milner, Mike Carlton and Victor's old friend Roger Barby all in attendance. Barby, who at one time had been a criminal barrister, urged Lee Goldsmith to get a copy of the search warrants the police had used to gain access to Hamilton Terrace and the Linhope Street office. He thought they were probably illegal unless they could prove Victor was some kind of international drug dealer. "In due course, I went voluntarily to Charing Cross police station for an interview, which was totally pathetic. We sat and talked for about 10 minutes and then they said 'What else is there? Oh well, we'd better keep you here for another half an hour for the sake of appearances.' And for the rest of the time we talked about racing. They asked me if I knew Osborne, Gallagher and the other jockeys, and I said, yes, of course I did. It was an extremely sociable sport back then. How could I not know them? They'd picked up this letter I'd written to James Osborne, George Osborne's uncle, who is actually a punter and John Aspinall's half-brother. There was also an invitation to an exhibition at the Osborne Gallery in Motcomb Street. The detective seemed to think that James, and Jamie Osborne the jockey, were one and the same person and that the letter proved a sinister link between us.

They asked me if I knew John Matthews, and I said 'yes,' I did. He'd been a customer of ours for four or five years. Then they wanted to know if I knew Brian Wright, and I said 'yes,' he'd been a customer of the firm for over 30 years, going back to my father's day, and I'd known him ever since I'd been in racing. All the big bookmakers knew him, and half the racing fraternity knew him too. He used to hold court at Newmarket, sitting outside on those benches by the rails. He had his coterie of admirers, like Waggy and 'Jimmy The One,' and all the top jockeys used to come out and talk to him. He was someone you couldn't miss. He never put his bets on in person. His son, Brian junior, or Jimmy or his son-in-law would come up and do it for him.

We'd even see him at Annabel's during Royal Ascot week. But in all that time, I never saw him at a jump meeting, and as far as knowing him socially, I never had breakfast, lunch, tea or dinner with the man. In 1994, I had a horse in training with Alex Scott in Newmarket. We were in the Hole In The Wall pub near Cambridge one evening and he (Wright) was there and he came over to ask me if I'd heard that Alex had been shot by a groom at his stud. But that was it. When it came to his betting, he used to lose far more than he won, and I often used to have enormous trouble getting paid by him. When someone like Michael Tabor backed a winner, you didn't get it back, but with Brian Wright, you'd know he'd back another two or three losers that day or the next. But he still kept on betting, because gambling was his life. No one immediately thought of drugs, though. There were so many people around at that time with loads of cash from property, the City, advertising, or whatever. But if he was really worth hundreds of millions, I must have been worth billions."

The police confiscated security tapes from the phones at Linhope Street and loads of diaries. 'You'll get all these back again,' Victor was told, but he never did. One or two of the items eventually finding their way, via Roger Buffham, into the hands of a BBC *Panorama* team. "They had taken away all kinds of odd things too, including some photographs of me on a boat in Hong Kong, and another of me and Richard Thomas together in an Italian restaurant along with two waiters and the chef. I'd got up and gone into the kitchen to thank them for the dinner, and the staff were all in there watching the racing on TV. The police seemed to think this was some sort of top-level confer-ence. It was all incredibly worrying and unpleasant for the staff who'd been frightened to death when they turned up, and it was extremely upsetting for my mother."

Not that Victor was just sitting back and taking it. Lee Goldsmith found that Roger Barby was quite right and that the search warrants were illegal and could only be obtained if the suspect was believed to be a drug smuggler. "Lee took counsel's opinion, and the QC Alun Jones said that we could sue the Metropolitan Police. But they'd taken Carole's car keys too, and as well as the money in her knicker drawer, they'd found a can of Mace in the glove compartment, which they said was the equivalent of having a firearm. The woman who lived opposite us in Hamilton Terrace had recently been mugged and beaten up, and the thieves took her car. One of my friends who lived locally had heard about it and bought these cans of Mace in Paris and handed them out to his women friends. The police said that they'd arrest Carole for possession if we didn't drop the charges against them. Nonetheless, the search warrant was a big issue, and Alun Jones was adamant. 'I want an apology from them,' he said, and we got one. I spent the most nerve-wracking day, sitting in Alun Jones's chambers, waiting for the Crown Prosecution Service to arrive at their decision, but when they did, I was told that I was only the second person ever to get an apology from the Met. They also returned the personal photographs and share-dealing records, and a total of £49,000 in cash."

As well as his encounters at Charing Cross police station, Victor met Roger Buffham one-to-one in the Churchill Hotel, not far from the Jockey Club headquarters in Portman Square. It brought back memories of Ted Robertson and Norris Butcher. "He spoke to me as if I was a naughty schoolboy. I'd like to have strangled him. There was all this talk about money laundering, but the sort of figures they were going on about couldn't possibly have gone through any book-maker's book. I'd had guidance from Lord Hartington [now the Duke of Devonshire and the former Jockey Club Senior Steward and first Chairman of the British Horseracing Board] and he'd been more than sympathetic and could see how stupid it all was. There have always been loads of grey areas in racing, but what really worried me was that someone like Buffham had got into such a powerful position in the first place. He was going around telling Christopher Spence (the JC Senior Steward) that we were all criminals and that racing was one big con-spiracy to cheat the punters. He (Spence) was very anti early on, but much more understanding once Lord Hartington had talked to him."

Victor may have been out of the security team's clutches, at least for the next 18 months, but the wider inquiry ploughed on regard-less. In the summer of 1998, Roger Buffham positioned himself in the commentator's eyrie at the top of the grandstand on Newmarket's July course in order to survey the betting ring through a high-pow-ered lens. Bill Tye remembers the bookies looking up and waving at him. But that August, the amiable starting price reporter Neal Wilkins, who had spent 25 years working for the *Sporting Chronicle* and the Press Association, became the latest man to be arrested. The dapper and moustachioed Wilkins, who felt his "only crime was to wear smart suits and smoke a nice cigar," used to make his own tissue, or form guide, on the day's racing, and sell it to bookmakers who hadn't done their homework. He was also accused by Buffham of inflating returns for bookie-punters when they were trying to execute a knock-out (forcing a horse's odds out and then attempting to back it at the bigger price with a rival firm), and simultaneously deflating starting prices at the behest of the big high street betting shop chains for whom no SP could ever be short enough.

Wilkins, who had suffered a brain haemorrhage the previous year, was charged with conspiracy to defraud, and bailed for six months, even though no evidence was presented to establish his guilt. After spending what he described as "a year in the wilderness," he was told that the case against him had been dropped and that he was official-ly discharged. By this time, he had lost his job with the Press Asso-ciation and was offered the post of racecourse PR man for the Victor Chandler firm in the UK. Companies like Ladbrokes, Hills and Coral all had their representatives who could be found in the press room and the unsaddling enclosure, distributing their firm's latest prices after every big race. Wilkins, nicknamed 'Lord Melbury' by Butch (due to a "nonsense moustache," which lent him an unfortunate resemblance to the aristocratic conman Lord Melbury, played by Michael Gwynne in *Fawlty Towers)*, joined their ranks. To Roger Buffham, this was proof of his collusion with Victor, who was meant to have employed him in order to shut him up.

August 1998 also saw the arrest of Adam Hodgson, a gardener who had been seen "acting suspiciously" at Exeter races on the day of the Avanti Express doping. Then a month later, on September 16th, the detectives heading the investigation brought in the man presumed to be their number one suspect. Brian Wright. The 52-year-old gambler, Irish born but London raised, who, as a shocked but enthralled racing public now discovered, rejoiced under the nicknames 'Uncle' and 'The Milkman', was officially arrested at Charing Cross police station. But only three months later, in the midst of fevered speculation on course and off, he was ruled out of the inquiry. There was a reason for that, as would become apparent three years later.

In October, Jamie Osborne was airily informed that he too was to be released without charge, but Dean Gallagher and the other five were bailed until December and then again until March 1999.

The millennium began with yet another slew of dramatic and contradictory developments as Sheriff Buffham's round-up continued. On January 8th, 2000, the jockeys Ray Cochrane and Graham Bradley were arrested. The 38-year old 'Brad' was a consummate rider and a cavalier, like Osborne, and had been involved in numerous run-ins with the authorities. Punters had a rather ambivalent attitude towards the Yorkshireman. They liked his cheek and applauded his style, especially when he was winning big races like the 1996 Champion Hurdle on Collier Bay. But some of them remembered his 1986 clash with Barney Curley, when the gambler accused him of stopping a horse called Robin Goodfellow at Ascot, and there were invariably mutterings when he was beaten on a short-priced favourite.

Also arrested, in an increasingly surreal climate, was the sociable ex-trainer Charlie Brooks, who had gone to Charing Cross police station of his own volition. He thought he might be able to help clarify a few details regarding Bradley, who was his former stable jockey. He was thinking in particular about a two-horse race at Warwick in November 1996, when Bradley rode the odds-on favourite Man Mood but pulled up halfway through, leaving the only other runner, Drumstick, to win at odds of 5-4. Man Mood had been booked for a wind operation the following week and they had tied his tongue down at Warwick, but it hadn't worked. Brooks explained that he had been out of the country at the time, only to be told that he too was being added to the charge sheet. (Some years later, Victor had an amusing encounter with Brooks in the French Horn in Sonning. "People must think I lead an eventful life," joked the Old Etonian, as he reminisced about his experiences in police custody. He was referring to the second time he was arrested in 2012 along with his wife Rebekah, the former News International chief executive and editor of *The Sun*. The couple, who were accused of conspiracy to pervert the course of justice in relation to the phone-hacking investigation, were acquitted at their trial in 2014. But not before Brooks was forced to explain why he had hidden a laptop and assorted DVDs in the underground car park at his London house. He said they contained his porn collection and that he was worried that they might be found by the police and leaked to the press, further embarrassing his wife).

The first intimations of alarm were now beginning to appear in the ranks of the Turf's ruling bodies, and four days after Brooks had been arrested, the British Horseracing Board, acting independently of the Jockey Club, wrote to the Crown Prosecution Service urging a speedy conclusion to the investigation. Later that month, concerns over the damage the inquiry was doing to racing's image were aired in a debate in the House of Lords.

On March 10th, 1999, on the eve of the Cheltenham Festival, Ray Cochrane and Dean Gallagher, who by now had been under arrest for nearly 14 months, were both released without charge. (Gallagher went on to win the 2002 Champion Hurdle, but also was subsequently banned twice for testing positive for cocaine. He retired from race riding in 2009). But Graham Bradley was re-bailed until April, while Butler, Hodgson and the three punters were officially charged with "conspiracy to defraud by administration of a performance-inhibiting drug."

Still the game of musical chairs continued. In April, Charlie Brooks was released without charge, but Bradley was formally accused of conspiracy to cheat in the Man Mood race, and the Jockey Club promptly revoked his licence. But then, like some plot reversal in *Alice In Wonderland*, the narrative changed once again, and on June 9th, it was reported that all charges against Bradley were to be dropped. What's more, he was informed by the JC that he was free to apply for his licence again.

By now it wasn't just racing's traditional supporters who were demanding answers. There had been 18 months of lurid headlines and arrests, with five jockeys charged at one point or another, but all of them eventually released without charge. Buffham's sack wasn't entirely empty, but the pressure was mounting on the bomb disposal expert, with the Jockey Club Senior Steward Christopher Spence and his colleagues beginning to shift uncomfortably in their chairs, anxious for the threat to be defused. Somebody had to end up behind bars, if only to justify all the trouble and expense, but Buffham presumably never thought it would be an ex-Metropolitan policeman.

In February 2000, Bob Harrington, a former Detective Sergeant turned private eye, was jailed for 18 months after being found guilty of trying to obtain money from Jamie Osborne in return for ensuring that no further action would be taken against him. Harrington had been in touch with an old colleague, DS Richard Wall, who was also part of the racing investigation and had leaked information to him. Wall left the Met himself a few years later, joining Roger Buffham in the unhappy, parallel world of Jockey Club security.

The Harrington case received front-page coverage in the *Racing Post*, and in January there was a banner headline proclaiming that Victor Chandler was "linked to the race-fixing plot." The story reported that Victor had been named in court as connected to both Dean Gallagher and Brian Wright, and that he "was supposed to have run a false book," on the Man Mood race. It was only when you read the whole article that you realised this was a claim by the accused, Bob Harrington, as part of his defence, rather than an undisputed statement of fact, but the initial impression was a damning one. Victor had no doubt that it was one of a series of stories fed deliberately to journalists who were already convinced by Roger Buffham. There was a particularly acidulous character working for the Post at the time called Andrew Sim, and Victor believed "Sim was Buffham's tool, and the police and the Jockey Club were leaking him stuff, and then he was writing these semi-snide articles."

Within 12 months, other journalists would be writing openly critical articles about Roger Buffham. On September 25th, 2000, Ray Butler, Adam Hodgson and the three punters – Jason Moore, John Matthews and Glen Gill – went on trial at Southwark Crown Court. It was the culmination of the longest-ever police and Jockey Club investigation into alleged racing corruption, and it ended ignominiously after three and a half weeks. The Judge, Christopher Elwen, ruled that there was no case to answer and set all five defendants free. The proceedings had cost an estimated £3 million.

Knowledgeable betting and racing figures following the progress of the trial and, expecting theatrical revelations, had been amazed by the flimsiness of the prosecution case. No concrete evidence was presented linking the defendants together in a conspiracy, and negligible proof that any of them had gained financially from the results. The impression most people took from the affair was of a police force painfully ignorant of the subject matter they were trying to investigate. Detective Constable Peter Kelly in particular was comprehensively filleted and barbecued in a masterful cross-examination by Jeremy Gompertz QC, who was representing Gill. The silver-haired barrister, who would go on to represent Dr David Kelly's family at the Hutton Enquiry, drew an admission from DC Kelly that his knowledge of racing matters was limited to say the least. Kelly's view, Gompertz advised the jury, seemed to be that anyone who opposed an odds-on chance in a three-horse race must be "either a lunatic or a fraudster." A position any sane bookmaker and gambling man would know to be imbecilic. Mr Justice Elwen clearly agreed. Significantly, Gompertz also reminded the jury that the indictment alleged a conspiracy to dope not "a conspiracy to back horses which someone else has doped."

The outcome was a huge blow to Roger Buffham's credibility and prestige. He may not have been responsible for the ignorance of the Metropolitan Police, but he had, as yet, failed to persuade the wider world to share his black and white view of the infamy rife throughout racing. Many in his position, chastened by such a setback, might have been expected to follow the post-war Prime Minister Clem Attlee's advice to a colleague who was told, after a series of annoying interventions in 1946, that "a period of silence on your part would be welcome." Buffham, though silent, was far from inactive.

At the end of December, the Jockey Club announced that it wanted access to the phone bills and betting accounts of all licensed individuals. Yet, in a rider seemingly designed to rein in their zealous security chief, the Club stressed that the use of any information gleaned was to be policed by a committee overlooking Roger Buffham's department.

The publicity that racing had been getting during Buffham's eight years on the job had been almost universally bad, with little in the way of positive gains to compensate for it. By this time, anyone with a cynical view of power politics (or who has read a few Shakespearean history plays) could have been forgiven for thinking that the high and mighty grandees of the Jockey Club were growing weary of their troublesome hitman and might have welcomed any developments that hastened his departure.

Was it entirely coincidental then that on July 1st, 2001, the man who seemed to be without a single ally or friend left on the racecourse was made aware of a serious, though as yet unspecified, allegation against him? Could it be that the old Ulster secret agent had fallen victim to precisely the kind of black op he might once have been responsible for devising? But if racing and the Jockey Club thought they'd heard the last of him, they were wrong. Less than 12 months later, race-fixing was back in the headlines against a backdrop that Roger Buffham claimed provided, at least, a partial vindication of his, so far, spectacularly unsuccessful pursuit of wrongdoers.

Chapter Twenty One

The Milkman

On June 14th, 2002, reporting restrictions were lifted on the trial of 16 men accused of cocaine smuggling. It was the conclusion of a six-year Customs and Excise investigation entitled Operation Extend, which had begun with the discovery of 599 kilos of coke with an estimated street value of £80 million on a fishing trawler called the Sea Mist in Cork in September 1996. A further 472 kilos of cocaine were seized three years later in a lock-up in Essex and on a farm in Middlesex.

In May 2000, seven men went on trial at Woolwich Crown Court accused of conspiracy to import and supply the drug. One of the accused was Brian Wright's son, Brian junior, or 'Briany' as he was known, who had been arrested at his home in Weybridge on February 12th, 1999. His father (who had been called into Charing Cross police station in connection with the race-fixing enquiry the previous September, only to be discharged three months later) was abroad at the time and, as of June 2002, was believed to be living in Northern Cyprus.

At a separate trial at Southampton Crown Court in 2001, the jockey Barrie Wright, no relation to Brian, was found not guilty of conspiracy to import cocaine with some of the Woolwich defendants. But, of serious interest to the racing community, his old friend Graham

Bradley, appearing as a character witness, testified that he and Barrie Wright had regularly passed on "privileged and sensitive information" (meaning news about horses' fitness, gallops and general stable wellbeing) to Brian Wright in return for money and other rewards.

The exact nature of those rewards, shocking to some, understandably tempting to others, included being entertained in Wright's box at Ascot and other racecourses, in his flat in Chelsea Harbour, at the adjoining Conrad Hotel, and at assorted West End nightclubs. These weren't monastic all-male occasions either. The hard riding boys from the weighing room, some of whom had played in a 1998 golf tournament Wright organised in Spain, could count on the presence of girls, sex, champagne and, if they so desired, stonking great lines of white powder. A very late 20th century spin on the kind of excesses that have tempted not only jockeys, but many other ordinary fallible human beings since time and horse racing began.

The Jockey Club Senior Steward Christopher Spence linked the revelations to the Roger Buffham race-fixing inquiry. He hoped people would now "appreciate why we did what we did….we couldn't publicise why we were taking the action at the time for obvious reasons." Yet, even at that moment, the Jockey Club's ex-head of security was subject to a judicial gagging order sought by the Club in relation to his involvement in an imminent *Panorama* exposé of horse racing.

Anticipating the BBC programme's main thrust, the JC confirmed they believed that Brian Wright had been behind the dopings at Doncaster in 1990. They also identified the so-called 'Needleman' as the disgraced ex-jockey Dermot Browne, who was regarded by some in racing as a 'dodgepot' and congenital liar. Shortly afterwards, Browne popped up in a *Racing Post* interview claiming to have doped a total of 23 horses on Wright's behalf in the 1990s.

The Jockey Club went further, giving their backing to the assumption – that had clearly originated with Roger Buffham – that Wright hadn't just entertained jockeys and shown them a good time in return for tips and information that would help him improve his strike rate as a professional gambler. The prosecution case was that the dopings, including the Exeter and Plumpton races, along with other suspicious instances of beaten favourites, were all part of a grand design to enable Wright to launder the proceeds of his drug deals through the betting ring.

A cunning masterplan? Or another product of Roger Buffham's overheated imagination? Victor Chandler, implied by Buffham to be a tool of the plot, was scornful. "When you're talking about money laundering, you're talking about drug money running into millions. I can tell you, it would have taken them a bloody long time to launder a million at places like Plumpton and Exeter. Yet Buffham was inferring that all the SP men were crooks – he got Neil arrested on trumped up charges – and that all racecourse bookmakers, rails and boards, were involved in this giant conspiracy."

That wasn't just Chandler's opinion. Any racecourse bookie with experience of the gaffe tracks on a routine weekday in the 1990s would testify that, by comparison with the previous decades, attendances were often sparse and the market chronically weak. Mysterious punters suddenly sticking thousands of pounds on something other than the favourite in three or four-horse races would immediately draw attention to themselves.

Of course, a bookmaker or a gambler can try and fix a race, especially if the jockey is in on the plot, but it's an expensive racket. As well as all the cash you have to pay to straighten out the various participants, you need putters-on – not directly traceable to the originators of the plot – who will have to back other runners in the race to force your horses odds out to avert suspicion, as well as backing the 'good thing' in numerous, necessarily small wagers. Even then, racehorses, not being able to talk and therefore not privy to the plan, can let the side down. In Lively Knight's race at Plumpton, Glen Gill had a number of reverse forecast bets on the other two runners but, in spite of the doping, Lively Knight still managed to finish second, so the bets came to nothing. Would sophisticated big-time criminals, playing for the highest stakes, really rely on such a method to launder their profits?

What was not disputed, and never has been, was that villains, often charming and generous with their hospitality, were still as naturally attracted to betting and racing and as much a part of the whole gambling scene as they had been in the 1920s and '30s. It was an open secret that Victor knew one or two of them and, as Richard Thomas puts it, "sometimes it suited him not to discredit the stories for the sake of his image." There was one character who came in to pay his account at Linhope Street one day, tossed a sackful of cash onto the desk and left. "There must have been about £85,000 there, and when the office manager Mick Saunders looked in the bag he found there was another £15,000 in the bottom the punter had forgotten. He wasn't the sort of man you didn't tell but, when he came back to collect it, he said he'd been so stoned that he thought he must have left the money in the taxi. We didn't mention that, as well as the cash, there had been a pair of surgical gloves in the sack too. We thought it best not to ask what he'd been doing with them."

Then there was the punter who walked into Victor's box at Ascot one day in the 1980s, saw a man with a shoulder holster and was about to draw a gun of his own, until it was pointed out to him that he was looking at one of the Queen Mother's bodyguards."

A spiritual relation of the Ascot gunman was Frannie Butler, a haulier's son from the East End who "used to come up to us on the racecourse wanting £50,000 on a horse. You didn't ask where the money came from." A huge man weighing 17 stone, and over six-foot four, Butler went inside for a spell in the 1980s and had the distinction of sharing a cell in Highpoint Prison with Lester Piggott. "I'm the only Essex boy who's ridden a Derby winner," he joked when he came out.

Before Butler, there had been the celebrated conman 'Brian the Swan,' who once needed someone to look after some money for him while a friend was in prison. The Swan decided to leave it with Guy Packer (the former jockey who'd introduced Victor to Lucian Freud) at his house in London. "Guy was another wonderful character and he knew my father long before he knew me. He came from an old Newmarket gypsy family and he too was painted by Lucian. He'd always hunted, and he rode as an apprentice when he was very young.

THE MILKMAN

He won the 1945 Cambridgeshire on a horse called Esquire, who was returned at 40-1. The bookmakers' Briggs and Berman, who were known as 'Bugs and Vermin,' always said it bolted with him at the start. He went on to train horses unofficially while doubling as an antique dealer, and at one point he got into a bit of trouble with the law and changed his name to Guy Hart.

Well, in the late Seventies, he was living in this lovely big house in St John's Wood and racing and gambling people were always passing through. But, for some reason, The Swan hated Guy, so when he came to collect his money, he left this trick cigar, shaped like a Churchillian Havana, behind in the cigar box. Guy didn't realise it had deliberately been left for him, and for a day or two it just sat there unsmoked. Then the following week, the punter Sandy Cowley and his brother went round to Guy's house. Sandy had just come out of prison too, and he said he was taking a couple of girls out to dinner that night at the Connaught. So, as a friendly gesture, Guy invited him to take a couple of his cigars along with him. Of course, unbeknown to Guy, one of them was the Swan's Churchill.

Well…. later that evening at the Connaught, Sandy orders a brandy, pulls out the cigar and asks the waiter to cut it and light it for him at which point it explodes in their faces. Sandy's furious. 'You fucking dog,' he starts shouting at the waiter. 'What have you done to me?'" When the waiter protested his innocence, Cowley became convinced that Packer had set him up on purpose and Guy needed all of his considerable charm to persuade him otherwise. But then skating on thin ice was Guy Packer's speciality, and the skill with which he managed it only added to his allure.

Packer's heyday was in the 1950s and '60s, when toffs and spivs still travelled the same primrose path, and hard riding cavalier jockeys – like Ronnie Cornwell's friends – were in the thick of it. And whether in restaurants, clubs or private houses, they were as likely to encounter villains as they were bookmakers and members of the aristocracy, and sometimes the villains were their biggest fans.

Graham Bradley's autobiography *The Wayward Lad*, published in

2000 was a throwback to those days. In it, Bradley was quite open, ill-advisedly as it turned out, about his friendship with Brian Wright, describing him as having "been a very good friend of mine for 15 years...I've always prided myself on being a good judge of character, and after a couple of beers in Brian's box, I just knew he was my kind of person." But then it wasn't just a case of The Wayward Lad and his fellow riders being dazzled by Wright's hospitality. The Milkman was flattered and excited to be around them, because whatever he became, Brian Wright indisputably started out as a passionate racing enthusiast and punter. One who regarded rewarding jockeys and other insiders for information as being as natural a part of the game as it was for the bookmakers he was trying to beat, and as it had been for other big professional gamblers for the past 150 years.

Splashing the cash when he had it, and bringing gratification to those less fortunate, boosted Wright's image and self-esteem. He was like a Mafia made man going to the Copacabana in New York and ostentatiously over-tipping the hat check girls and the doorman. Bill Tye tells a story about the Milkman being on the way to the races one day and his chauffeur-driven car being held at a red light by some road works. "He looked out of the car window and saw a workman digging a trench. 'How much do you earn for doing that?' he called out. '£100 a day,' says the man. So Brian takes £200 in cash out of his pocket and chucks it over to him. 'Give yourself a day off,' he says."

The road mender was understandably impressed, as were many of the jockeys and other courtiers attending on Wright on those benches at Newmarket. But what Graham Bradley and some of the riders didn't realise, or chose to ignore, was that their starstruck benefactor was also mixing and doing business with people whose professional activities went well beyond plotting up the occasional horse race. Men like Roy Adkins, a racehorse owner and career criminal who, in September 1990, was shot dead in a hotel bar in Amsterdam where he had been waiting to talk to two Colombians. As you do. His murder was allegedly connected to the earlier death of the former Great Train Robber Charlie Wilson, who was shot at his home in Marbella in April

1990. It was said that Wilson had encouraged another man to name Adkins to the police as the head of a major drug-smuggling ring.

Wright's criminal associates and their connection with racing were meant to provide the main thrust of the *Panorama* report, which went out on Sunday, October 4th, 2002, the evening of the Prix de l'Arc de Triomphe. 'One of the biggest scandals in the history of British sport,' claimed a BBC press release in advance of transmission. Viewers were promised the story of how 'a whole generation of National Hunt jockeys had links to organised crime,' a phrase almost certainly penned by the programme's advisor, Roger Buffham. The film featured an interview with Dermot Browne and shadowy glimpses of Brian Wright in Northern Cyprus, as well as unintentionally comical moments like the death stare that Kieren Fallon, not a jump jockey but nonetheless accused of 50 shades of skulduggery, trained on a reporter who tried to accost him on his way back to the weighing room at York. But thanks to Buffham, the biggest talking point became not so much the corruption of the riders as the perceived incompetence of the Jockey Club and the extraordinary lengths their former head of security had gone to in his efforts to embarrass them.

Buffham's successor at Portman Square was Major General Jeremy Phipps, an ex-Special Forces officer whose skilful behind-the-scenes planning enabled the SAS to break the 1980 Iranian Embassy siege. The General's appointment seemed to be a continuation of the Jockey Club's military fixation, going back to the Peaky Blinders era of Majors Wymer and Bebbington. But Phipps came highly recommended, having gone, like Roger Buffham, from the army into the private security business. Unfortunately, his special skills were not matched by comparable worldliness or knowledge of horse racing. *Panorama* had secret film of Phipps meeting Buffham in a London wine bar supposedly to talk about racing issues and the JC's deficiencies. Phipps, unaware that Buffham the ex-spook had come to the supper wired up and riskily concealing both video and audio equipment, quickly agreed that his employers lacked "the backbone" to tackle corruption. Subsequently, a *Panorama* reporter confronted Phipps with the damning tape and footage at Newmarket racecourse just before the appalled Jockey Club PR man John Maxse could drag the General away.

The *Panorama* producer, Stephen Scott, claimed afterwards that it would be "absolutely ludicrous" if Phipps became a fall guy, while the Jockey Club insisted that he had simply been trying to ascertain what Buffham knew. But the Major General's naivety had been exposed as ruthlessly as Buffham's devious methods and determination to get back at the JC, and within a week, he'd resigned. There was speculation about whether the Jockey Club itself could feasibly carry on in the face of such embarrassment, and Claude Duval in The Sun predicted that the Club was "doomed."

The Senior Steward, Christopher Spence, explained that he hadn't seen the programme because he'd been away in Greece, though he did describe Roger Buffham as "a snake." The Secretary to the Jockey Club, Christopher Foster hadn't seen the programme either. He'd been in Paris at the Arc, and 'no,' he wasn't resigning. Ex-police officers, "expert in intelligence gathering," had supplied the Club with prima facie evidence of something criminal, he said, but despite all that, and a 12-month investigation, Greg Wood in the Guardian felt that *Panorama* had turned up "little that was either new or contemporary." David Ashforth, while observing that racing tended to close ranks at moments like these, also questioned why *Panorama* had been happy to broadcast some of Buffham's claims unchallenged. Claims including what the producer Stephen Scott described as "quite serious allegations about a leading bookmaker."

There had been no attempt to link Victor Chandler's name directly with his former punter, but thanks to a couple of old letters that had been confiscated by Buffham and then passed on, illegally, to the BBC, the programme still managed to make Victor look shady. Back in 1993 and 1996, he wrote to the trainers Jimmy FitzGerald and Gay Kelleway offering them free bets up to a limit of £2,500 if they chose to open an account with him. The motivation was simple. Intelligence gathering. 'Fitzy' in particular was an extremely shrewd operator who liked a bet, as did a number of his owners. Encouraging him to put his money on first and foremost with the Chandler firm would give them an early warning of the horses in his stable he was particularly keen on, enabling them to shape their book accordingly. Punters not party to this kind of inside information were understandably indignant, and the Jockey Club ruled the practice illegal in December 2000. Victor, who had tried and failed to get a court injunction preventing *Panorama* from using the letters on the grounds that they had been taken from him illegally by Roger Buffham, put out a statement after the programme saying that he had discontinued the arrangements as soon as the new ruling came into effect.

One or two other bookmaking firms issued hasty denials of ever having sullied their hands with such devious practices, though not everyone believed them. Off the record, it was widely accepted that all of the big operators used to try and wheedle out sensitive information. Especially if they were sponsoring a big handicap, when they might ring up certain trainers in advance and offer them a free ante-post bet up to a certain limit and at favourable odds on a runner of their choosing. The bookie sponsors would then use that intelligence, indicating stable confidence in certain horses but not in others, to price up the race to the general public and to try and pick off any value bets with their less well-informed rivals.

Panorama went big on the two letters, and there was some film of Victor looking dodgy in a flat cap at Goodwood and rather more artistic *The Long Good Friday* shots of him getting out of the Mercedes, with Everton holding the door open. Recalling the incident made him laugh. "I was actually on my way to do a radio interview and they just turned up on the pavement as I got out of the car. It never really worried me, other than the spin that some people put on it. We had one account closed, but the customer reopened it after two months. The worst thing was my mother telling me that on television I looked about 70. That and a cab ride I had out to Heathrow one day after a lunch meeting at the Carlton Towers (Hotel). The driver had a *Racing Post* on the seat beside him and he started telling me how impossible it was to win at betting anymore. 'I've had them all in this taxi,' he said. 'But what chance have you got when bastards like that Victor Chandler are stopping horses and fixing races.' When I got out at the airport to pay the fare, he looked at me and suddenly realised who I was. 'Oh, fuck,' he said. 'I suppose a tip's out of the question?'"

Then there was the day at Newmarket races when Victor was a guest in a box along with the notorious freeloader and ex-*Daily Express* racing correspondent Charles Benson. The mischievous Benson, well lubricated after lunch, asked the company if they knew the connection between Jamie Osborne and Victor Chandler. "They both work for Brian Wright," he said. "I said to him, 'I'll sue you,'" says Victor grinning.

VC may have laughed it off, but others weren't so happy. "Victor may have been a bit of a desperado," said Carole, looking back on the almost three decades that they spent together. "But in all the years I lived with him, I think he only ever tipped me one winner and, from his experience, I'd say the last person who ever knows if a horse is going to win is the trainer. The fundamental thing about Victor is that he's totally honourable. He gives everyone the benefit of the doubt and, if anything, he's too kind and too generous. He's given fortunes to both racing and non-racing charities, and lent money to all kinds of people without notes, proviso or anything. The slur on his character really was a travesty."

That autumn a book was published called *Racing In The Dock*, written by the former *Racing Post* correspondent Richard Griffiths, who had followed the race-fixing and Brian Wright stories in the paper and now attempted to draw all the strands together under one cover. There was a distinct feeling that legal niceties had prevented him from saying certain things up front, but the book still engendered plenty of gossip and speculation in Turf circles. One experienced journalist confided how he'd been told by a colleague that "Victor was up to his neck in it. He was laying dead meat (horses he knew in advance couldn't win)."

If any journalist like Andrew Sim did indeed believe that Victor was acting in collusion with Brian Wright, in the sense of being party to corrupt acts before the event, they didn't have the nerve or the evidence to say so in print. But then the full logic of the accusations – strenu-ously denied by Chandler – is hard to credit. In the past decade, Victor had been trading on a colossal scale in the Far East with Swordfish and others, while simultaneously investing millions with Michael Tabor in their new offshore business in Gibraltar. Would he really have put all that at risk and jeopardised the firm's prestigious sponsorship at Ascot, as well as of the British Masters golf tournament at Woburn, in order to stitch up a Mickey Mouse race at Plumpton with Brian Wright for £6,000 pounds?

Roger Buffham, a man with no time for the betting ring's colourful history, seemed to think that if a bookie like Victor laid a bet to a villain like Wright, that automatically made him an accomplice in The Milkman's crimes. But, as Butch observed at the time, "when you're a bookmaker, you get the chance to walk on both sides of the street. But just because you lay a bet to a gangster, that doesn't make you a gangster yourself." He could have added that unsavoury characters come in all guises in racing, some of them outwardly, ever so respectable. Victor, John Banks, Stephen Little, Michael Simmonds and their colleagues were not in the habit of asking their customers at Newmarket or Ascot where exactly they'd got their money from before accepting a bet, or turning them away if they weren't completely satisfied as to their unimpeachable integrity. If they had been, a great many well-heeled 'gentlemen' and City fraudsters would have struggled to get on just as much as the Guy Ritchie types with the shades and the Marbella tans.

Victor's grandfather laid bets to men who worked for Darby Sabini and his brothers, and to Prince Aly Khan and Lord Rosebery. Victor's father laid bets to Albert Dimes and Bert Marsh, and to Jim Joel and the Duke and Duchess of Norfolk. VC laid bets to Brian Wright and assorted other 'faces' with form, and to the Queen's racing manager. And when a profligate client like Wright suddenly started making money from backing a string of second favourites, Victor Chandler – like any other bookmaker – would monitor those betting patterns and adjust his prices accordingly.

Within a few years of Wright's suspicious wagers, modern technol-

ogy extended the opportunity to make a profit from inside information to thousands of online speculators. Some of them attempted to
narrow the odds in their favour. If you were the owner or trainer of a
fancied runner and you knew for certain that it couldn't win, maybe
thanks to a recent injury or a compliant rider, you could try and enlist
your friends to lay it for you, or back it to lose, on Betfair. But the
self-same technology, a far cry from the old word in the ear, nothing
written down days, also gave the authorities the opportunity to trace
winning punters' identities and connections should they be alerted to
any suspicious results.

It's not just the exchanges that made things harder either. With
relentless observation from social media, terrestrial and satellite television coverage and dedicated trade paper columnists, there aren't many
plots or strokes that go unnoticed these days. In some ways, the effect
on racing's spivs and chancers has been similar to the impact that the
invention of the telegraph and the automobile had on the outlaws in
the dying days of the American West. In one of the most memorable
scenes in *Butch Cassidy and the Sundance Kid* – one of Victor Chandler's
favourite films – Sheriff Jeff Corey tells the train robbers that "your
days are over, gone, and you should have quit when the rest of the boys
did…you're going to die and die bloody, and all you can do is choose
where."

Victor, always smart enough to know when it was time to move
on, had no intention of dying, literally or metaphorically, by Sheriff
Buffham's hand or in a hail of Bolivian gunfire. But Graham Bradley,
who many believe stopped Man Mood at Warwick in 1996 to enable
Wright to scoop enough money on the winner Drumstick to pay his
betting ring creditors, paid a high price for enjoying The Milkman's
company, not wisely but too well. A 'sly bugger' and double-dyed villain
to some, a tarnished but still gifted jockey to others, he was warned off
for eight years by the Jockey Club following his courtroom confession
to passing on information to Wright for reward. He appealed at length,
but unsuccessfully, to have his sentence quashed, but he did succeed in
getting it reduced to five years. Victor always thought Bradley was "a

very bright man who'd be dangerous with an education. He had a very good eye for buying a horse. But when he gave evidence at the trial in Southampton, it seemed like he was pointing a gun at his own head. Wouldn't he have sat down and gone through it all beforehand with his lawyer?" The answer may be that the barrister was unable to restrain his client, who enjoyed flaunting his risqué connections just as much as he was determined to speak up for a friend.

Perhaps even Bradley's flaws should be seen in context. The non-racing, non-gambling Roger Buffham deplored the Jockey Club, not just for what he called their "moral cowardice," but for being imbued with "the same values" as the suspicious characters in the weighing room. But was that so surprising? The best, or most enlightened, officials understood that the bone-rattling dangers and neurotic wasting of a jockey's life had taken their toll of better men than Brad the Cad. Most of the greatest riders in history have had a devil in them. Fred Archer – the Lester Piggott of the 19th century – was a gambler and manic depressive who took his own life at the age of 29. The great Australian jockey Rae Johnstone was another compulsive punter. Lester was prosecuted for tax evasion and went to jail. Steve Cauthen suffered from bulimia. Walter Swinburn, Johnny Murtagh and Kieren Fallon all struggled with drink or drugs, or both. But would they have been half so compelling if they had not possessed what John Arlott called "the salty quality of human nature," and all been unclouded beacons of virtue?

As for the great corrupter Brian Wright, he was arrested in southern Spain in the summer of 2005 and extradited back to England. In April 2007, he was convicted – on a majority verdict – of drug smuggling at Woolwich Crown Court and sentenced to 30 years. It was said that he expected to die in prison but, in April 2020, he was released after serving 15 years. Roger Buffham's appeal against his dismissal was settled privately by the Jockey Club, which paid him compensation. He continues to serve as a magistrate in Lincolnshire.

Chapter Twenty Two

New Deals

I t was towards the end of the 20th century when Victor Chandler
first seriously considered selling up. Not to retire altogether. Not in
his early fifties. But he had been in the bookmaking business non-
stop for almost 30 years and suddenly, with all the new overheads
and responsibilities of the Gibraltar office, the idea of taking a profit
on what he'd achieved up to that point and letting someone else run the
show was an attractive one. He would become a non-executive director. He would spend more time in Britain and he would be able to go
racing again regularly, returning like a lover who has strayed, to his first
and dominant passion.

There had already been a couple of unorthodox approaches in the
1990s from foreigners who wanted a share of the business. One of
them was from a Californian bookmaker called Pete Johnson, whose
nickname was 'Snakey Hips Pete.' Slim and very dapper, he told Victor
he represented "some people" who would like to enter into a partnership with him and bring him some high-rolling American clients. One
of them was a punter called Steve Carson, "who started betting big
with us on the tennis at Wimbledon, but then decided not to pay."
'Leave it to me,' said Snakey Hips when Victor told him about the
problem. Carson's debts were settled within days but, feeling uneasy
about the precise identity of Johnson's 'people,' Victor declined to

accept any more of his customers and the connection fizzled out.

There was a not dissimilar offer shortly afterwards, when a mysterious Italian rang Victor one day at the Linhope Street office. "We had started advertising in the Italian sporting papers and on Ceefax there. The journalist Carlo Zuccoli, who followed all the big British race meetings, was our representative and we were employing six Italian-speaking telephonists, and it was going very well." The man on the phone, whose name was Rodolfo, said that he and his associates were coming to London the following week and that they'd like to take Victor out to lunch and discuss a business proposition. "There were three of them and their minders, and they were all beautifully dressed. They wanted to take over part of our office at weekends and bet on football. They said they'd bring their own staff and that they'd let me have 25 per cent of whatever business they did." Victor was understandably puzzled as to why he would want to take 25 per cent of the Saturday and Sunday trade when he was currently getting 100 per cent, but the Italians urged him to consider their offer carefully and invited him down to Portofino to stay on their yacht. He never went to Portofino and he never accepted their proposal, but soon afterwards, Ceefax and the Italian papers dropped his advertising and the unfortunate Carlo Zuccoli was arrested. It wasn't hard to conclude that 'Rodolfo' and his friends were emissaries of the Mafia.

In the summer of 1999, a more respectable outfit, the English National Investment Company, or ENIC, began talking to Victor with a view to them taking a 25 per cent share in his business. ENIC's managing director Daniel Levy and Michael Tabor, who was a close friend of the company's founder, the Bahamas-based billionaire Joe Lewis, flew out to Gibraltar for a meeting. Nothing much happened that day, but a few weeks later, Joe Lewis invited Victor to be a guest on his yacht. A relatively modest eight or 10-bedroom affair, moored, at the time, off the coast of Majorca.

The 62-year-old Lewis grew up in a room over a pub on the Roman Road not far from Michael Tabor's childhood home in Forest Gate. A self-made Croesus, like Victor's grandfather in the 1930s, he shared

Tabor's love of racing and used to "come up and have a few bets with us in the old grandstand at Ascot," said Bill Tye. "He was very shy to begin with, and was sometimes accompanied by his grandchildren." Shy he may have been but, as Victor discovered, he would always try and beat the bookie down when it came to the odds he was offered about a horse. "I used to go up and see him in his box before racing. He'd have his man Charlie Smith, a semi-minder with a pointy beard, with him and he'd keep me there for some time until he got the prices he wanted."

Meeting Lewis at the races in England gave no real indication of his wealth, and life on his boat was hardly Russian oligarch style either. But there were still staff on hand to cater for every need. "All my clothes were laid out and put in cupboards or taken away and pressed. The discussions with Joe took place on deck in shirts and swimming trunks. Then, when we were having lunch, the purser asked me 'What time will you be leaving the boat, sir? Only there appears to have been a slight accident with your trousers.' It seems he'd burnt a hole in them with an iron. The next thing I knew, he'd taken them away too. I jokingly said to Joe that I felt as if I was a sort of hostage for as long as they wanted to keep me."

Lewis and Chandler ended up playing Kaluki together until well after midnight. "He loves cricket and golf, but it seemed that all he wanted to talk to me about was slow horses and fast women." There was a definite rapport between the pair, and if the negotiations had been left to the two of them, the sale would probably have gone through. But back in Gibraltar and London, Victor had to contend with Daniel Levy, "who was quite a difficult man to deal with even then," and, despite a farcical press release with pictures of them standing on the runway at Gibraltar airport with the Rock in the background and Levy holding a football in his hands, progress proved elusive. The root of the problem was a dispute over the precise value of the Chandler firm. "There was a lot of money involved, and I was to have 'an executive position' and a 30 per cent stake. But we ended up having to re-write three years of accounts due to what Levy called 'a lack of clarity.'" Perhaps that top-floor room at Linhope Street, with its cigars and bottles of claret and old boxes of Christmas crackers, didn't quite match up to Daniel Levy's notion of company assets.

There was an attempt at arbitration in a meeting at Les Ambassadeurs in May 2001 but, after 18 months of discussions, the two sides agreed to break it off.

The ENIC marriage may have been aborted but, in the buoyant financial climate of the period and with the Far Eastern business growing, there was talk of other deals. In 1998, during Mike Carlton's first year with the company, Sagitta Asset Management – the investment vehicle set up by the banker Bob Michaelson and the Lebanese racehorse owner Wafic Said – discussed joining forces with Guinness Mahon to finance a Victor Chandler takeover of Coral. There was also talk of Victor acquiring Zetters Pools and the old Zetters building in Clerkenwell, which is now a hotel. Neither of these projects came to fruition, but in June 2003, the company opened their first new betting shop for 14 years. In keeping with the affluent era and taste for bespoke, concierge services, this was no run-down haven for rheumy-eyed small-change punters either. Number 4 to 6 Deanery Street in Mayfair was the smartest betting office in Britain, complete with a uniformed commissionaire (Tony), marble floors, soft brown armchairs, giant state-of-the-art plasma TV screens and Molton Brown toiletries in the loo. It even had its own private smoking area.

The grand opening, followed by a lavish buffet dinner at Les Ambassadeurs, was attended by, among others, Sir Peter O'Sullevan, Lester Piggott, Pat Eddery and John McCririck. Everyone was impressed by the club-like ambience and setting, which was as central to the shop's concept as the ultra-modern technology and reflected the style and chutzpah of the emcee – Mr Peter Beaton-Brown, or 'Mr West End,' as Victor had started calling him. Butch had come a long way since his nervous debut making small talk with Lester in Hong Kong. Now he could be seen every week taking lunch in Les A, drinks in Motcomb Street and dinner at the Wolseley, where the famed doorman Sean O'Driscoll (who later moved to Scott's in Mount Street) was as well informed a racing fan as anyone in London. These eminently enjoyable pit stops were all part of Butch's job description, which was to press the flesh and meet and charm customers old and new.

Mayfair was home to a dwindling number of old-school gentleman punters who came out of hibernation at the start of the flat racing season each spring. It was also where many of London's leading hedge-funders and Russian billionaires had set up base, resulting in no shortage of rich, testosterone-filled young men and women on Butch's doorstep. Deanery Street was created, in part, to appeal to this new generation, who were as likely to be interested in football, rugby, cricket and golf as horse racing. But the majority of the shop's punters were traditional racing big hitters, mostly Middle Eastern or Greek, though JP McManus used to pop in to check the results when he was staying at the Dorchester Hotel across the road.

The shop was situated on the site of a former massage parlour and some punters still turned up looking for services that even an upmarket bookmaker couldn't provide. Butch joked that, thanks to the award-winning designer Steve Hatfield, they turned it "from a knocking shop into a betting shop inside six weeks." Critics of gambling may see a seedy and satisfying symmetry between the two professions, but Deanery Street was nothing if not tasteful with pastries from the nearby Café Richoux at coffee and teatime, and lunchtime sandwiches to order.

Victor recruited the manager and assistant manager of the nearby Ladbrokes branch in Curzon Street, and they brought in new customers. Some of the profits were reinvested in tilts at the ring, with bets placed with rival bookmakers in the area. The wagers had to be placed within a tight timescale in order to get the best odds and, as Butch put it, "you needed a decent pair of running shoes if you wanted to work there." One of the best days was when Victor had £100,000 on a Robin Bastiman-trained gelding in a race on the all-weather at Lingfield. Maramito, who was named after Victor's favourite horse in Spain, went off at 4-5, having opened up several points bigger, and won by three lengths. "Robin said beforehand that it would be four lengths clear after 50 yards and as far ahead as it wanted to be by the time it crossed the line. Everton (Victor's driver) put the bets on for me, and nobody saw the connection. I watched the race on the TV in the shop. You can imagine the party we had afterwards."

All of Deanery Street's customers had their own quirks, and it was their body language that gave them away. "We used to get so many Greeks in there and they were fabulous punters," said Butch. "'Come on baby,' you'd hear them cry. 'On you go.' The sick ones, the ones with a disease, would lean into the TV screens as if the closer they got to the picture the more chance they had of influencing the result. But then there were others who would never say a thing, never even blink, whether they won or lost. Generally speaking, we'd not beat the three-times-a-week punters. It was the ones having 20 bets a day that gave us a chance."

But with each passing year, the 20-bets-a-day men were more likely to be wagering online, instead of at the track or in the betting shop, and in this strange new world, many professional gamblers preferred staying at home and betting on the exchanges to actually being there. The Victor Chandler office in Gibraltar was fielding hundreds of thousands of online bets on a typical Saturday afternoon, and many of those punters were playing online casino games too. If big money poker tournaments were the sexiest gambling craze of the early 21st century, playing cards online alone in your bedroom late at night must, along with virtual racing, be the most soulless. But for bookmakers like the Coates family, owners of Bet365, and Victor Chandler, who launched VC Bet in 2004 along with the VC online casino and VC Poker.com, it was hugely profitable. One regular client, holidaying in Barbados, lost nearly £2.5 million with the firm in a fortnight playing solitary online roulette in his hotel room between the hours of 11pm and 2am.

Old family retainers were horrified when Victor dropped the iconic Chandler family name from the new brands. Deanery Street and the racecourse pitches continued under the old banner, but commercial logic insisted that the firm had to be in step with changing fashions, and that included broadening their sponsorship portfolio too. Between

1999 and 2002, they backed the British Masters golf tournament at Woburn, and in May 2000, they signed a five-figure deal with Kieren Fallon, who was to wear their logo on his breeches when he was riding. It was also agreed that he could go up to the Chandler box before racing and brief the company's guests about the day's card, but the relationship didn't last long. In Victor's words, it "suggested a dangerous cosiness which could alienate the punters." There was also the question of Fallon's volatile and unpredictable temperament, which made him a headache to look after for anyone closely involved with him.

When Victor was at York in August during the Ebor meeting one year, he got talking to the diminutive trainer Dandy Nicholls, who had a new story about a leading rider. Two nights before, he had been at home asleep at his stable near Thirsk when he was woken up by a phone call at four in the morning. It was a famous jockey. He said he was in a spot of bother and he needed Dandy to come and pick him up. In Leeds. He also asked the trainer to bring him some clothes. Like a pair of trousers, for example. A sleepy and exasperated Nicholls, who had been in this situation before, reluctantly decided to put loyalty before comfort. He got up, got dressed, threw a tracksuit in the back of his Range Rover and set off in the direction of Leeds. The street name the jockey had given him turned out not to be in the city centre, but in the respectable western suburb of Headingley. As Nicholls cruised along, passing row upon row of dark and sleeping houses, he suddenly saw a familiar figure dart out from behind some bushes on a corner and run towards him. He was stark naked, but covering his modesty with his mobile phone. "What the hell happened?" asked Nicholls as he opened the passenger door. "Her husband came back," said the jockey.

On another occasion, also during Ebor week, the same rider went for a night out after a good day at the track. It began with dinner in the Mount Royale Hotel, where the jockey had a steak with mashed banana on top, and half a bottle of vodka, and continued in a pole-dancing club. The evening ended when a bouncer threw the jockey out for reaching out towards one of the girls, running his credit card up and down the crack in her bottom, and calling out, "will that get me more? Or will that get me more?" The answer was "No, it won't. And it's way past your bedtime." The following morning, Victor and Bill Tye were discussing the day's card over breakfast in their hotel and Bill pointed out that the same jockey had three or four fancied mounts. "He couldn't possibly ride a winner today," said Victor. "He was so drunk last night that he couldn't stand up, and passed out in the taxi coming back." Needless to say, that afternoon the jockey rode a treble.

The trainer Jeremy Noseda had good cause to be frustrated by the same character when he put him up on a horse that was owned by Victor and Edward St George. The well-backed colt hit the front too soon and was overtaken in the closing stages. "If I'd ridden him on the gallops as I'd been asked, I'd have known he had to be held up," explained the jockey afterwards. To which Noseda retorted that the pilot had been "too hungover to turn up on time."

Jockeys were not the only big sporting names at the time whose racing and gambling excesses were arousing comment. The quick and easy nature of online betting contributed to some ruinous addictions, and the former England midfielder Paul Merson and Chelsea's Icelandic striker Eidur Gudjohnsen were among the casualties. Other footballers gambled regularly, and not especially profitably, but kept within their limits. Michael Owen's losses were leaked to the papers and he was unfairly vilified for his gambling, which was a secondary pastime to his passionate love of racing. He has invested millions in Tom Dascombe's state-of-the-art stable in Cheshire and become a popular and respected owner-breeder. Other players knew little about racing lore or form and were just looking for a good time. One year, a group of Premiership big names decided they'd like a day out at the Cheltenham Festival. "There were about 20 of them," said Bill Tye. "Victor chartered two helicopters to fly them down from London and organised a box and a gourmet lunch for them when they got there." They didn't like the food it seems, and at one point Victor's staff had to send out for hamburgers to keep them happy, but "all of them were punting and their total losses on the card came to about half a million pounds."

An altogether shrewder punter was the ardent racing lover Sir Alex Ferguson, who Victor first met in the company of Lester Piggott and Sir Alex's old Mancunian friend Sotirios Hassiakos in Les Ambassadeurs in the 1990s. "Alex might have a bet on the football before the start of each season, but then he liked to ring up from time to time and have something on the racing too. He was incredibly knowledgeable about it, and I think having a bit of a financial interest was a release for him. The job put him under such immense pressure. I'm glad to say we became good friends, and it's great to see him better and back racing again."

By the early 21st century, Victor was going racing less and less, his time monopolised by Gibraltar, the Far East and billowing domestic and emotional turmoil that had yet to fully reveal itself to the world outside. But there were still a few colossal plungers around who wanted the bookmaker's personal attention. Men for whom a day at the races was never complete until they'd managed to lose most of whatever they'd won earlier on. Men like Billy Sodha (not his real name), "an Asian businessman from Leeds who was dapper, well spoken and entirely convincing. He came and put some money in the Indian Lottery with me. He owned property in the north of England and he had investments all over." Sodha was a casino gambler as well as a racing punter and, over a period of time, he lost over £10million in cash at Aspinall's, Les A and elsewhere. "He could lose up to a million a night. Every casino in London was desperate to have him. Of course, they treated him like royalty. Their food was better and their customer service more obsequious than any bookmaker could manage."

One night Sodha turned up at Les Ambassadeurs in his Range Rover and saw "a fellow in a smart grey suit standing on the pavement. Assuming he worked for the club, he handed him his car keys. 'Park it for me,' he said. There was over £100,000 in cash in the car along with two Rolex watches. He never saw them or the Range Rover again."

Sodha may have had a flamboyant lifestyle with luxury cars and matching £150,000 watches for his girlfriends, but Victor felt that, where his betting was concerned, "the only kick he really got was losing.

After Cheltenham one year, he was on a run with us and winning big, but he couldn't stop. There was a Friday evening meeting on the all-weather at Wolverhampton. 'Can you send someone up there with me?' he said. We did as he asked and he lost everything he'd won at Cheltenham on six very poor races."

Even Billy Sodha's gambling paled by comparison with the high-stakes excesses of Nigel Palgrave-Brown, an Admiral's son whose family home was Redisham Hall, a massive red-brick Tudor manor house near Beccles in Suffolk. He also owned two houses side by side in Hampstead. "His capacity for drink was unbelievable, and he was as thin as a rake. When he walked into a restaurant, people would do a double take. You'd think he'd just come out of Belsen. Gambling was his life. He had a million on Frankel at even money ante-post in the 2,000 Guineas, and then he turned up at Newmarket on the day with half a bottle of vodka and another £300,000 in cash in a plastic bag, and he put all that on it too."

One year, Victor invited Palgrave-Brown to the firm's box at Royal Ascot. He turned up with his driver, an ex-policeman, who had tattoos not only on his body, but all over his face. VC and his other guests were horrified by the driver's appearance, which was widely noted, his picture appearing in the *Daily Mail* the next day. "Fortunately, the badges he was wearing were the wrong way round and you couldn't tell from the photo whose box he was in."

In 2010, Victor and Michael Buckley were part of a syndicate called 'Men In Our Position,' which owned the Cheltenham Triumph Hurdle winner Zaynar. The trainer Nicky Henderson had "come up to our box at Ascot on Victor Chandler Chase day the previous year and I said to him, 'Can you buy me a horse to win the Triumph?' 'Okay,' he said. 'Oh, I'll be in on that too,' said Michael and another friend of mine, Graham Porter." The grey gelding Zaynar, who was bred by the Aga Khan's studs, was purchased that summer, and at Cheltenham in March 2009, he won the four-year-old championship by three quarters of a length. The following year, Zaynar was one of the ante-post favourites for the Champion Hurdle, and a few weeks before the Festival, the trainer sent it up to Kelso in the Scottish borders for a prep race in the Morebattle Hurdle. It was only a four-horse race, but the going was heavy and Zaynar had to concede weight all round. He was beaten a length at odds of 1-14, making him one of the shortest-priced losers in recent racing history. Beforehand, Nigel Palgrave-Brown had wagered £60,000 on him to win £5,000. But Victor was charitable. "The race in that ground half destroyed the horse," he said, "and so I told him we'd write it off."

In October 2018, the 64-year-old Palgrave-Brown was knocked off his bicycle by a car in London and never recovered from his injuries. Bill Tye went to his funeral in Suffolk. "I'd never seen anything like it," he said. "We were all sitting there in the crematorium when suddenly two blokes rode in on Harley Davidson's. They put pictures of race-horses on the top of Nigel's casket along with a bottle of red wine, a gin and tonic, an ashtray and a copy of the *Racing Post*. It was quite a way to go."

Racecourses are full of ghosts. The spirits of old punters, bookmakers, owners, trainers, jockeys and horses continue to haunt the party long after they are gone. One of Nigel Palgrave-Brown's last days at the races was a trip to France as Victor's guest. By then the bookmaker had drastically reduced his attendance at ordinary weekend meetings in the UK. But from time to time, when the racing calendar reached those still points in the turning world, those essential unmissable afternoons, he dropped whatever he was doing in Gibraltar or Spain or the Far East and returned briefly to the great stages once graced by his father and grandfather before him.

To Cheltenham… or Ascot…or Longchamp.

Chapter Twenty Three

The Valiant Cowboy

A jet-black Mercedes was gliding through Paris on a sunlit Sunday morning in October. The atmosphere was gently autumnal. The leaves on the horse chestnut trees were beginning to turn and Choucroute and Boeuf en Daube had started to appear again on the lunchtime menus. Despite the sunshine, there was an underlying feeling of summer drawing to an end and of shorter, colder days ahead.

The mood inside the car was tense, eager and expectant. It was Sunday, October 7th, 2007, the day of the 87th running of the Prix de l'Arc de Triomphe, one of the most famous and prestigious horse races in the world. With more than £750,000 in prize money to the winner, and a glittering supporting card featuring five other Group One races, it was the climax to the European season. All of the big owners were in Paris – the British, the Irish, the Arabs, the Japanese – and Victor Chandler, bookmaker and high-rolling gambler, was on his way to do battle with the punters.

Victor's annual pilgrimages to Longchamp, French trips on an altogether different scale to those summertime visits to Deauville, were designed to mix business and pleasure in equal measure. Which is what the French racing authority, France Galop, objected to.

One of Victor's happiest memories of his time in Paris as a young man were those invitations to eat lunch or dinner at Patrice des Moutis' house in Saint-Cloud on Sundays. "Patrice was tall and handsome and extremely well dressed. He was also the biggest illegal bookmaker in France. He used to go jogging in the Parc de Saint-Cloud. The chauffeur would drive along in front in the Mercedes, and he'd run along behind. As soon as he got tired, he'd order the driver to stop and take him home."

Des Moutis, whose clients included many of the top French owners, trainers and jockeys, laid off regularly with the leading British bookies of the 1950s and '60s, including Victor's father. Betting with anyone other than the state-run Tote or Pari-Mutuel was officially prohibited in France, but as Patrice's success testified, numerous French citizens preferred the better odds and more flexible markets offered by an independent operator.

Des Moutis was a brilliant mathematician who gambled heavily in his own right, pulling off a series of audacious coups on the PMU's big Trifecta bet, the Tiercé. The more he won, the more the PMU and the French government changed the rules surrounding Tiercé betting in an attempt to stop him, eventually criminalising his activities and driving him into the arms of the underworld. When a Tiercé race was blatantly fixed at Auteuil in December 1973, the police moved in, and with the law on one side and the gangsters on the other, 'Monsieur X,' as Des Moutis was known, ran out of road. In October 1975, the postman found his body lying in the back garden of his house in Saint-Cloud and, tragically, his son François killed himself with the same gun a year later.

Victor had held Patrice in high regard, and every October in Paris, he saluted his memory. The big race also reminded him, more light-heartedly, of the 1969 Arc – the year when Bill Williamson riding Levmoss narrowly got the better of Lester on the Duke of Devonshire's mare Park Top – when his father was arrested and charged with illegal bookmaking. He'd been socialising with Patrice des Moutis the night before, an association that hadn't escaped the notice of the authorities, and he was caught bang to rights, much to the amusement of his son, who was so often accused of irresponsible behaviour and was living in Paris at the time.

Patrice's and Victor senior's experiences didn't in the least put VC off from running a covert odds-making service of his own when he started taking parties over to the Arc from London in the 1980s. The Société d'Encouragement, though, had long memories. "I used to have a group of about 30 people at a big table in the panoramic restaurant. Then, in 1989, the year Carroll House won, I suddenly got a letter from the Société a few days before the meeting telling me not to go. I was in my room at the George V when there was a knock on the door, and when I opened it, the concierge was outside. 'This has just arrived for you, sir,' he said, handing me an envelope. 'I'm told it's rather important.' It was a bit like getting a warning from Inspector Clouseau." But the guests had already been invited, and the table paid for, and they couldn't just cancel the arrangements at short notice. Victor found a way around it. "There were no mobile phones back then, so a stockbroker friend of mine, David Gallyer, had to run the betting side, while Carole hosted the lunch." VC, though forbidden to attend, was skulking down below in the Horse Racing Abroad tent in the old Longchamp pavilion. "I was surrounded by all these non-racing people and somehow trying to run messages up to David and back in the restaurant. It wasn't easy."

Fortunately, the Société lifted their embargo a few years later and Victor became accustomed to renting a box in the Horse Racing Abroad Pavilion in order to entertain the mixture of old friends and Chandler account holders who joined him in Paris for the weekend. At the insistence of France Galop, who succeeded the Société as French racing's ruling body in 1995, there had to be an automatic PMU machine or guichet in each hospitality area. And whatever business Victor and his guests did on their mobile phones with the office in Gibraltar, he was not allowed to lay cash bets to them there and then on French soil. Which, of course, he fully intended to do, only discreetly and without being caught.

The Chandler party for the 2007 Arc was about 60 strong, mostly from the UK, but also with a couple of Indians and a Spaniard. It included Butch, Lester, Sotirios Hassiakos and the still unfailingly charming Gerry Albertini, Victor's one-time Ibiza host who had been a good friend and client of three generations of the Chandler family. Bill Tye, Ashley Woodford and Steve Ridsdale (known in the firm as 'Certainty,' due to his fondness for declaring certain horses to be bankers) were travelling over for the day to do the clerking and settlement of bets. Bill's companion on the Eurostar was the actor and racing lover James Nesbitt, who had been betting with Victor for several years and embraced Arc weekend with a storm of energy and enthusiasm.

The core group assembled on the Sunday morning downstairs in the lobby of the Hotel George V. Lester, all alone and in shades, lurking behind a pillar like some professional assassin; Butch talking on his phone in the café bar, fielding bets and making dinner reservations; waiters still serving silver pots of coffee and plates of croissants with little bowls of strawberry jam; some racegoers hungover from Saturday night and drinking mineral water, others preferring a Bloody Mary or the day's first bottle of champagne. Gerry Albertini was comfortably ensconced in an armchair and reflecting on a lifetime of elegant racing jaunts to Paris, going back to the days of the £50 foreign travel limit imposed by Harold Wilson's government in 1964. One year, in an attempt to get round this tiresome restriction, Gerry had the tyres removed from his Hispano-Suiza before he left London and a hefty roll of banknotes tucked in under the hubcaps. But when he got to Paris, having driven down to Dover and then on from Calais to the French capital, and had the tyres taken off again, he found that his readies had shrunk to a small bundle of useless paper.

Gerry was not the only old-school gentleman gambler staying at the George Cinq. Also waiting for their rides out to the course, were famous racing aristocrats: English, French and German, titled men and women whose families had been guests at the hotel for the Arc in October, and the Prix du Jockey Club at Chantilly in June, since before WW2. Then, too, there was a recognisable complement of gigolos, conmen and shifty 'international financier' types, whether from Mayfair, Monte Carlo or Marlow-on-Thames, still clinging to the kind of 1970s safari jacket look that Roger Moore used to favour in The Persuaders. Victor, as usual, was the last man down, but he was looking immaculate today in a dark suit, white shirt, dark tie and dark glasses, and by 11.30am, his convoy was ready to move off. The smartly suited hotel drivers heading up the Rue Vernet and along the Champs-Élysées, past the Arc de Triomphe – the real one – on down the Avenue de la Grande Armée to Porte Maillot and then turning left into the leafy greenery of the Bois de Boulogne. Overtaking joggers, equestrians and Sunday-morning cyclists before hitting the race-bound traffic at the bottom of the Allée de Longchamp.

As the great stands of the racetrack drew near, they joined the shuttle buses from the Metro stop and passed row upon row of parked coaches that had brought punters over from countless British towns and cities, from Edinburgh to Eastbourne and Dunstable to Devizes. The Mercedes drew to a halt in front of the black wrought iron gates and Victor and his companions joined the estimated 30,000 other cross-channel visitors swelling the ranks of the local Turfistes. There were bloodstock advisors, racing managers, racing correspondents and senior officials from at least 20 different countries. There were ex-footballers, football managers, actors, restaurant and nightclub owners, and celebrity chefs. Awaiting them all was one of the most exciting and spectacular days racing of the year, and in a setting to match. The horse chestnut trees around the paddock were glinting russet and gold. Conkers and fallen leaves lay on the brushed gravel. French Jockey Club members in their distinctive grey bowler hats – a Marquis here, a Comte or Chevalier there – stood around importantly and tried to ignore the barracking of a regular Longchamp heckler. And around the weighing room and in the bars, and among the crowd on all sides, there was talk, talk, gossip, speculation and intrigue.

This being the eve of Paris fashion week, there was no shortage of feminine glamour and hauteur either. One woman was wearing a hat with a Salvador Daliesque apple and snake on the crown, in a miniature replica of the Garden of Eden. But the truly chic – less attention-seeking yet so much more noticeable – were wearing plain black. Black Chanel suits, black designer sunglasses, black boots like the actress Emanuelle Beart. The men accompanying them appeared to be very rich, very famous, or both. Like Alain Delon, still oozing charisma, in spite of puffy cheeks and a slight stoop. A junior Agnelli slicking back his black hair and eyeing Beart wolfishly, and a waxed and pomaded French industrialist bowing unctuously to Mrs Aga Khan the third.

The chic women and their escorts disappeared up the escalator towards the private loges and the panoramic restaurant as racegoers without bookings joined the queue for tables in the overpriced brasseries behind the stand. But Victor's guests, the party from the George V and others who had just arrived, made their way to the pavilion just beyond the horse walk to and from the paddock to the track. The British travel firm Horse Racing Abroad had the entire ground floor. Victor's and other private parties were in the capacious boxes on the top floor. The rear windows looked back towards the racecourse stables, and steps led up to a balcony and outdoor viewing area at the front. It wasn't always so luxurious. "The first few years we used to sit on our raincoats on the terraces and have champagne and sandwiches," remembers Carole. "If Victor backed a winner, he'd send someone like Jeffrey Bernard off to the bar with the money to buy another bottle. He didn't always return, though, sometimes preferring to pocket the cash."

Jeffrey Bernard died in 1997 and there was no need to rely on an impecunious journalist to fetch the refreshments 10 years later. Lunch in the box – with super-smooth and bow-tied French waiters in attendance – was a delicious buffet comprising oysters, langoustines, crevettes, wedges of paté and foie gras, thin slices of cold roast beef with mayonnaise and a mouthwatering selection of French cheeses and desserts. The lucky punters quaffed champagne as they arrived and then Claret, Chablis and Sancerre as the afternoon wore on. Some of them may have realised that they were on the menu too, just as much as the Chèvre and the meringues and Crème Chantilly. Others, high rollers used to winning four and five-figure wagers, were hoping to eat their host's food, drink his wine and pick his pocket before it was time to go home, and it all promised to be an awful lot more fun than betting alone at home on a computer.

Victor had begun the day nearly £10,000 down after treating a dozen clients to an eve of Arc dinner in the Tour d'Argent overlooking the Seine. The guests included Matthew Green, son of the art dealer Richard Green, who was a punter with Victor's father "for years and years, going to the wall and coming back again depending on how his fortunes went." Matthew Green would end up being targeted by the FBI, accused of fraudulently selling millions of pounds worth of art he had previously used as collateral to secure loans. But that night, he was one of the lucky ones, feasting on the Tour d'Argent's acclaimed pressed duck and enjoying the equally memorable view from their table of the Île Saint-Louis and the floodlit Notre Dame.

Eating alongside them was a large and very formal party of Japanese racehorse owners, one of whom got up and did some private business, big business, with the English bookmaker before the evening's end.

Now, with Sunday's first race imminent, the cameras of the French Equidia TV channel were roaming around the course, lingering over the Presidential Box with its' impressive array of red velvet chairs providing comfort – in the absence of Nikolas Sarkozy – for the ample bottoms of assorted France Galop and government figures. Down in the paddock, the Belgian-born jockey Christophe Soumillon, so cocky but so talented, was posing with Yves St Martin, the great French champion of yesteryear. The old master, looking tanned, if slightly mottled, in retirement, was once the undisputed Roi de Longchamp, duelling every year with his English contemporary Lester Piggott. At the request of a photographer, Lester, still in his trench coat and shades, half smiling but otherwise impassive, joined the line-up, and watching the old rivals standing side by side and shaking hands made the hair stand up on the back of your neck. What Arc memories they shared. Of glorious triumphs and heartbreaking defeats. Sassafras and Nijinsky. Rheingold and Allez France. Alleged. Sagace. Akiyda and Ardross. Names and days that will endure for as long as there is racing.

Other jockeys and trainers bustled in and out of the weighing room. An unsmiling Kieren Fallon, who had a date at the Old Bailey the next day, where he was due to face serious race-fixing charges of which he was subsequently acquitted; 'Aidan Patrick O'Brien,' as the French commentator called him, for whom Fallon was due to ride the battle-hardened Dylan Thomas in the big race; Michael Tabor and John Magnier, the co-owners of Dylan Thomas and half a dozen other Coolmore runners on the card – Magnier, in the same distinctive trench coat and brown trilby hat that he used to wear at Cheltenham, adjusting the glasses on his nose, and making a quick call on his mobile –and Derrick Smith, the former Ladbrokes Trading Director and newest member of the Coolmore syndicate – a man who Victor remembers with "fingers in lots of pies and ins with just about everyone," in the days when he represented the Magic Sign on the rails. "'I don't even know what my Ladbrokes salary is,' he said to me once."

The French owners and trainers stuck to their own cliques. Captain Pompous, Francois Doumen. Pascal Bary. Alain de Royer-Dupré. His Highness the Aga Khan, looking as if he was putting up a few pounds overweight. And the master craftsman Andre Fabre, a veritable Napoleon of the Turf, displaying his unsurpassed ability to smile unsmilingly while turning his back on those French – but not English – owners, trainers and racing correspondents he despised.

Around half the occupants of the Chandler box came downstairs to look at the runners in the Prix de l'Abbaye in the paddock. The low murmur of English and French voices around the Bar des Anglais. The scent of money, Gitanes and expensive colognes. The glistening coats of the thoroughbreds strolling beneath the trees. A hypnotic blend and a setting that resulted in a near-death experience for Victor's friend Alan Kinghorn, who had talked VC out of selling the Chandler business to Playboy Bookmakers back in 1977.

Kinghorn was an incorrigible philanderer. 'Take a walk on the wild side, Victor' he used to say. One year on the eve of the Ebor meeting, he told his wife he was travelling up to York on the Monday night, whereas he was really with his mistress at her flat in Lisson Grove. The couple had a fight and the mistress left the next morning, locking Kinghorn in. The flat was on the first floor and he had to jump out of a window to try and escape, but in the process he injured his ankle. Worried that his wife would ring the hotel in York and discover that he wasn't there, he took a helicopter up to the Kavesmire, where he'd arranged for an ambulance to meet him and take him directly to a local hospital. When his wife did catch up with him, he told her that he'd hurt himself falling down the hotel stairs.

There were similar antics one year at Longchamp. Kinghorn had travelled over with another woman who was not his wife, and they were enjoying themselves, posing hand in hand around the paddock, Kinghorn ducking whenever he saw a photographer. But the weekend's undoubted pleasures turned to ashes back home in England a month later when a friend cheerfully informed him, 'there's a very nice picture of you and your girlfriend in Paris, Alan, in the latest issue of Tatler.' Aghast at the news, and with intimations of marital meltdown, Kinghorn dashed round all the newsagents in Mill Hill where he lived and bought up every copy of Tatler he could find.

"He was terrified his wife would still see it," said Victor. "So he nonchalantly asked her where she was having her hair done at the time? Then, the following morning, he raced round to the salon to see if they'd got any copies of Tatler there. He did the same thing at the doctor's and the dentist's surgery. In the end, he had enough copies of the magazine to fill up his entire garage." It was all to no avail. On the night of his son's 21st birthday party, Kinghorn had "overindulged in just about everything," and his Catholic guilt convinced him he should confess to his wife, and own up not just about the Paris episode, but a whole lifetime of indiscretions. She listened patiently to his account and then threw him out.

By now, the racing was in full swing. The Irish-trained Benbaun, ridden by Pat Smullen, won the Prix de l'Abbaye at 13-2, with the

5-2 favourite Kingsgate Native in second place, and Fallon and Dandy Nicholls back in fourth with Moss Vale. The Aga Khan's two-year-old filly Zarkava scored a scintillating victory in the Prix Marcel Boussac, flooring Frankie Dettori on the favourite Laureldean Gale, but then Dettori and the Godolphin stable comfortably landed the Prix Jean-Luc Lagardere with the odds-on favourite Rio De La Plata. The balance so far was about 50/50 between Victor and the punters, with the Oaks winner Light Shift, trained by Henry Cecil, coming up next in the Prix de l'Opera at 3pm, and then, 40 minutes later, the Arc.

It was just before the Prix de l'Opera when the police turned up. Four or five of them in plain clothes. Some with jackets and ties. Others in leather jackets and open-necked shirts. They walked into the box without knocking and fanned out around the room. Les Flics of the French gambling squad. The Police des Courses et Jeux. Something about their inherently non-racing persona immediately setting off alarm bells in the mind of Ashley Woodford, who made a quick getaway before he was noticed. Victor, conscious of the sudden intrusion, attempted to confront the leader and ask him in French what they were doing there, though he already had a good idea. "You couldn't make it up," he said. "It was almost dreamlike, though I'd expected it to happen one day. I think Louis Romanet (son of Jean, who had caught his father at Longchamp in 1969) was behind it." The lead detective explained that he and his colleagues were there to make an arrest. Several of them. 'An arrest for what?' asked Victor, innocently. The detective said he believed that illegal gambling had been taking place contrary to French law and in defiance of warnings by the racing authorities and the Ministry of the Interior.

Bill Tye reckoned that one of the PMU officials who had been coming and going since lunch, supposedly to check the smooth working of the guichet, had been a Romanet plant effectively spying on the party from the outset. Five races in, they'd decided they had enough evidence to make a case and had alerted their police colleagues, who duly made their move. The police wanted to know who was the bookmaker and his employees, and who were the guests and, in short order, separated

Victor, Butch, Bill and Steve Ridsdale from the others and corralled them to one side. The doors were closed and everyone was told to turn out their pockets for inspection, women being made to open their handbags to check there were no incriminating VC betting slips inside. Bill was carrying what was meant to be the day's cash float in his trouser pocket, including cash bets from the losers at Newmarket the previous day. As instructed, he'd been placing occasional bets in euros with the PMU to give the appearance of normality, but he still had a sizeable wedge on him and his heart was beating faster than most. In a mumbled conversation with Victor, he was advised to keep quiet about the money unless he was forcibly searched.

Preliminary questions complete, Victor, Butch, Bill and Steve were led away down the stairs, out through the Horseracing Abroad tent and around the back of the paddock to the weighing room. Their temporary destination was to be the racecourse lock-up. A small glass box into which the four Englishmen were herded. Curious spectators, including British and French racegoers who knew Victor by sight, stopped to stare, some of them pressing their noses right up against the glass. By this point, the Prix de l'Opera was over, victory going to the French filly Satwa Queen, with the favourite Light Shift unplaced. The runners in the Prix de l'Arc de Triomphe itself were beginning to enter the paddock, the 12 horses accompanied by a great procession of 'grands propriétaires' – owners, trainers, breeders and connections – with cameramen in close attendance and the jockeys following, and the Coolmore entourage taking centre stage and looking like a cross between the Mafia and the Papacy.

Victor pleaded with the detectives to let them out to watch the race, but his request was denied. The police wanted them to hand over their passports and other forms of identification. Bill and Steve had their passports on them, as they had just come over for the day on the train, but Victor's and Butch's were back at the hotel. The police noted that they were staying at the George V and said that they would all have to remain in Paris that night and report to the Police des Courses et Jeux headquarters in Clichy at 10am the following morning. They were warned that illegal bookmaking carried a sentence of up to seven years imprisonment in France, and that if any of them tried to make a run for it, the penalties would be even more severe.

The arraignment, such as it was, took nearly an hour, so of Kieren Fallon's sensational Arc win on Dylan Thomas – taking it up a furlong out and just holding off the fast-finishing Youmzain, the yelling of the crowd building to a crescendo in the stands – they saw nothing. Neither were they aware of the 30-minute Stewards Enquiry into possible interference by the winner that preceded the sight of Fallon, Aidan O'Brien, Derrick Smith and Michael Tabor and his wife Doreen mounting the podium in front of the stands. The connections ascending the steps rather like expensively dressed victims on their way to the guillotine. Baron de Rothschild and assorted France Galop bigwigs shaking everyone by the hand. The French Prime Minister Francois Fillon and the model Adriana Karambeu presenting the trophies, and the band of the Republican Guard striking up the Irish national anthem.

Back up in Victor's box, all those racegoers who had not been arrested, and were still talking about the dramatic events, were encouraged to fortify themselves with the teatime tarte au citron with raspberries, blueberries and fresh cream. There was still more great racing to come too, with Coolmore's Ascot Gold Cup winner Yeats lining up in the two-and-a-half-mile Prix du Cadran. But Victor saw nothing of that race either. Once freed from the glass box, he had called up Mike Carlton in Gibraltar on his mobile and told him to find a good English-speaking lawyer in Paris who could meet with them at the George V that evening. He also called to book hotel rooms for Bill and Steve, and by 5pm he was in the black Mercedes and riding back into the city.

The driver took the route along the Seine this time, the illuminated Eiffel Tower looking down and the lights coming on all over Paris. It reminded Victor of scenes, escapades and characters from his younger life: Patrice des Moutis, Gisèle Cesar, Jean Bouquin, Fernando Ponce-Torré. Their faces flashing past the car window like snatched images from a dream. There was a day, a long time ago, when Victor stood a horse at Longchamp to lose so much money that he would have been ruined if it had won. But it didn't win. And perhaps that made all the difference. But had he finally overreached himself and gone too far?

The police were waiting at the George V when they got there, and they wanted to search both Victor's and Butch's rooms. Butch had another fat bundle of cash hidden in a briefcase under his bed, but he had the wit to claim he hadn't got his key on him and, while the detectives were talking to the concierge, he slipped it to one of the hostesses who had been working in the Horse Racing Abroad tent earlier and asked her to go up to the room, pick up the cash and hide it somewhere until Les Flics had gone. The bi-lingual lawyer arrived soon afterwards, and Victor, Butch, Bill and Steve had a meeting with him in Victor's room to go through their situation and discover what they should say and not say in their interviews the next day. Butch was particularly worried about the prospect of spending seven years in a French prison. "Don't worry, darling," said Victor. "If you do end up spending seven years inside, you'll be able to learn the language." Butch said he was more concerned about some of the other things he might learn. By now Victor was meant to be downstairs hosting a dinner for 20, the climactic event of the Arc weekend's festivities. James Nesbitt, whose booked car back from Longchamp had been hijacked by an Irish imposter, had to take over the role for the first hour or two, and performed it with his customary panache. At one point, he got up from the table to go to the lavatory, and when he returned he'd rolled his trousers up and put his shoes on his knees and proceeded to launch into an impersonation of Dandy Nicholls.

Clean shirts and toothbrushes were found for Bill and Steve, and at 9.30am on the Monday morning, another black George V Mercedes swept the outlaws off to the police station. As Victor got out of the car, he turned to the driver and asked him to wait for them there, no matter how long, so that he could give them a ride back to the hotel later on.

Once inside, they were separated and cross-examined in different rooms. When one of the detectives, a new face who had not been at Longchamp, studied Victor's passport and realised who he was, he was elated. "It's him," he was saying in French. "It's Victor Chandler. We've got him at last." Other cops came in to celebrate Victor's capture as if they were the FBI and he was John Dillinger or Pretty Boy Floyd, and as the room filled up, he half expected them to ask him to pose for a photograph.

There was a translator present for Bill's interview, in which Bill came out with the approved story, as advised by the lawyer, about how he worked for the company, but all the bets had been on credit and none of them in cash. The detective scowled and exchanged a few harsh words with the translator. "What's he saying?" Bill asked. "He says you're talking bullshit," she replied.

The police kept them there all day, sending out for coffee and jambon baguettes at lunchtime. Once they were satisfied there were no French cash punters involved, "they were actually very polite," said Victor. "The chief flic, who arrived late, was very smart in every way. A mature man in his fifties who spoke good English. 'This is all finished,' he said as he walked into the room. 'I don't know what all the nonsense is about. I'm sure we're going to legalise it (bookmaking) soon.' Then he conducted me out of the building."

It was dark outside when the four passports were finally returned and they were allowed to leave. There had been warnings but no formal charges, and Victor Chandler, always more attracted to the forbidden, had got away with it once again. To Bill Tye's amusement, the only thing that seemed to be bothering Victor when they got outside the police station was that there was no sign of the black Mercedes from the George V. "We'd only been in there for about 10 hours. But 'where's that driver?' he says. 'I told him to wait.'"

The Rue De Clichy was not somewhere you'd really want to linger in, let alone celebrate, so they started walking south for about half an hour until they came to a more congenial area and found a decent café, where they all went inside and had a beer. They had made it. There had been no hail of Bolivian gunfire and no jail time either. Just another in a long line of brilliant memories.

Outside, the rain had begun to fall and the waiters were packing up the café chairs and tables. The latest edition of Paris-Turf was on sale featuring tomorrow's declared runners, and across the city, the last British stragglers were wending their way home by train and plane. Returning again to the familiar branch line of provincial racetracks. From Plumpton to Ludlow and from Hereford to Bangor-On-Dee.

When they got back to London, Victor ordered four T-shirts to commemorate the whole episode. They all bore the logo 'Free The Longchamp Four' on the front. Some of them were emblazoned with Steve Ridsdale's catchphrase 'Certainty' on the back. Others, in honour of Bill Tye and Butch, proclaimed them to be 'Billy The Kid' and 'Butch Cassidy;' the rest were named after VC, the 'Valiant Cowboy.'

It would be appropriate, really, if Victor's story ended there on that high note in Paris. But behind the scenes, "the great adventure," as Mike Carlton called it, had become embroiled in greater troubles than a close shave with the French gambling police. Victor's personal and professional life undergoing a series of upheavals that even the most melodramatic scriptwriter might have baulked at.

The great days of racecourse bookmaking were drawing slowly but irrevocably to a close. The face of gambling changing to an almost unrecognisable degree and not to Victor's liking. "The happiest days were the 1970s and '80s. I'm not saying I was some kind of Robin Hood, but I was trying to win money off rich people and they were trying to win money off me. It was a mutual agreement. You never felt as if you were taking advantage of them. But by 2007 it was becoming so impersonal and once you went to Cheltenham and saw people standing in front of you and having bets on their mobile phone, you knew that it was over."

In an increasingly censorious age, anti-gambling zealots hold forth with as much righteous fervour as the temperance movement a hundred years ago and the view that backing a horse – or a football or cricket team or a golfer or a tennis player – can be a harmless, enjoyable and even thrilling experience, risks instant condemnation. There are a few gentleman bookmakers left like Balthazar Fabricius at Fitzdares (who acquired Pat Densham's firm Sunderlands in 2016) and the dapper Irishman Justin Carthy, while the Deanery Street shop was bought by Ben Keith, a one-time Chandler employee and founder of Star Sports. But otherwise, all the big characters seem to have left the stage. Unloved corporate brands, selling betting to those least able to afford it, now dominate the horizon and most of the stroke pullers, rogues and chancers have been ridden out of town.

A lot of people who sorely miss the old atmosphere and the style that went with it, going right back to Victor's father's era and his grandfather before him, wish VC had never moved away in 1999. But he's in no doubt that, even if he hadn't gone off-shore and to the Far East "it still would have happened. The camaraderie of that old world was at an end and it's no good thinking you could have stopped it. After all… the Wild West only lasted about 40 years."

The challenge in future would be to try and hold on to a share of that vast new global gaming market in the face of intense competition. A battle set to heat up like a no limit poker game with the stakes getting higher every year. Maybe luck and good friends would still be enough to see Victor through? Or maybe he'd used up his final get out of jail free card in Paris?

If so, what next for the Valiant Cowboy?

To be continued…

Index

INDEX

INDEX

INDEX

INDEX

INDEX

Wimbledon *(tennis)*, 302
Winter, Fred, 153
Wolseley Restaurant *(London)*, 305
Wolverhampton Racecourse, 311
Wood, Greg, 296
Woodford, Ashley, 316, 322
Wright,
  Barrie, 289-290
  Brian, 18, 278,-283, 286, 289, 291,
    294-95, 298-301
  Brian Jnr, 280, 289-290
Wrighton, Nigel, 115
Wu, Jimmy, 273
Wymer, Major George, 72

Y

Yarmouth Racecourse, 71
Yeats *(horse)*, 324
York Racecourse, 111, 150, 169, 207,
    229, 295, 308, 321
  (Races) – Nunthorpe Stakes, 229
Youlneverwalkalone *(horse)*, 27-29, 149
Youmzain *(horse)*, 324
Young American *(horse)*, 37

Z

Zarkava *(horse)*, 322
Zaynar *(horse)*, 311-312
Zetters Pools, 305
Zuccoli, Carlo, 303
Zurich, 122, 131